SPIRITUAL AUTOGRAPHS
SOUTHERN WOMEN
TELL THEIR STORIES

AN ANTHOLOGY

EDITED BY
Jane Purtle, Mary Brown,
Shirley Matthews, and Twyla Wright

CHICAGO SPECTRUM PRESS
LOUISVILLE, KENTUCKY

CHICAGO SPECTRUM PRESS
4824 BROWNSBORO CENTER ARCADE
LOUISVILLE, KY 40207
1-800-594-5190

For additional copies of this book, contact:
Spiritual Autobiographies Association
703 S. Main Street
Jacksonville, TX 75766
Fax: (903) 586-2412

Printed in the U.S.A.

10 9 8 7 6 5 4 3 2 1

ISBN: 1-58374-003-1

Photographs in this book are provided as a courtesy by the contributors.

Cover design by Melissa Britton-James

ACKNOWLEDGMENTS

We are grateful to Lon Morris College, a small United Methodist College in Jacksonville, Texas, which encouraged our project and to the Summers A. Norman Foundation which supported our vision with grants.

We called on many individuals for special help and expertise. We owe our gratitude to Linda Ward for transcribing interviews and other clerical chores; Carol Ochs, Dana Green, Jimmie and Shirley Reese, Rhonda Taylor, Jerry and Katherine Green-Ellison, Marcy Lang, Bonnie Wheeler, Kathrine Newton, Nancy Lowe, and Betty McLane as readers of our stories; and David Stone, Kay Keller, Judy Nemer, and Gordon Thrall for legal and business advice. Gerry Draper and Pat LaVigne, original members of the group, dropped out of the project along the way as their lives took them into directions which no longer allowed such a time-consuming endeavor. We are grateful for their time, creativity, and friendship.

Our families deserve special thanks, as they have allowed our stories to be told and supported us through this long and sometimes stressful project.

CONTENTS

For Those Who Come After

PREFACE

Sitting in the mellow light cast by Jane's skylight on a late fall Sunday afternoon, we first voiced the idea for this book. Five of us—Jane, Shirley, Mary, Pat, and Gerry—had spent the afternoon talking about our own spiritual autobiographies. We had met together weekly using the exercises in *The Story of Your Life: Writing a Spiritual Autobiography* by Dan Wakefield and pondered our childhoods, relived our adolescence, and struggled with our present. We told our stories, some of us for the first time, to each other and to our families. From this experience and the insight gained, our stories took shape on paper.

It was in the telling that we began to reflect and understand our stories. From our common reflections, we saw parallels of events and emotions even though our individual stories were different. We saw, felt connections we had not known were there. As we voiced these feelings, other women came to mind with whom we had similar ties. Our small circle of five expanded before we left Jane's living room as we began to understand the connections we were discovering. Moved by discovery, we voiced the possibility of gathering other women's stories with ours. We began to ask, "What if?" What if we could widen this circle to include women everywhere by gathering our stories with those of other Southern women?

Twyla soon joined the project from long distance through tape recordings, letters, and phone calls from her Arkansas woods. Jane evolved as the natural leader because of her knowledge of writing and publishing and from her long-time commitment to helping people—women especially—tell their stories.

After compiling our list of storytellers, we wrote letters inviting them to participate in this experience. Our simple project of helping women tell their spiritual stories and expand the circle of connection was not so simply accomplished. We could not do it alone or quickly. The process of collecting, writing, rewriting, editing, and publishing took more than seven years. Our contributors spent many hours searching their hearts and recalling the events of their lives before putting words to their stories.

Until now, they had not heard their stories and some did not realize they had stories to tell. As they listened to their voices, many told us that they knew and understood them for the first time. So the first speaking and hearing of the stories were for our autobiographers themselves. As one says, "That is what I am trying to do—to find my spiritual voice." Having found their voices, they join with others in this first collection of soul-stories of Southern women. A simple "thank you" seems inadequate to express our deep appreciation to these women and their families for their contribution to this book and our lives.

We have chosen to group the stories in this collection into four modes representing the contexts in which Southern women find or take the opportunity to tell their stories: oral storytelling, testimony, dialogue, and crafted autobiography. Though reproduced here in written form, the orality of some of the stories distinguishes them. It is as though we hear the writer say as she swings back and forth on the porch and shells peas, "Let me tell you a story." A second group has the distinct flavor of a testimony. Whether the woman rises in a revival meeting or speaks out at Al-Anon, her story has a rhetorical purpose, to tell of a way of life which may lead the listener or reader to follow her path. Dialogue is not unique to the South but a favored mode among women who find collaborative, conversational storytelling compatible with their natural bent. The interviews in section three illustrate an emerging, autobiographical mode among women, while the formal autobiographies of the last section follow the historical precedents of spiritual autobiographers over centuries.

Most of our contributors grew up Baptist or Methodist, listened to hell-fire-and damnation sermons, went to Sunday School, confessed their sins and were baptized, and only occasionally questioned, as one biographer says, "why the Methodists have more fun than the Baptists." Yet a significant minority experienced a different soul-shaping. One is Jewish and another, Native Ameri-

can. Three are Catholics who have struggled to define their relationship to their tradition; another grew up in an abusive home
and discovered the Salvation Army as a haven in her young adulthood; and two had little formal religious training, discovering their
spirituality in a personal search among the people and events of
their lives.

Five of the thirty autobiographers are under forty; these
women tell of the struggle to discover a voice. They want to know
who they are as spiritual beings, and most feel less sure than their
older counterparts that they have found their spiritual identity. As
one says, "There are times when I feel I am going to fall back into
a spiritual void." Six are past sixty; all of them speak confidently
when they say, "As life is winding down, I shall retain my youthful
spirit . . . . I shall laugh a lot as I reach out to others" or "I don't
waste time feeling sorry for my losses or worrying about things I
can't do."

The large middle group describe themselves as sometimes articulate, sometimes inarticulate. Individual women describe the
daily struggle to say with surety: "I know," while others tell of the
desire to make their voices heard in the political arena. They listen
to the past, and they catch the cadences of their mothers, their
grandmothers, their mentors, or the holy voice. Then, after telling
their story, they say, "The best has already been done for me. When
I told my story, something happened within me." They have begun to claim their true place in the divine scheme of things.

Thirty stories are shared here, including four of the nucleus
which began the process in 1991. We told our own only after we
understood that we had stories to tell.

Yet so many stories remain unspoken, like this story of an
Ozark Mountain woman, now dead:

> *There is a seventy-year-old woman who lives alone
> in a hut in the Ozarks. Each day she toils in an aban-
> doned cemetery grown wild in the woods. None of those
> buried there belong to her, yet a resolve grips her—she
> will turn this tangled mass into a beautiful resting place
> for three babies whose fallen headstones she has stumbled
> upon.*

Slowly, with handsaw, shovel, and pick, she cuts away vines, poison ivy and leaning trees. She struggles through heat and cold, ticks and chiggers. She uncovers long forgotten graves and embraces them all. She plants, waters, prunes. She transforms the remote cemetery, closed around by woods, into a garden of blossoms and flowering trees.

Few have seen the beauty she creates, but those who have are astonished and nourished by her devoted work—her spiritual autograph.

We trust this book will help more women to claim their own stories and give them voice, further expanding the circle of experiences that bonds us all together.

FROM THE PORCH

FROM THE PORCH

We remember, as Southern children, sitting on the south porch on a warm summer morning shelling peas or snapping beans and listening. On the east porch after supper, our elders spoke of the stirring breeze, and we watched the crochet needles in our grandmothers' fingers move in hypnotic rhythm, and again we listened. The stories seemed simple and forgettable, but today they linger in our memory.

The oral storyteller keeps her story alive in cadence and gesture, in place and emotion. She makes us immediately present to the memories of people and places she loves. Drawing on folk wisdom and emotion, she spins the story of her life and her place until we hear the beauty and feel ourselves quicken to the transforming power of the story.

The orality of Southern storytelling dates to the years of slavery when black and white storytellers used stories to pass on their values and traditions and to create community. Oral storytelling is vital in the South where skill with the spoken word has always been emphasized. The stories many of us treasure are still shared orally at family reunions and social gatherings. At Fourth of July celebrations where one family has gathered for more than seventy-five years, they once went to the river in wagons; today everyone meets outdoors under the oak trees. There they share the stories that grandmothers, grandfathers, uncles and aunts have told through the years. Like parables, the stories communicate the spiritual values and meaning that keep the family coming back each year to the oak trees to tell the stories again.

Today, we are recording these oral stories on video and audio tapes or asking a skilled storyteller to write her story so that the words and style of her telling are preserved on the written page. The stories in this section have been crafted for reading, which is not the same as hearing the story told. Yet the test of traditional storytelling is the bond created between the teller and the listener. Readers can judge for themselves if these storytellers weave a tale so as to make that bond.

Mary Carter Smith and Njoki McElroy travel over the country telling their stories to all kinds of audiences, as does Mary Elizabeth Thunder who tells her story through the ritual of her sundancing and as a teacher of the Seneca Wolf Clan Teaching Society. We are fortunate to have them write, each in her unique style, the story that focuses what she understands to be the core of her spirituality. Eula Williams, Lois Rippetoe, Merah McCullough, Donna Suter, and Shirley Boykins are of the folk—country women who celebrate their heritage of simple beginnings, hard work, and lasting connections to the land. Their stories carry us back to the porches of our childhoods and forward to the patios, decks, and poolsides where we expect our daughters and granddaughters to tell their own stories.

MARY CARTER SMITH

As Maryland's official Griot (African folklorist), Mary Carter Smith has strong ties to the South. Born in Alabama of Baptist background, she resides now in Baltimore, Maryland. Mary is a poet, storyteller, historian, philosopher, and preservationist of African-American tradition.

She has been a full time professional storyteller for twenty-one years and is co-founder of the Association of Black Storytellers. She has appeared at the Smithsonian's American Folk Festival and the Kennedy Center for the Performing Arts and had a sixteen-year radio ministry in the Baltimore area. She has traveled to Africa, Europe, the Caribbean, and Canada to tell her stories as a "Christian who uses her gifts to witness."

CHRIST AND A GRIOT

by Mary Carter Smith

M y family is the soil from which I grew. And in that soil I grew to love stories—all kinds of stories. As a small child I often stood at my grandmother's elbow, while she opened the big family Bible and read to me in her soft voice. The stories I loved best, though, were about our family, about my grandmother's earlier years.

I called her Mama, but her name was Mary Days Nowden. She and my grandpa, Joe Nowden, had once lived in and around Lowndes County, Alabama. Papa Joe had been a successful farmer who employed others. In those days some sharecroppers who lived nearby secretly brought him some of their cotton to sell. That way they could get some cash, for they were always in debt at the end of the year. One of them, a Judas, told the boss-man about Papa Joe selling for them.

The boss-man yelled at Papa Joe, "Nigger, you've gotten too big for your britches. By tomorrow night, either you or me will have to get the hell out of Lowndes County! It was Papa Joe who had to leave, of course, and Mama had to sell the farm at a great loss. Papa Joe died soon after, Mama said, of a broken heart.

They had six children who survived infancy. The family moved to Birmingham and lived in a section called Groveland during World War I. Mama took in washing from white families. The children found jobs wherever they could. Mama was a strong woman, a good mother, and a devout Christian.

Her daughter, Eartha, fell in love with a young man named Rogers Ward. He asked Mama for permission to marry Eartha, but Mama saw him as a spoiled only child and forbade the marriage. Soon after, the Ward family moved up North. Mama had no idea that Eartha was pregnant with me and was dismayed when she found out. It was considered a disgrace to bear a child out of wedlock, yet Mama accepted the fact, and the whole family treated Eartha with love.

On February 10, 1919, I was born into the center of the devoted Nowden family and named Mary Rogers Ward. I remember well the little house where we lived in back of Groveland Baptist Church. It was there that my mother rocked me to sleep as she sang the first song I remember, "In a lonely graveyard, many miles away, lies your dear old mother in the cold, cold clay—memories oft returning, of her tears and sighs. If you love your mother, meet her in the skies."

My mother was a tall, dark, slender woman with a quiet face and a gentle manner. She was a stammerer. When I was about three, she married a man named Earl Knight. Seeking a better life, he moved to New York City and sent for Mother after he found a job. She wanted to take me with her, but Mama asked her to wait until they were more settled. Later, I found a letter she had written to Mama and the words, "How is my baby? She is the darling of my life."

My uncle, Anderson Nowden, moved to Youngstown, Ohio, along with his older brother, Jackson. Although he was only sixteen, Anderson was a dependable worker in the steel mills and soon rented a house and sent for Mama and me to join him. I was living there when I was four and the news came from New York City that my beautiful mother was dead. Her husband had killed her, shot her in the head. I remember someone holding me up to look at her body. She was as pretty as I remembered her, but so still.

Later, we moved to Wilson Avenue in Youngstown, and I attended Shehi School. In those days we were called "Colored," and I was the only one in my class. When I was in the second grade, an Italian boy told me on Columbus Day, "We Italians discovered America. All you people did was pick cotton." Not knowing a good reply, I hit him in the mouth, and a fight ensued.

Soon after that, a substitute teacher came to our class, Miss Showalter. All of our teachers were white. She was short, balding, and—to me—beautiful, for she told the class the story of Booker T. Washington and George Washington Carver. That was the first time I'd heard of anyone my color doing anything worthwhile. This started me visiting the public library. I was a good student and an avid reader. Soon I was reading several books a week on many topics. I especially loved *The Bobbsey Twins* and *My Little Spanish Cousin*. I also discovered Black writers, for my Uncle Anderson had books at home written by A.J. Rogers and others.

Shortly before Christmas vacation the next year, my class decided that each of us would bring a gift to school and present it to our teacher. Mama gave me a whole dollar to spend for Christmas presents, and I went down to the five and ten cent store to do my shopping. I bought a white handkerchief with lace in one corner for my teacher, wrapped it carefully in tissue paper and tied the package with a bright ribbon. I was so excited.

On the special day, at a given signal, all of us slid out of our seats, lined up in the aisle, walked up to her desk and handed her our presents. She smiled and thanked each child—then it was my turn. I handed her my present. Her smile vanished, her features froze, and her face turned a deep red. She took my gift and held it between her thumb and forefinger as if it was something filthy. Slowly and deliberately, she held it high above the wastebasket, then dropped it. She looked over my head and smiled at the child behind me.

I stumbled to my seat. Since Mama had taught me never to leave church or school until I was dismissed, I sat there until school was out. Then I ran most of the way home and burst into the house sobbing, "Mama, Mama, why'd she do that to me?"

Mama put her arms around me. "Child, you are Colored, and that makes a big difference to some people."

I learned many lessons from my dear grandmother. She'd tell me, "Child, learn that book. Nobody can take that away from you." She also taught me to share, to help others, "Mary Rogers, if God blesses you to get a good education, then you help the younger ones in the family to get theirs." And, "Mary Rogers, you never take the last biscuit off the plate. If the three of us are eating, each of us gets a third of that biscuit."

Because of Mama, I grew up in the Baptist Church and loved it. On Sunday afternoons we told stories, during literary time. Best of all was B.Y.P.U. (Baptist Young People's Union) on Sunday evening. There we'd recite poems, present plays, have Bible quizzes. On Wednesday nights we had prayer meeting, and I learned the "lining out" of hymns and old-time praying.

God used stories to nurture me during those years in Youngstown, Ohio—stories in church, stories at school, stories in library books. And then, all those stories started flowing out of me. I gathered the neighborhood children around me in the playhouse that we had built of scrap boards and told them stories and more stories. I became a storytelling teacher.

In the summers my cousins and I went to visit our three aunts in Pennsylvania and West Virginia. Aunt Booby was a quiet, churchgoing woman. Aunt Cookie and Aunt Tete lived "the good life" available on the coal fields. They were both energetic, aggressive, attractive, business minded, but worldly women, who made lots of money. With the cooperation of local sheriffs, they made and sold the ever-popular moonshine. They also ran a gambling game called Georgia Skin, and took a cut from every pot.

Oh, how I admired and loved them. They loved me dearly and called me, "my dead sister's child." They shopped for me, and wore beaded dresses and carried beaded handbags. On their heads they wore large hats with drooping feathers. They allowed me to go to their parties, and I danced! The crowd encircled me and threw money on the floor for me. I loved it. But after collecting the money and eating as much as I could hold, I was sent to bed. In spite of their worldly ways, they made sure that I went to Sunday School, church, and choir practice when I stayed with them.

When my uncles moved to New Jersey, Mama and I moved back to the old house in Birmingham, Alabama. Climbing roses covered one end of the old porch, honeysuckle covered the other, and in between hung a porch swing. Mama and I were very happy there, but this peaceful phase of my life lasted only a few months. Mama became ill with cancer. Aunt Tete and Aunt Booby packed us up and took us to Aunt Booby's house in Edwight, West Virginia. It was here, in 1932, when I was thirteen, that Mama, the person I loved so dearly, passed way.

If anyone had asked me if I was a Christian then, I would have answered, "Yes." I had joined the church when a child, and I had been baptized, and I was an obedient, studious child. I loved words—Biblical and all others—and could use them well.

This part of my life ended when Aunt Booby's husband moved to Idamay, in the northern part of the state, when the local mines began working poorly. There I became active in church work, choirs, and teaching Sunday School. By this time I was in ninth grade and was bussed from Idamay to Dunbar High School in Fairmont, Virginia.

I met a girl there who greatly influenced my life. Her name was Elsie Williams. She was a teenager like myself, but different from anyone I had ever met. She was a preacher in the Church of God. Elsie was loving, human, pleasant, godly, yet not a "holier-than-thou" person. She had a certain kind of serenity, and a kind of power, about her. We were different in our spiritual lives. While I wanted to be like her, I did not really hold to some of the precepts of her church, such as—no make-up, no movies, longer dresses, much church-going. Yet, we were fast friends.

When Aunt Booby suddenly lost her sight, we moved to Baltimore. There, we visited Elder Phillip's Holiness Church and attended Israel Baptist Church. I searched for what I'd seen in the life of Elsie Williams. Finally, I decided to join the Apostolic Faith Church. When I went to the altar, they told me I had to speak in tongues to show that I had the Holy Ghost. A dear lady with unpleasant breath kept repeating "Hallelujah" in my ear. I didn't feel any emotion; I just wanted that dear lady out of my face. So, I cried out some gibberish so they would think I was speaking in tongues.

I loved the people in that church and the pastor, too, but I did not like having the church set rules for my life. I read the Bible and decided some of the church's ideas did not always agree with it. So, I continued to search.

Later, I joined Waters A.M.E. Church, still sincerely searching. That evening, as I walked down the aisle, my heart sang the old hymn, "Is your all on the altar of sacrifice laid?" That same Sunday night I went with some of the other young members to the nightclubs. I felt confused and mixed-up. I wondered what was right and what was wrong.

At Coppin State Teacher's College in Baltimore, I began to tell stories to adults as well as children. Soon churches and other groups asked me to do recitations and tell stories. I performed dramatic sketches but became known for my funny stories and monologues.

After I finished college, I became an elementary school teacher and later a school librarian. Then I met a handsome young man just returning from the Army, Ulysses Carter. After a brief courtship we married, when I was twenty-seven. I knew nothing of what marriage was really about. I didn't know marriage took hard work. I was a reader, a believer in fairy tales, in "living happily ever after." I didn't have the patience, knowledge or maturity to be a good wife. It was my fault the marriage did not last. However, we did remain friends. We had one child, Ricardo Rogers Carter. Ricky was the apple of my eye. I loved him beyond the telling. My only fear was that something would happen to him.

All this time my spirit still searched. One day I met a man who finally enabled me to make sense out of my searching—Rev. Eugene T. Grove, Sr. For the first time, I understood the difference between being a church member and a Christian. He told me that to be a Christian I must accept Christ as my Savior. I finally realized that is what Elsie Williams had—a personal faith in Christ. I found the source of her power. Through the leading of the Holy Spirit, through the acceptance of Christ, through Pastor Grove's teaching and Bible study, at last I found what I had searched for—I realized I was a sinner saved by God's grace.

I wanted to put my new-found understanding and faith to work for Christ, to help others. I knew I had not received a call to preach. I wondered what I could do. And then one day Mr. James Rouse talked to me about a community he was building, Columbia, and a church there called Kittamaquandi Community. When it opened, I attended because its people worked with those in need. During one of our small group sessions, Mr. Rouse said, "Now, it's clear that Mary's mission is to tell and act out stories."

His words startled me. I knew I had the gift of telling stories, but had not associated it with a mission. I looked at others in the Kittamaquandi Community and thought about how they used their gifts as ministries. I saw that a person could serve God outside of traditional roles. And I began to see that storytelling was my ministry. I asked God to bless others through it.

One evening, as I arrived home after one of my presentations, I learned of some class and racial troubles at a Christian Decency rally. It upset me so much to see hatred between the two groups of young people—those from the churches and those who had come to hear a famous rock singer at the rally. And I said to God, "If I have any gift of communication, I have to do more to bring love and peace to people."

I went to the school board and asked for a sabbatical leave. They said it was too late to apply, but I did anyway. I thought if it was God's will, I would get it. And I did. I volunteered my gift of communication, free of charge, to schools, libraries, and churches all during that sabbatical year. In some of those audiences, I saw African-American young people who needed a connection with their heritage. More and more I thought of Africa. I have always been Afro-centric and proud of my heritage. I wanted to know that Motherland. I wanted to go see Africa for myself. So, I mortgaged my house and went. I learned from its people, its culture—and I learned its stories. After that visit, I returned to Africa seven times. I began to incorporate some of the African folktales in my performances. I wanted to enrich all children's lives and to provide fine role models for African-American children, roles in which they could feel comfortable.

I had tried to be a good parent to Ricky. I had brought him up in the inner city because I wanted to stay and work with the people there. And I took him to church, as Mama had done for me. Ricky was a good kid, a smart kid. He attended church camps and witnessed to his faith in Christ. But, after he graduated from high school, he rebelled. He wanted to be like the other kids in the neighborhood. After some trying times, he turned his life around, finished college with honors, and started work on a master's degree in art. I was so proud.

Then, in 1978, he went into a tavern with a friend on his way to see his girlfriend. While he was there, a young woman did a terrible thing to him. (Later, she said Ricky touched her behind as he passed her. But several who were there said she lied and was angry because he didn't respond when she flirted with him.) The young woman reached into her bag, grabbed a knife, and stabbed Ricky to death. She killed my child, my only child.

If I could have gotten my hands on her at the time, I would have killed her. Later, I thought of the woman's mother and the pain she must be suffering, and I remembered that I was a Christian. So, I went to her mother's house and saw the sad condition of her family. We talked together of our losses. A few months later, the court found the young woman guilty of manslaughter and sentenced her to ten years. I pushed her out of my mind. I turned even more to my storytelling ministry.

Three years later, I was scheduled to speak at a pre-release center for women prisoners in Baltimore. The woman in charge told me the one who had killed my son was there. She wanted to see me. When I sat down with that young woman, I saw that her arrogant attitude had disappeared. She was a broken woman. Quietly, she asked if I would forgive her. Suddenly, I realized I had never thought of doing that. I had buried away any thought of her.

I sat there a moment and thought about Ricky. He was dead. I could not bring him back. I looked her in the eyes and said, "Yes, I will—because of Christ. He forgave the dying thief and the people who spat on him and those who crucified him. I can forgive you."

Two or three days later it came to me that the woman who killed my son was a godchild, sent by God to me out of all the pain. And so I did what I could to meet her biggest need—I helped her find a job, so she could be released on probation.

For the past twenty-two years I have given almost all of my time to my ministry as a performing storyteller. I try to speak the truth in beauty. People need to be told that hatred destroys, that love with self-respect is essential. They need to know that God loves us all. I use stories from my own experience, from diverse cultures, and from many writers to speak this truth.

It was through an admired author that I came to know I was a griot. In *From Slavery to Freedom,* John H. Franklin described the African griot—a French West African word meaning "folklorist-storyteller." He said griots took bits of history and traditional stories and wove them into songs and poetry, which they sang or read before kings as well as common people down through the generations. It amazed me that the thing I had been doing all my life had an African name!

Alex Haley also talked with me about griots. He came to speak at Kittamaquandi Community in 1975, and I picked him up at the airport. He was writing *Roots* then, but it was not yet in print. One evening on that visit, I prepared dinner for him in my home, and we talked. He told me that it was through an African griot that he was able to make the connection between the stories his aunts had told him of his ancestor, Kunta Kinte, and Africa. The griot remembered Kunta Kinte. At the conclusion of our conversation, Mr. Haley affirmed my storytelling ministry by naming me his "American griot."

At times, God flows through me into the audience. I can feel his spirit moving. The best word to describe it is "vibes." Once, in a Mississippi high school, as I was dramatizing the funeral sermon "Go Down Death," God's spirit rose like a wave through the audience. It brought the twelve hundred students out of their seats together, stood them up in awe. It happened in Liberia, too, during one of my presentations. At times like these, I know the Holy Spirit is working through the stories. It is Christ, not I.

I thank God daily for his gift to me—for story-telling. He has guided me in all my public presentations. He has given me the love of Christ to spread, bridges of understanding to build between groups and between individuals. And in the quiet of morning, when I pray and read the Bible, God gives me strength to grow more like our Lord.

I am alone now and growing tired. I am not afraid of dying. For a time, though, I was afraid of having a stroke. I didn't want to be helpless and drooling and a burden to someone. And then it came to me that if it happens, it will be part of God's plan and be used for my good. So, I stopped dreading it.

All that I have is a gift from God. He has blessed me with people to love and a ministry to share. I'll continue that ministry as long as I can. For, like Paul, "I count not myself to have apprehended, but this one thing I do, forgetting those things that are behind, and reaching forth unto those things which are before, I press toward the mark for the high calling of God in Christ Jesus." (Philippians 3:14 KJV)

And some wonderful day God will take me to heaven to be with Ricky and Mama and Aunt Booby and Elsie and all those other loved ones gone before me. Perhaps, after I have filled my eyes with them, we will sit down together at the feet of the Master Storyteller. I will look up into his face and drink in his words, his parables, his wonderful stories.

EULA LEWIS WILLIAMS

Eula Lewis Williams always lived in the South and made her home in Batesville, Arkansas, for most of her life. She was the mother of seven children, grandmother to fifteen, and great-grandmother to five. When she was widowed, she moved into retirement housing and lived alone. Quilting was a favorite pastime, as was writing, painting, and volunteering in her United Methodist Church and community.

"I write for the pleasure of expressing myself, but I have had two books published on a small scale. I feel honored to be included here," she said. Eula died on her eighty-first birthday, April 5, 1998.

A TIME TO FLOWER
by Eula Lewis Williams

I was born into a Methodist minister's family, the fifth of nine children. My father was a big man, weighing over two hundred pounds with a loving gleam in his eyes. He guarded us with an iron hand, keeping us from the impurities of life. I didn't have the freedom that my friends had, and that hurt me and made me feel that I wasn't one of them. When our family went to church, we had to sit still and be perfect or Papa would call us down from the pulpit, which was very embarrassing. He taught us children that we were watched by our church members daily, and we were never supposed to do anything wrong. This was very hard on me, since I was full of mischief just like any other child. But I didn't want to hurt Papa in any way, so I tried to abide by his rules.

In those days there were not enough ministers to supply all the churches in Northern Arkansas, so Papa had to preach in five small ones. People didn't have much money, so they paid him in things they did have—canned goods, home-cured meat, chickens and garden produce. Sometimes we didn't have much to eat, but we always bowed our heads and gave thanks for what we did have.

Papa had a way with children. He loved them and expressed it. Children responded to him quickly. We moved often, from one church assignment to another, and everywhere we were sent it wasn't long before our yard was full of children who had come to play. Mama and Papa watched, and sometimes took part in the fun. They taught me from my earliest years to love God and follow his ways.

In 1935 I married a young farmer, Ross Williams. He was faithful in the church and had a good singing voice. He was an honorable but poor man. Soon after our marriage we moved into a house with another couple, whom we had known for a long time. We made a garden together and shared the vegetables. I divided these just as fairly as I could, but the woman accused me of stealing and spread her accusation all through the community. My parents had taught me to be honest and to respect everybody. To be accused of such a thing was about more than I could bear.

I hurt so badly that I couldn't hold up my head around other people. I thought everybody hated me. Finally, I knew I had to talk with somebody who could understand my hurt and help me. I went to old "Aunt" Lina. She was a hard-working, simple woman, and I always loved to visit her. When I went to her with my problem she listened to me and talked with me in a soft voice. She assured me that I was not hated, and that my accuser was acting in such a way that others would soon see the wrong. I felt such great relief.

My married life was filled with seven children and hard work. As a farmer's wife I had jobs to do the year around. My babies took up a big part of my life, and on top of that I took care of the house and garden, milked the cows, and canned everything I could. We raised nearly everything that we ate. If we hadn't, we would've gone hungry. The children soon learned that they had responsibilities and to carry their part in making a living.

We had many joys together. One afternoon in late summer Ross said he was going fishing in the White River, and that we could all go with him in the wagon. It was our first vehicle and all of us were so proud of it. At the river I watched over the little ones as they played in the sand, while Ross and the older boys baited the trotline. As dark approached we loaded everything into the wagon and the kids settled down. Before we got home it was so dark Ross couldn't see the road, but he wasn't worried at all. He just gave the horses free reign and said they would take us home safely, and they did, too. Late that night Ross and I cleaned and salted the fish down so they would keep until the next day. I fell asleep feeling grateful to God for all my joys.

We taught the children to have respect in all their dealings and especially toward God. We worked together and played together and went to church together. Each Sunday at Campground Methodist I worked with small children and learned as much from them as they did from me. Kindergarten was my favorite age to teach. They were in their formative years, and I prayed that I could plant a little seed in their minds that would grow to produce a Christian person.

At home, while I took care of my six boys I often dreamed of having a baby girl, too. So, when I found I was pregnant again, I began to pray for a little girl. Every day I asked God to grant me one. In the first moment after the baby was delivered the doctor said I had another boy. And then he turned it over. It was a girl! I laughed and cried at the same time. I loved to cuddle and hold her close. As she grew she helped me in everything I did. When I washed dishes she would prop a song book up and we sang together, even though she couldn't read. I will always believe that God meant for me to have Darlene, although I had to wait a long time for her.

As the years rolled along, the children all grew up and married. I filled my days with gardening and canning and church work. Our children and grandchildren came by regularly. Many Sundays after church they all gathered at our house to eat dinner together. All but our son David, for he had married a fine girl in Illinois and worked in her family's business up there.

Then in 1974 tragedy struck. Doctors found a tumor embedded deep in David's brain. We waited by the phone after the surgery, but when his wife Peggy called she had bad news — they couldn't get all the cancer. It just broke my heart. The doctors did all they knew to do, but he got worse. Ross and I drove up there to help Peggy, and took turns going to the hospital to be with David.

He was soon helpless. When I fed him and could get him to eat a few bites, I was overjoyed. I just knew he was getting better. I kept praying, and wouldn't let myself see him changing from a big, healthy, strong man to one who was so weak he couldn't even move by himself. Every night I begged God for a miracle. I knew he was able to do it and would do it, for David was a young father with years ahead of him. God would give back his healthy body. But David got weaker and weaker until his life was gone.

At the funeral home I looked at my beautiful son for the last time, and everything he had done in his life passed before me like a movie. It was nearly more than I could bear. I stood there paralyzed and couldn't move away. Why had God taken him? It wasn't fair! It just wasn't right. I had thought God was a just God, but he wasn't.

After we returned home I kept David's pictures with me every hour of the day. I looked at them all the time, trying to imagine that he was still a big, robust healthy father to his two children. I wouldn't talk about his death, and couldn't bring myself to cook any of the foods he had liked so much. I just couldn't. My hurt was too deep. I couldn't pray as I always had, for I was bitter.

I struggled a long time, until one day I simply told myself that I had to face the fact that David was gone and life was going on as usual. I put his pictures away and turned my thoughts to my living children. I realized that I was hurting myself and everyone around me. Nothing could bring my son back, but I could live in sweet memories of him while getting back to those around me. Once I had made this decision it was easier to talk of my loss, and finally I could cook the dishes that David had loved. At times my grieving caught up with me again, but then I would have a good cry and get it out of my system. I felt easier toward God.

A few years later, while I was in my sixties, I became ill. After many examinations the doctor still couldn't find out what my trouble was. I got worse and couldn't be up very long at a time. As I got weaker I lost interest in whether I lived or died. My thoughts sank to a low ebb.

One afternoon as I lay on the couch, it suddenly came to me that I was trying to do everything myself. I began to pray for God to take my life over. I gave myself completely to him, telling him he could do whatever he wanted with me. If I died it was okay. If I lived it was okay. I was in his hands. Immediately a peace washed over me. It was wonderful and filled me up completely. I thought I had lived a Christian life, but I had never experienced such a peace before. It stayed with me, and any time I felt discouraged I thought back to that wonder.

Soon they found what was wrong with me. I had Cushings Disease, a tumor on my pituitary gland, which was very serious. But when I went into surgery I was as happy as I could be. I wasn't worried about a thing. I knew God was with me whether I lived or died. The surgery was successful, but I was left with a weak leg and had to walk with a cane.

However, I stayed busy cooking for Ross and putting up food from the garden. Like always, he tried to shield me from the problems and concerns that came up. He took care of everything. He was wise and steady and worked happily around the place, pruning fruit trees and tending the blueberry patch.

Sometime in 1988 I noticed a mole on Ross' shoulder was changing size, and asked him to see a doctor. When he did go, the doctor said it was a fast-growing cancer. After they removed it, he worked outside for a time, but soon felt very sick. He lay on the couch and talked with the children when he had the strength. Then he was in such pain that he stayed in bed with his eyes closed and didn't talk with anyone. He didn't fight to live, but realized that he couldn't get any better, so he waited for his time to go. A nurse came every day to check on him. I knew he was in God's hands.

Some of the children, and daughters-in-law, helped take care of him, for I could not help at all. Back pain, which ran down my leg, kept me in bed in another room. The pain grew more intense every day until I thought I couldn't stand any more. Nothing I took relieved me from the pain. I wanted to be with Ross but couldn't get out of bed. It seemed that I was suffering right alongside him.

One day I couldn't stand being separated from him anymore. I had to tell him that I cared that he was suffering so much. So I got the family to help me into a wheelchair and roll me into his bedroom. There he lay with his eyes closed, not saying anything. I rolled over close to the bed and reached for his hand. He clasped mine and we stayed this way for a long time; neither of us could say a word. It wasn't necessary—our hands touching said it all. He knew I cared. It was the last time I saw him alive.

For weeks after the grave side service I felt guilty over not being able to take care of him in the last weeks of his life, but the children kept telling me he had understood. The house was so empty without him. Gradually, my back got better, but I was not able to do all the housework. What would happen to me now? Here I was, living out in the country, not even able to build a fire in the fireplace. My family disagreed about what was best for me.

For some time, even before Ross died, our family had begun to have trouble. We had always been close and loved each other, but I saw the children turning against one another. To see the ones that I loved having trouble among themselves broke my heart. I cried, and prayed for help in getting my family back together. No matter what I did, though, it didn't work.

Some time before, one of our sons had agreed to give Ross and me a payment on our place each month to help us meet our living expenses, in exchange for the deed to our place. But after Ross died our son stopped making payments. He told me I could stay in my house if I would do what he wanted me to, and that he would take care of me. However, because he was angry with his brothers and sister, he told me that as long as I lived there the other children could not come on the property.

I wanted my home to be a place where all my family could come together again, and I also wanted to be able to make my own decisions. What was I to do? Where was Ross when I needed him the most? I was alone and confused. I prayed and cried.

For days I paced the floor, supported by my cane, and prayed. Then one day I suddenly heard God's voice inside of me say, "Move out." Again, he said, "Move out now." That afternoon I began to pack a few small things. It broke my heart to leave. Ross had built that house with his own hands, with the help of our boys. We had celebrated our fiftieth wedding anniversary there. I would be leaving so much of him, and happier family times. But I knew I was making the right choice, God was leading me to move. My confidence grew.

My son was furious when I told him my decision. I continued trying to reconcile with him, but he would not. Finally, I sadly accepted that I could not make him understand that I had to take charge of my own life now.

Another of my sons asked me to stay with him until I found a place to live. My daughter helped me find a vacancy in a housing addition at the edge of town. It was small and just right for me!

Yet, it was strange to live in a new place. I missed the open farmlands and my old neighbors, although I got a ride out there each Sunday to attend my church. Living in town, I found I had a lot of time on my hands. I busied myself with quilting and different kinds of handiwork. Soon, I learned that a bus came to pick up the senior citizens in our housing addition. It took them downtown, or to the Senior Center on the other side of town. I started asking questions about what there was to do at the Center. And my life began to change. To my surprise, I found that a writing class was starting at the Area Agency on Aging complex, and that the bus would take me there. I got all excited.

And then, there I was sitting in the class with a wonderful instructor. In class we wrote on subjects that were sprung on us at the spur of the moment. I really enjoyed this and found that I could express myself in what I wrote. I also made new friends who had the same interests that I did. We all became very close —like family. We greeted each other with a hug, and when our class ended we hugged each other again. Everyone needs love all the time, but when we advance in age, and are more or less alone, love means so much, both to give and receive. I could feel God loving me through all those people around me.

This writing class was, and still is, an influence on my life. My new friends' writings are an inspiration to me. Because of the class, I entered a Senior Citizens' essay contest that included the whole state. It was a new experience for me, but I won third place in the state with my essay. It was the first award I had ever been given. Two of my sons took me to Little Rock, where I went up on the stage and received my certificate. Everyone applauded. But I think the most important effect of my essay was the help it gave me in dealing with my grief over Ross' death. I had titled it "Death: New Life," and talked about new beginnings.

The next year I entered the contest again and won first place for my essay titled "My Mother's Hands." After I received the award, it came very clear to me that if I stop trying new things, I may miss the blessings that God offers me.

Other opportunities have opened for me, and I try to do everything that comes my way. I joined a drama group which performed skits for local nursing homes, community centers, and schools. We wore red shirts printed with our logo, "I Can Do That!"

I also joined an art class. I wanted to learn to sketch in order to draw illustrations for books I plan to write. I started out sketching with a pencil, and enjoyed it. I'll never be an artist, but I hope to get better as time goes on.

I get to travel some now, too. For months and months I saved for a dream trip on Amtrak last year. My eldest son went with me. We rode from Chicago to the northern states and on to Washington, Oregon, and down the coast in California. I nearly wore my eyes out from looking so much. It was amazing to see all those wondrous things God created. Sometimes the beauty brought tears to my eyes.

The senior citizens in my town make short trips together, and I go on every one. This summer I also made a six-week-long trip to visit kinfolk, which took me to Kentucky, Illinois and Iowa. What a vast, beautiful world God has created for us to enjoy.

Since I lost Ross and moved into Batesville, I have found there is no one but me. I don't want to sound selfish, but all through my life I had others to consider and take care of. Now they are all living productive lives on their own. I can do a little living for myself. I grab every opportunity that comes my way. I don't waste time feeling sorry for my losses or worrying about things I can't do.

I believe God wants me to live and learn every day. And he wants me to have faith in myself, so I can do things I never dreamed I could in my younger years. Each day is a gift. How I use this gift is left up to me and I want to live it to the fullest. Someone may be looking my way, and I want to show them how good life is with God.

Njoki McElroy

Njoki McElroy, Ph.D., is a storyteller, folklorist, university adjunct professor, playwright, poet, and short story writer. A mother and grandmother, she is a fifth generation Texan. She was born, bred, and educated through Dallas public schools; moved north after obtaining a bachelor's degree from Xavier University-New Orleans; and returned to the South as a resident in 1985. Njoki is president of Black Fox Enterprises, Founder/Director of Back Home with The Folk Festival, and co-founder of "Let's Talk: The Real Deal," storytelling workshops for teen girls at risk.

"'Keepers of the Faith' was written in honor of my ancestors who lived in an oppressive reality of hostility, indignities, and terrors, yet managed to keep their journeys on course. I can therefore stand tall because their strength, wisdom, and endurance provide the shoulders that I now stand on."

KEEPERS OF THE FAITH

by Njoki McElroy

I've been sick but God bro't me.
I've been in trouble but God bro't me.
I've been friendless but God bro't me.
Don't believe He bro't me this far
    Just to leave me.
I don't feel no ways tired
I come too far from where I started from
Nobody told me the road would be easy
I don't believe He bro't me this far
    To leave me.

                      –Negro Spiritual

The Santa Fe train glided into the Gainesville, Texas, station and huffed to a stop. I was traveling with my three little sons—David (six months), Phillip (two years), and Ronald (four). We had ridden all day and all night, confined in the FOR COLORED ONLY car. The porter was now on the platform helping me down the iron steps and into the warm embraces of Mom and Dad and an entourage of family friends. In the middle of January, the strong Texas sun embraced us, too.

A fire had wiped us out in Chicago, and I was seeking temporary refuge with my folks. We would spend some of our sojourn in Dallas at my parents' home but most of our time at "Granpa" Jeff and "Granma" Julia's in Sherman.

It was 1951, and I had been living in Chicago five and a half years. In 1945, I had received a B.S. degree from Xavier University in New Orleans. My graduation present from Granma Julia had been a round trip ticket from Dallas to Chicago to visit my Xavier roommate and her parents, Mama T and Papa T. I was to visit two weeks and return home. At the time of my departure, Dad was in a veteran's hospital at Muskogee, Oklahoma, and Mom suffered from severe migraines. I was their only, and very protected, child. On one level I wanted to be there for my parents, and on another level, I wanted to flee the nest and the mean-spirited South and fly to freedom in the North.

Mama T and Papa T were considered upper class. They lived well, due to Papa T's job as a head steward for the Illinois Central Dining Car Services. His run was between Chicago and New Orleans. When he was home, he prepared special gourmet meals and entertained us with lively repartee. Mama T had a social agenda that included bridge, poker parties, and frequent free trips to anyplace she wanted to go. They were all convinced that better opportunities awaited me in Chicago, so they waged a serious effort to encourage me to stay.

At the time, Chicago's booming, unskilled labor market was pulling Black people from the rural South at a rate of over one thousand a month. Sharecroppers, who were being pushed from the land and being replaced by cotton-picking machines, came to Chicago looking for the promised land. Black female domestics, weary from years of cruel exploitation, shed their aprons and bandannas and joined the great migration. Since no members of my family had migrated, we really had no tangible evidence that life was better up North, but I believed it anyway.

Five generations back, my foreparents had become landowners during Reconstruction. Strongly rooted in Texas, they passed on these beliefs: deep roots make strong trees; rolling stones gather no moss; Blacks should not move away from their spiritual centers, their southern roots; the North was too fast, too worldly; Blacks did things in the North that they would never think of doing in the South.

I wore those values like a second skin until the summer of my graduation from Xavier, the heat of Texas oppression finally stifled and overwhelmed me. Mean-spirited whites focused heavily on ways to deny Black people their human dignity. FOR COLORED and FOR WHITE signs placed at every turn were ugly reminders of white supremacy and Black subjugation. It troubled me to see that no matter how hard all my family and friends worked to be faithful servants of the Lord, there was no glimmer of hope that matters of race and color would change.

After my two week visit in Chicago, I decided to remain there. I knew that only my promise to pursue graduate studies would soften the blow for my family. At the time, Texas had a program which paid for Blacks to attend out-of-state universities. It was a compensatory program to keep them from trying to enter Texas institutes of higher learning, but it did provide low-cost educations for Blacks. Dad had introduced me to this plan before I graduated from Xavier. He believed the prerequisites for Black success were education, more education, and delayed sexual gratification. I held fast to Dad's admonitions until the day I met Clenan McElroy. He was tall, handsome, witty, brilliant, and charming. He had just returned from serving in the all-Black Tuskegee Air Force unit. He wore an officer's uniform, decorated with gleaming airplane wings and insignias. He was such a marvel that he attracted a following of neighborhood kids like the Pied Piper. Six months after meeting, we married. My Dad was absolutely crushed. "What about your graduate studies? And why the rush to get married?" he asked. We didn't dare tell him that six months later he would be a grandfather.

Granma Julia always said that if you make your bed hard, you have to lie in it. It wasn't long before I understood the meaning of the proverb very clearly. It was my quick decision to get married instead of pursuing graduate studies that forced me to lie in a very hard bed. Social and economic constraints also put rocks in our bed. As a civilian, Mac had high hopes of becoming a commercial pilot, but it was to be many years later before Blacks were hired as pilots.

The worst constraint we suffered was the lack of decent housing. Chicago's segregated racial policies held the majority of Blacks in a tight vise of crowded ghetto conditions. Slum landlords cut large apartments into small kitchenettes where five to six families shared one kitchen and one bath. Our first apartment after our marriage was in a dilapidated two story house which violated every health and safety code on the books. Three years later in 1949, we "progressed" to a basement apartment which was situated next to the furnace room.

Around 6:00 p.m. on a frigid evening in the middle of December, a fire spread from the furnace room and engulfed our apartment. A fire is a disaster anytime of year, but absolutely devastating in a sub-zero Chicago winter. Mac was at the barber shop, close enough to hear the fire trucks but unaware it was our catastrophe. Fortunately, I was able to get our three little fellows out safely through the one exit in the front of the apartment.

We received kindness from a stranger that night when Mrs. Alexander took us into her home. A single parent who supported six children with an abundance of faith and a domestic's meager salary, she shared her limited resources with us expansively and graciously. In the evening we gathered around the big dining room table, and she lifted our spirits with her wonderful stories of surviving in Chicago.

Up to the time of the fire, Mac and I had been working very hard to develop a radio and television sales and repair business. We had financed the enterprise from our own resources. I worked through each pregnancy as a substitute teacher in the Chicago schools, taking little time for the frequent births. We deposited my checks and lived on Mac's earnings. We used our savings to open the business. Our decision to sell television sets in the late 1940s was somewhat premature. Most families, struggling to cover basics, could not afford the luxury of a television. Every day curious lookers came to our store, but sales were few.

In the meantime, we had invested all our savings in the business, and our financial future was indeed dismal. But Mac had a tenacious interest in entrepreneurship, probably as a result of his childhood membership in Marcus Garvey's UNIA, the Universal Negro Improvement Association. Mac believed intensely that as Blacks we had to work a long-term plan for economic success and freedom. He said that we would keep the faith—regardless of reversals and disruptions. Through the ensuing years we did.

Being home again with my parents and grandparents after the fire in 1951 was like waking up after a terrible nightmare. I savored the feeling of safety and security that my grandparents' home had always provided. I went through each room seeing, smelling, hearing vivid images from my childhood. As a child I had spent the school year with my parents in Dallas, but the magic and wonder of my life came from the summers I spent in Sherman with Granma Julia and Granpa Jeff.

They lived at 1012 Natchez off the main thoroughfare, accessible via foot bridge on one end and vehicle bridge on the other. Situated on three acres, their home was storybook beautiful, a big Victorian house with jewel-colored, stained-glass squares framing the door, and a wrap-around porch. The entire place was like a village, with Granpa Jeff the chief. "Brother Washington," as others called him, was advisor, counselor, mediator, et al. After purchasing the property in the late 1890s, Granpa Jeff had faced the terrorizing reality that whites placed a low value on Black life and property. Surrounded by such a hostile environment, he lived in a state of preparedness. It was no secret that he maintained ample supplies of ammunition and weapons. During the race riot of 1930, their home had become a refuge for all those who needed protection against the lynch mob.

In the late nineteenth century and prior to 1930, because of the excellent railroad system, cotton industry, and intellectual influence of three colleges, Sherman was designated one of the more progressive and civilized towns in Texas. A remarkable number of educated and professional Blacks were drawn to the town. They had journeyed through the difficult days of the Reconstruction Period, and they looked forward to the rewards of hard work in Sherman. Grandpa Jeff and Grandma Julia were the son and daughter of ex slaves. It was no small feat that in just one generation they had established a stable middle class family. Along Mulberry Street, near downtown, Blacks developed a vital business district which consisted of services, retail businesses, a theater, and professional services such as doctors, lawyers, pharmacists, and morticians. Segregation and racial policies forced Blacks to bond as a community and support one another. Prosperity in Sherman's Black community was obvious—they dressed in the latest fashions, lived in well-appointed homes, rode in beautiful horse-driven buggies and T-Model Fords. However, as the depression era approached, the cotton industry declined, and whites (particularly those from surrounding small farms) began to intensify their jealousies and hostilities towards Blacks. While I did not personally experience the events of the 1930 riot, the stories of what happened at 1012 Natchez have remained intensely vivid and formed a permanent part of my ancestral memory. 1012 Natchez represented what was for me the best of times and the worst of times. It was a haven of refuge—a beautiful safe place surrounded by a stifling, segregated, mean world.

When John Hughes, a Black man, was brought to the Sherman jail, accused of raping a white farmer's wife, the tension became palpable. On May 9, a mob gathered and attempted to take him from the courthouse. When that attempt was foiled, they returned after the courthouse was closed. They dynamited the vault area where John Hughes was locked up, pulled his body from the wreckage, tied him to the back of a car, and dragged him through the Black community. Later that night they hanged him from a tree limb on Mulberry street, castrated and burned him, and proceeded to torch all of the businesses, professional offices, funeral parlors, and surrounding homes.

As the mob turned Sherman into the lower level of hell, Granpa Jeff mobilized his forces, and the men guarded 1012 Natchez. His orders were to shoot first and ask questions later. The women prayed, sang, and prepared meals. The smoke house was well-stocked with meats, the storm cellar housed shelves of preserved fruits and vegetables, and Nellie the cow supplied plenty of fresh milk and butter. No one seeking refuge would go hungry or be turned away.

The Texas Rangers came into Sherman and restored order, but the Black community never regained its earlier pride and dignity. The Mulberry street businesses were lost forever. Dreams and aspirations, collectively and individually, vanished in the billowing smoke of the riot. Several years later when I was five or six years old, I began to spend long periods at 1012 Natchez and its neighboring community. At an early age I became aware of the enormous spiritual power in Black people's lives, no matter how diverse their religious beliefs and practices.

From my constant childhood companions Booder and Buddy, who lived in a three-generation matriarchal family, I learned about the Spiritualist/Sanctified religion. The oldest family member was Flint Mama, great-grandmother, who in her eighties and nineties went fishing every day, usually by herself. Perhaps the secret of her vigorous longevity had to do with the layers and layers of petticoats and odd assortments of clothes that she wore even in hot summers. She and the others who called themselves the Sanctified expressed their spiritual joy in holy dance and very loud music. I loved the spontaneity of their spirituality. At any time of day or night when the spirit hit them, the living room would shake and rattle, and the sounds would vibrate out of the house, out on the air waves over Natchez, across Travis Street, up, over and beyond.

Granma Julia, who was a Harmony Baptist, had doubts about the appropriateness of the Sanctified's use of secular-sounding music. She declared that she could not tell the difference between their emotional release and that of those who frequented the juke joint honky-tonk. The holy dances, she thought, were much too exuberant for *spiritual* joy. Instead, Granma Julia and her friends sang spirituals and call-and-response versions of the One Hundred Hymn Book. They always sang when they did chores, whether collectively or individually. They did not concern themselves with the key, nor were they self-conscious about their voices. In a high-pitched voice, Granma Julia would lead in a half-song, half-talk, and the souls of the faithful would be touched. Some cried or shouted:

> I heard the voice of Jesus say,
> Come unto me and rest
> Lay down thou weary one
> Lay down thy head upon my breast.

Granpa Jeff, on the other hand, was Payne Chapel African Methodist Episcopal. Every morning during the week he led family prayer in the dining room before breakfast. On Sundays, the parlor was the setting for family prayer. Wonderful smells of cornmeal, griddle cakes, home-cured ham, and coffee mingled with Old English-polished mahogany and leather. Then Granpa Jeff's deep melodious voice and the poetic imagery in his prayer would linger long afterwards in the recesses of my mind:

> Oh Father, we come this morning with our knees bowed and our bodies bent before the throne of grace. We come this morning, Lord, like empty buckets before a full fountain. We realize that many who are better by nature than we are by practice have passed on into the great beyond. But we are grateful to you, oh Lord, that we awoke this morning and our bed was not a cooling board and our sheet was not a winding shroud.

During my 1951 sojourn at 1012 Natchez, we followed Granpa Jeff's prayer rituals every day. As our stay lengthened, he added us to his prayers, imploring God's help to get us back on our feet. On my part, I began to wonder if God was listening, because our situation worsened before it got better. Two months after the fire and my departure from Chicago, Mac, who had stayed behind to try to keep the business going, began to suffer leg problems. Due to a delay in correct diagnosis and prompt treatment, he developed blood clots and ulcerated varicose veins. By the time he recovered, our television business had fallen into a state of non-recovery. After investing so much of ourselves in the enterprise, it was difficult to give up our dream. At the time there were no options available to us. With funds depleted and no income, I had to find work. Even with my college degree, the only job I could get was one as a part-time domestic, preparing noon meals for Ms. Wheat, an elderly white woman who lived on the periphery of Natchez. Humbled by earning only five dollars per week, I learned how to be grateful for small things and how to stretch a dollar—old Black magic tricks.

The boys and I had been in Texas six months when at last the time came to return North. Mac had recovered from his illness and found a job and a decent apartment in Gary, Indiana. It was the first week in May when we waved our last goodbyes from the windows of the Santa Fe train. Just like the Egyptian Phoenix, we had risen from the ashes, and we were starting a new phase of our lives. During our sojourn, the boys had thrived on plenty of space for play and discovery. We had also benefitted from the love and support of my parents with frequent trips to their home in Dallas.

Six years later, 1012 Natchez was designated for removal to make way for an interstate highway. Progress sans human concern kills. When Granpa Jeff was no longer able to defend his sanctuary, he joined the ancestors. Granma Julia lived a year after her removal from 1012 Natchez.

On occasion when I'm asked to name my role models, I invariably name my foreparents. It was their capacity to constantly go beyond themselves to help others that has most profoundly influenced my spiritual journey. Consequently, I experience the strongest sensations of transcendence when I reach beyond the concerns of my own life to help a fellow traveler. For instance, a friend since childhood recently suffered a brain aneurysm which resulted in impairment of vision, motor, speech, and cognitive skills. After releasing him from the hospital, the doctor recommended twenty-four-hour rehabilitation center therapy. With my belief that healing is much more than mechanics, I altered my calendar for six weeks and brought my friend to my home. In the role of twenty-four hour caretaker, I was cook, nutritionist, therapist, teacher, poet/storyteller, and most of all, provided large doses of laughter.

In six weeks, my friend regained most of his brain connections. The doctors say his recovery has been remarkable. To those who say he was lucky to have me, I relate that the benefits I received were astonishing. For throughout the experience, I felt the spirits of Mom and Granma Julia supplying the fuel to energize my spirit. It appears that as we (Mom, Granma Julia, and I) helped my friend heal and recover, I was able to reach beyond the usual definition of myself. As a result I have been restored physically, emotionally, and spiritually. This for me is the essence of spirituality.

Lois Gill Rippetoe

Born into a family of Southern heritage, Lois now lives in New Mexico. She is a member of the Conservative Baptist church, and has experience in a variety of volunteer positions. A retired homemaker, she now lives alone in an independent-living apartment, and has a grown son and daughter. Her son, Dexter, is a deacon and teacher in his church. Her daughter, Twyla Wright, also has a story in this collection. Lois says, "I have always found life exciting and adventurous."

I WILL LIFT UP MINE EYES
by Lois Gill Rippetoe

My grandparents owned a ranch on Antelope Flat, under the West Texas caprock. There, in their ranch house, I made my appearance on earth, one of twin girls. Three years later my father moved us to Colorado to homestead a half-section of land.

We lived in a tiny shack while Dad and the boys dug two large cellars, covering them with cedar poles and two feet of dirt to make a snug home for us. Soon, we moved into the larger one. A pot of beans brought all six of us children around the family table in the evenings. A kerosene lamp threw shadows on Dad as he bowed his head before supper. "Lord, receive our thanks for these and all other blessings," he said, his voice steady and humble. He never varied this simple prayer during his long life. After supper we always gathered around Dad to hear him read a chapter from the Bible.

During one of those readings, I discovered I had a personal guardian angel. At four years of age, I was sure that Dad was my protector, sure that God listened to him, and now I was sure that I had an angel to watch over me, even though I didn't know where it was. Each night Dad ended the reading with the same heartfelt prayer, "Lord, keep us through the night. Amen."

Over the next four years we all worked to clear the sagebrush, plow the land, and plant the crops. A huge garden fed us. There were no stores or telephones or schools or churches within twenty-five miles of us. But by the time I was six, Dad and neighboring farmers built a school house for the twelve students in the elementary grades. Church, though, was foreign to me.

My spirit continued to be fed by my dad. But most wonderful of all—I had located my own guardian angel. Even though I couldn't actually see it, I felt its gentle, protective presence like a warmth on my shoulder. It came to light there each time I felt afraid. This friend did not fail me.

Just before I turned eight years old, Dad decided to go back to Texas for an extended time. He rented our Colorado homestead to a neighbor. On the last day of April, 1923, neighbors from miles around gathered at our farm for an auction of farm equipment and household goods. Our two covered wagons stood in the yard, filled with trunks of clothing, dishes, pots and pans, and feather beds. But many of our precious things had to be sold.

I picked up an old purse which held the few personal treasures I was allowed to take and hid in an old cedar tree, away from the milling people. I clutched my treasures and called to my angel. When I felt its comforting presence, I hummed to it, which was the language I used to tell my feelings; I half-sang my words in a low voice. And like always, my angel calmed my fear.

A day later we took to the road, traveling about thirty miles a day. My twin and I ran beside the wagons until we grew too tired, then climbed up in the wagon with Dad and Mom. I loved every mile. We passed through Durango, Pagosa Springs, and over Wolf Creek Pass at a 9,000-foot elevation. The horses snorted and stomped as the wagons slowly wound around the knife-edge dirt road.

For the next month we traveled like early pioneers, stopping each Sunday to rest. We camped at sunset by a stream of water wherever possible. Mom cooked supper for all eight of us over a campfire, and baked biscuits in the Dutch oven covered with hot coals. When she called us to eat, we gathered around the fire with plates in hand, while Dad took his hat off and said, "Lord, receive our thanks. . . ." I hugged myself with gratitude and felt my angel sitting soft on my shoulder. My world was still safe, even if it was contained in two wagons.

One month after leaving the homestead, our wagons lumbered into Antelope Flat, Texas—the place of my birth. Relatives of all ages ran to meet us. After a month-long visit there, we once again climbed into our wagons, this time heading east toward Dad's parents' home in Wellington.

On the second day out, we pulled into a Primitive Baptist Associational Camp Meeting at Shamrock, Texas. I had never seen such a thing. People and wagons and cars were everywhere! A large brush arbor shaded long benches; big iron pots hung over camp-fires, boiling with beef stew and corn. Bowls of food dotted a long table.

That afternoon I sat on a bench under the brush arbor and listened to the preachers speak. In between the sermons, people sang hymns. The songs drew me like a magnet—most sung in the minor key, without musical instruments, their words sounding like the words my dad had read to us from the Psalms. I had never attended a religious service before in all my eight years.

And then a young preacher named Wyatt Smart got up to preach—quiet, sincere. Suddenly I knew that God, Almighty God who listened to my dad, must be near. He was more than my angel. Brother Smart's gentle, loving, and sure voice captivated me. He was speaking for God! He became my spiritual mentor right then in that arbor and continued to be from then on.

After we reached my grandparents' home, Dad rented a cotton farm four miles from Wellington. It was there that my Grandma Rhea died from a stroke. They laid her out in our living room. Family members arrived, but I fled to the yard.

Mom came out to get me. "Come in and tell your grandma goodbye," she said. I dared not disobey, but, oh, I did not want to go see a dead person. Slowly, I moved near the casket. My grandma lay chalky white, still and dead. An older cousin of mine stroked her white hair and kissed her cheek. I shuddered. I could not feel my angel's presence, and I asked inside, "God, where are you? I'm scared!" There was no answer.

After four years on the cotton farm, Dad decided to move us back to the homestead in Colorado, and Wyatt Smart was going to move his family there, too. We would have a church! When we arrived on the homestead, Dad once again put in crops and expanded the frame farmhouse. We got up at sunrise, ate breakfast, and did our chores. As a young teen, my summers were filled with field work, canning hundreds of quarts of food, and cooking for harvest hands.

After I finished my work and put the dishes away, I often slipped away alone to sit on the west porch just as the sun went down over the Blue Mountains. The sky turned from one brilliant color to another—mauve, pink, apricot and gold. I sat still, lost in joyous ecstasy, for without a doubt God was alive in the sunset. My spirit soared.

As if from a distance I could hear sounds inside the house—the creaking of my dad's rocking chair, the turning of Mom's quilting frame, and the noisy laughter of my brothers and sisters. Family security framed me while I worshiped God on the horizon.

On Sundays we hitched up the horses to the light spring wagon and drove to the school house where Brother Smart preached. Neighbors came from miles around. One Sunday when I was fourteen, just after the sermon began, I suddenly felt a joyous touch—like the touch of God. I went to Brother Smart and asked for baptism. The church members all rode over to our stock pond, where they stood on the dirt bank and sang hymns. Brother Smart immersed me in the muddy water. I prepared for a joyous euphoria to descend from heaven. But it didn't. I just felt wet. It bothered me.

Over the next few years I often slipped off to the large, flat rock that hung over the canyon rim north of our homestead. I would sit there and dangle my legs over the canyon. Below snaked the wild Dolores River, flowing to somewhere I could only imagine. I talked out loud to God there. My guardian angel had gradually disappeared with the years, but God had grown more and more real to me. "Oh, God, what is out there in the big world? I want to fly away and see," I prayed.

Whether I was harnessing a team of horses to harrow a field, riding the cultivator in the corn field, or cooking breakfast, I sang my prayers to God. I didn't have a particularly good voice, but it came natural for me to sing my words to him.

He never spoke to me, and I never asked him to, but I knew he was with me in that place. He was God Almighty, God of Love, not just over my shoulder or beside me, but surrounding me with his invisible presence. He was my best friend.

After I was baptized and joined our Primitive Baptist church, I felt confined by its strict rules. Although they believed salvation was predestined, they excommunicated members for what they considered unseemly behavior, such as dancing, bad language, and visiting another church. I loved to attend the neighborhood play-parties and regretted joining the church.

At the end of my teen years, Paul Gill came from Texas to visit his cousins, who were our neighbors. Soon he and I fell in love and decided to marry, but there wasn't much romance. We made our first home in a half-dugout on the edge of Dad's homestead. Within a few months Paul decided to move north, to some unchosen, unknown place. He traded a horse and cow for an old Roosevelt car, and I packed our few things into it. As we drove away from my folks' place, the security of my childhood slipped away, and I felt a need for God's assurance. Softly, under the rattle of the car's engine, I hummed to God, "Lord, take this car where you want us to go. Take us safely on our way." I looked over at Paul, but he didn't seem to hear me, so I continued to hum my prayer.

We arrived in Winchester, Idaho, a small sawmill town. God was good to us there, giving Paul a job, and—a year later—our own baby girl. I was so full of joy that I named her Twyla Joy. We returned to Colorado two years after we left. Paul built a house from railroad cross-ties and worked at various jobs. Two years more and God gave us a baby boy—Clay Dexter. My heart was complete.

During World War II, Paul worked in the shipyards in Richmond, California. No housing was available, so we moved into my sister's tiny garage near there. Then I looked for a church. But there were no Primitive Baptist churches to be found! I searched and prayed. Over and over I remembered my parents' teaching that all other churches were of the world, not God's choice for his elect. For two years I constantly asked God to show me which church to attend. I wanted to be sure it was the right one.

One night, I got up to quiet the baby and returned to lie down. Suddenly, a man appeared beside my bed—a shadowy man. I felt no fear. The man held out a hand for me. I looked down at my sleeping husband and hesitated, then rose and reached for the outstretched hand, which led me across the room. There, covering the entire wall, was a scene—a rolling green meadow, trees, and a flowing stream of water. Cattle grazed in the pasture. A white cloud of light filled the ceiling. From it a mighty voice said, "The church of the Living God!" Gradually, it disappeared.

I found myself sitting back on the edge of the bed—but I wasn't the same person. Joy filled my whole being. I could not contain it.

I woke my husband and told him what had happened. He looked at me for a moment, then said, "Go to sleep," but I couldn't, for the joy consumed me.

The joyous euphoria gradually quieted after two weeks, but I can still feel it anytime I say, "The church of the Living God." The assurance stayed with me. God was alive. He cared for me. And I knew there was no single, right, denomination.

We returned to Colorado before the end of the war and then moved on to Arizona where we joined a Northern Baptist church. During our five years there, I began a closer walk with God in the fellowship of Christian friends. I gained a bit of self-confidence and lost some feelings of inferiority from earlier years.

In 1953 we moved to the timbered hills of Prescott, Arizona; I was thirty-eight. My spiritual and personal development reached a high point there. I loved sharing activities and feelings with my two teenage children. These years were fulfilling "Mother Years." Our family attended a Conservative Baptist church, which enriched my life. I reached out to new friends and found many avenues of service, filling positions as deaconess, member of the Christian Education Committee, and—most fulfilling of all—leader of the church Pioneer Girls.

In the girl's club work I began timidly to pray aloud in a group. Although I had learned in the church of my childhood that women should not pray in public, these girls needed leadership, and I needed to be their help. The girls became my stepping stones in prayer. And what fun I had with them—picnics, slumber parties, service projects!

Life in Prescott was gratifying and busy. Yet I often walked a tight rope in my marriage. My husband and I could not communicate. The need for quiet and for God often called me to the porch, where I looked at the setting sun evening after evening. The reds, golds and purples quieted my soul—a reminder of my childhood when I had watched that same sun give those colors to the sky and mountains.

Paul retired from his building business in Prescott, and we moved into the Arizona desert hills. Our marriage continued to be strained. One evening my heart began to race out of control. Pressure, tight and constricting, bore down on my chest. Paul put me in the car and raced the forty miles to Phoenix to the nearest hospital. Calm, I told him not to drive too fast, that I was in God's hands—perfectly safe. I thought I was near death, and it was okay. I had prayed to die in that manner. I did not call out to God or pray. Quietly, I gave my sister, who rode with us, messages for my children and friends. I closed out my life.

By the time I reached the hospital the tachycardia had lessened and I thought, "Oh, no, I'm not going after all." I was disappointed. The doctor kept me in intensive care for a couple of weeks, saying I had suffered a moderate heart attack. Back at home I recovered slowly, feeling increasingly depressed. Within the next few years I also had serious back surgery. My health declined, both physically and emotionally. Tension hung in our house.

Months later after the back surgery, I flew to my sister's home in Idaho to recuperate. I stayed for two months. One morning as I watched a flock of white geese circle the land, flying high against the snowy mountain peaks, I felt God near. I knew he would direct the way my life must go. I prayed that when I returned home, I would receive a happy greeting. But upon my arrival, Paul was silent, removed from me.

We moved to Emmett, Idaho, and built a nice house, but a continual feeling of vacancy kept me in constant conversation with the unseen presence of God. Paul and I both needed tender loving care, but with no communication between us, we could not meet each other's needs. The anger that had built over the years could not magically disappear. Darkness loomed ahead. I do not enjoy remembering this period of my life. I have blocked a large part of it from my memory by choice. When it does surface, I feel devastation all over again.

It was noon one sunny day. Lunch lay ready on the table when my husband spoke. A quiet man, he rarely shared his thoughts, but now he said, "I want a divorce. I want to leave." Shock ran through me.

How does this happen to a Christian marriage of forty years? It can, and it does. It left me feeling like an unwanted failure, like dirt swept under a rug. For months I was adrift, lost in depression, trying desperately to keep afloat. I wrote in my diary every day, and when I look back at the entries now, I remember this dark time.

December 10, 1975

Paul left today. My forty years of marriage is a failure. I walked to the window, pulled back the curtain, tried in vain to watch the tail light disappear through the thick fog. I can't stop crying.

December 14.

Today is Sunday. I went to church. How thankful I am for Christian friends. My mind hurts. Did you ever realize that a separation after forty years together is like dying? Really a death would be easier, far easier. That way the children and family and friends would be here for support. A divorce goes on forever, no end. You fight the loneliness, the guilt, the blame, the anger, all by yourself. Just you and God. I'm so thankful for God. But I need a human hand to hold mine.

May 5, 1976.

I sit on the porch tonight, totally alone, listening to life around me. There is momentary peace. I must move toward a growing edge. Take my hand, Lord, make something beautiful of my life.

May 10.

The Lord visited me tonight. Walking across the room I suddenly felt an uncontrollable joyous song in my heart. I threw my head back and sang a praise to the Living God. But, I could not sustain that happy joy the whole evening.

Gradually, I made plans to move to Colorado to care for my aged parents. Dad was one hundred years old, and Mom ninety. Being a caretaker brings a feeling of worth, which I needed desperately. It helped me begin to heal. Months later, I held Dad's hand as he quietly left this world; and still later, I smoothed my mom's forehead and whispered love to her as she reached for heaven.

At age sixty-three I remarried, which brought new challenges. My husband and I moved to a lovely mobile home park in the

Verde Valley in Arizona and made many friends. As I near age eighty, my son and daughter and my grandchildren are quiet blessings which have come my way, enriching my life and causing my gratitude to reach heavenward.

Sitting on our porch in late evening, I watch the sun set over Mingus Mountain behind our home. The red rock formations far to the east blush pink and apricot. My heart sings a favorite Psalm again: "I will lift up mine eyes unto the hills, from whence cometh my help. My help cometh from the Lord, which made heaven and earth."

As I settle down for a night's sleep, I repeat the Psalm, "The Lord is my Shepherd . . . ." And if my sleep is disturbed with concerns, I sing an old chorus, "God knows the way through the wilderness, all I have to do is follow."

My life has traveled up hills and down valleys. God has been the glue of my life. I have, all through the years, retained the Calvinism of the Primitive Baptist church. I believe that God draws and secures all those who will love him.

My private companionship with God's Holy Spirit is supreme, yet I have the need to attend worship service each week. Without that fellowship, I am not fulfilled. When I walk into a quiet sanctuary where soft devotional music is sung or played, my innermost self goes out to meet God.

As life is winding down, I shall retain my youthful spirit, indifferent to the ravages of the body. I shall laugh a lot as I reach out to others. I shall live life to its fullest, confident I will be met by heavenly angels as I fly upward.

Mary Elizabeth Thunder

Mary Elizabeth Thunder lives on Thunder Horse Ranch with her husband and ranch crew which she considers to be an "extended family of choice." Her ranch is open not only to buffalo and peacocks but to elders and teachers who come regularly to share ceremonies and teachings.

As president of Blue Star, Inc., a non-profit church and spiritual university, Mary shares her way of life as a spiritual advisor, author, and sundancer. Recently she was in France as a delegate of the Spiritual United Nations (S.U.N.) where she discussed women's roles in traditional religions with a crowd of eight thousand.

In addition to her three children and eleven grandchildren, she has heart connections with many other people. "I like to consider that I am living in the family of the world, striving to be aligned and in touch with all life and the Great Spirit."

LESSONS FROM GRANDMA GRACE
by Mary Elizabeth Thunder

I'm telling my story to shut up Grandma Grace Spotted Eagle. Grandma Grace was a traditional Lakota Elder, deeply alive with the spiritual heritage of her people, always walking at the side, and in the shadow, of her half-side, Wallace Black Elk. She keeps talking to me from the Spirit world as if she were here on this planet in the physical body. When she was alive, she never hesitated to tell me what to do, how to do it, and how I'd done it wrong.

Grandma Grace was my role model and mentor. Her teachings would often be accentuated by the beat of a drumstick pounding away on the top of my head. Setting up the most outrageous, impossible situations, she would fling me in the deep end and order me to fix it. Once I got past total panic, confusion, embarrassment, or fear for my life, I would hear Spirit or find the golden lesson buried in each circumstance. Grandma was a teacher of how to live and how to love. She would bring me to my limits and with humor, love, and the drumstick, show me that there were no true limits.

It is all a mystery to me today why she chose me to be one of her many adopted daughters. Perhaps she realized that if I did not learn how to live, I would die. For many of the half-breed and Native American people learning how to die is not difficult; learning to live is.

Grandma Grace was like a portal or keyhole from which I, angry and dissatisfied with life, could receive glimpses of beauty and grace. She helped me to access the cellular memory that activated in me a state of knowing. This knowing, or remembrance of what a woman is, helped me rejoin the Dance of Life. Grandma provided a way, through Spirit, that helped me to let go of rage and despair, shame and anger, and begin to walk the path of gratefulness and beauty of life. To me she was a Goddess/Medicine Woman/ Mother. She said, "Thunder, this time around, you're living life for all people, especially learning and teaching women things. This just might be a completion of many lifetimes for your soul."

In recent years I have been close to many examples of the Goddess. However, Grandmother Grace Spotted Eagle was always the one leading me on with her drumstick and her curt words, in my quest towards being a woman, toward nurturing and gratefulness, toward living creation principles of beauty on his planet!

As I write these words, I find that I am crying because I miss Grandma so much. She was quite a woman. Some saw her as scary, but I always saw her as a spiritual master hidden and living in a physical body. At times she was unreasonable and explosive, but these blow-ups were always well-timed to illustrate or catalyze a universal lesson or truth. To me she was warm, funny, cagey, shrewd, and real.

On one of many visits that I made to her home over the years, I was at a point of total exhaustion. She said, "Sit down," and started talking to me about eagle feathers. She said that a long time ago, if a person had identical twin feathers with the same markings, that person would hold those feathers until the time came that a bonding between two humans needed to take place. A mother would give one to a daughter, a father to a son, a mother to a son, a father to a daughter, a man to his wife, or a wife to her husband. She took out two very beautiful, identical spotted eagle feathers and told me that she had planned to give one to her daughter, but she had died soon after birth. Now she was going to give this feather to me.

Grandma said that sharing this feather meant that she loved me, that she was old and unable to fly on her own and needed me to help her out. She said it was only when we joined hands and hearts that either of us could enjoy the soaring flight of the eagle. "Wherever I am," she said, "whatever I am doing, I will always be with you. As long as you have this feather in your possession, it will protect you from harm and will comfort you in loneliness." I still have the feather. It is placed on a staff that Grandpa carved for me and goes with me everywhere.

Late one night Grandma was talking to me about the energy of the body, what others might call Chi. She took her hands and formed a ball of energy that shined very brightly in the dark. She placed it in my hands so I could feel raw, body energy. Mystified, I handed her back the ball. When it reached her hands, she took the ball of energy and placed it on my chest so it would go into my heart and heal the places she said hurt so bad. But her story to the public would always be that she was not a medicine woman, that you could not be a medicine woman until you could grow plants out of your body like Mother Earth. Mother Earth was the only true medicine woman.

In the honoring ceremony, during the four days right after her passing, I was given special things to do. I was to help Grandpa Wallace Black Elk, her beloved half-side, with several tasks, one being to clean out all of her possessions from the home they had shared together. "Whatever you do, daughter, don't let anyone see my old clothes," she said. Grandma always wore the simplest clothes, usually those which were given to her. I always thought she was beautiful in whatever she wore. Another vow was to write a book about her. And she wanted me to Sundance for her the following year to help her spirit make its transition.

A Sundancer is what I am. I had to die to be able to write those words. I remember when Leonard Crow Dog introduced me to some of his friends one time after I had danced for many, many years, "This is my niece and she is a Sundancer." The words kind of flipped back and forth in my mind. I had never really considered myself a Sundancer until that moment. I looked at him, and he looked at me and I truly believed that he knew what it meant—but did I?

Before I became a Sundancer, I was a woman who was disillusioned and unhappy with myself and the world around me. Life had not measured up to my expectations. I felt alone and put down. I had eaten myself up to almost three hundred pounds, somehow trying to find nourishment in life. I just wanted to leave the planet, to die. I found myself as the servant to everyone—husband, children, family, jobs, life.

This was not a good way to live and something had to happen. It did. I had a heart attack. Louise Hays says in her book, *You Can*

Heal Your Life, that a heart attack represents squeezing all the joy out of the heart, hardening it. My heart attack changed everything. It was as if I had died of the old and was reborn of new. A newness came over me that changed my thinking, being, and becoming. I became a Sundancer.

A Sundancer is a native person who has a prayer or vision to Sundance and who, according to tradition, must be accepted by a Council of Native Peers/Elders to be allowed to dance to the sun for four days without food and water, praying continually for the people so that the people might live. At the Sundance, we give to the Spirit all things that we have to give, our bodies and our Pipes in Sacred Prayer for All. As Grandma would say, "Just saying you are a Sundancer does not make you one or really anything at all! You have to live your prayer, become your prayer, remember your prayer, and most of all, don't walk on your own prayers. Some people pray prayers, then forget those prayers the very next day. That is what I call walking on your prayers!"

Sundance is an echo which comes to me like the voices of my ancestors, like old memories of other times and other loves, like the heartbeat of my Mother the Earth, the Great Drum, like the smell of sage and cedar, and like a morning prayer before sunrise when you can see the dew and smell the freshness of the world in its pristine perfection.

My Lakota Elders told me to go out on the road and follow the Sacred Pipe. So for most of the past decade, I have lived on the road, continually traveling across the United States. I have lived in my car and carried with me only those spiritual items and personal possessions that I needed. I have traveled alone, with my first husband and kids, with my Elders, and later with my second husband and students. I have walked in service to the Creator, always letting Spirit direct my steps and choose where I next needed to be. I have always loved God/Spirit/Great Mystery.

Now, you say, what is the Pipe? The Sacred Pipe is a wonderful instrument of peace that one can hold and pray with to the creator. The bowl is made from red stone and comes from and represents Mother Earth. The stem is made of wood from a tall tree that touched and represents Father Sky. When these two pieces come together, all life finds a Universal balance—stone and wood, male and female, heart and mind, body and spirit—a *oneness*, a union, together and inseparable, that which we as humans are striving to find.

The Cannupa Wakan (Sacred Pipe) is my life. When I pray with the Pipe, I stand at the center of the four directions, and the center of all things. Then the Spirit carries my thoughts and prayers to the Great Mystery through the vehicle of smoke. The Elders say that we were once like this smoke, without body, without form, and able to pass freely back and forth from this physical body/center of the universe to the Creator. When I hold the Pipe, I become part of the divine order of Creation. I pray for all things that have life.

On this Sundance walk, guided by a Sundance vision, I learned the lessons of the Five Directions—East, South, West, North, and in the fifth year, the "within space," or the center of all those directions and lessons. Each year I walked the way of one of the four winds, although not in the traditional E/S/W/N order. The very first year the Sundance Chief said that he knew from information the spirits had shared with him that I would start working on lessons of the West.

I walked to the West and learned about going inside myself to learn from the teacher within: the West is the place of contemplation. The walk of the East brought me to many Eastern and Tibetan masters, and I learned of enlightenment. The path of the South taught me pureness of thought, trust, and relationships. The last way was to the North, where I found lessons in the wisdom of the Elders and the children.

I walk from one year of Sundance season to the next. The calendar year for me changed to one based on the ceremonies and the seasons. Life for me became a ceremonial way of living twenty-four hours a day. I know when I walk into that "Great Mystery Circle" of the Sundance the prayers that all the Sundancers make seem to affect the whole world—my world and the world of others.

After being with my Elders for years, I was told I had the ability to see the "other world" with all my senses. The Elders told me that there were more senses available to each one of us than the ones we use. They said that a five-sensory person is crippled by the "today world," for they cannot see or sense Spirit.

Since childhood I've had an ability not only to "see" the spirits, but also to see the colors around a person's body, sometimes called auras. This ability I call Vision. My visions are not of the eyes; they are visions of spirit. I have been taught that there are two worlds, the one we live in every day and the spirit world. Some elders call the everyday world an illusion. Once as I talked with Swami Rami, a great Eastern master, he said, "Close your eyes, Thunder; now that is the real world. But just as soon as you open your eyes again your are back in the world of illusion that is of your making."

Some of my visions have come from Vision Quest, an ancient ceremony in which a person surrenders to the ceremony and receives guidance from the Great Mystery. On a quest a person sits alone on a blanket without food or water. It can be difficult, but Spirit's voice can shape a person's life and give it direction. Sometimes I have been rendered helpless or unable to drive or talk for the duration of the experience.

I realized that not a lot of people around me had similar experiences, so many times I would not share what I saw. Yet I knew that my experiences were special, and I also knew that I should act on the guidance in some concrete way. Sometimes my "visions" were only strong or strange images or intuitions, yet many times my own life or that of another was saved, or at least spared unnecessary grief, because I acted upon the information given to me in these "visions."

Once I received a vision in the Sundance, in the sacred Mystery Circle listening to the Never Ending Song. This vision was of a snake with four faces that turned into a two-headed snake. On about the third day of the dance with no food or water, and in the sun, I saw a coiled rattlesnake next to my foot. Its face changed from a snake's face to one of a young girl, then changed to an old Indian woman's face, then it changed to a young boy's face, and finally to an old man's face. After all the faces vanished, the snake's head split, creating two perfectly matched heads on one body. I watched for a long time as each head seemed to go its own way with its own thoughts. I continued to watch as the snake quieted itself and the heads slowed their hysterical pace of twisting. One head turned and just kept looking at the other head. Slowly, one head looked into the eyes of the other head. The two heads melted into one head on one body of one snake. The snake then disappeared. But what did it mean? Later in the home of a Cherokee chief, I saw a shield of a two-headed snake with neither head looking at the other. The chief explained that the self never wants to look at itself. We know about everything but ourself. When a person is willing to look at the self, the two-headed snake (or life force) looks into each others' eyes, and they become one with each other. That oneness is called Truth.

Some twenty-five years ago, my Elders shared an ancient prophecy with me, a prophecy that I feel strongly at work on the planet today. In February, 1987, as my Elders say, there was the "Day of Two Suns," The Supernova. This was the sign of the consummation of the love between Mother Earth and Father Sky. From their union, seeds of life, neutrinos, began to rain down on and through our planet, begetting changes in the consciousness of the people.

I believe that Mother Earth is now pregnant. When a woman is pregnant, she quickly learns that she must now take care of herself in a gentle, loving way. She must learn to love herself and pamper herself because she is responsible for new life. The only time I ever treated myself as if I really loved myself was when I knew I was carrying new life. Sometimes a woman wonders, "What am I bringing this child into?" That is what I am feeling now. Some elders say that as of 1994 we have eighteen years left to elevate our consciousness so our Mother Earth can bring the child, or a new way of being, to full term.

Recently, I made a trip to Geneva, Switzerland, to attend the United Nations Council of Indigenous Peoples. I shared the message that a gateway is now open, on a worldwide basis, to the Keys of Genetic Memory. This opening enables people to remember who they have been so that they can then remember who they will be. It is an opportunity to experience all that has come before us. It has been told to me that encoded in genetics is the entire knowledge and experience of all time. Through it we can remember when the Earth was one people living in peace and harmony. Once a person taps into this experience, the person is never the same. They can access their genetic memory, and Spirit will show them gifts for all of mankind—the use of plants and herbs; cures and healing for diseases; ways to get along with each other; ways to feed the world; and the will, power, and desire to work for good.

Indigenous peoples of the world have the knowledge needed to access this gateway. The energy behind the opening of the gateway is love, love between men and women, between humans and the spirit.

Mi Takaye Oyacin! Amen to all my relations and all things with life.

MERAH MADGE McCULLOUGH

      Merah Madge McCullough lives in Lubbock, Texas, with her husband, Gene. An alcohol and drug abuse counselor, she is Executive Director of the Lubbock Faith Center, a residential treatment center for alcohol and drug addiction.

      Merah's roots are in Alabama and Georgia, and she and her son, Alan, have published a family cookbook, *Cookin' With the Clecklers, From Alabama to Texas.*

Songs Along the Path
by Merah Madge McCullough

Our house was always filled with people—people talking, people singing. Gospel music wove its images into my early childhood. I could plainly see the pearly gates, the golden bells, and the railway into heaven. The singing made me happy as I heard "Bringing in the Sheaves" and "Standing on the Promises." Gospel music permeated our church services, also. I can remember myself at age six sitting on the front row at church, watching my father leading the songs and patting his foot. Words that were sung—words like "love" and "peace"—were connected to the feelings I had for my father and my older brother, S.D.

I saw God as a loving heavenly Father who sat on a golden throne somewhere far above the clouds, looking down and watching over all God's children. When I was very small, the prayer, "Now I lay me down to sleep" did not frighten me, since I did not understand the meaning of "death" and "soul." But as I became older and began to understand the preacher's hellfire and damnation sermons, I grew afraid I would die during my sleep. I worried especially about how God, my heavenly Father, might judge me. My reaction was to be in church every time the doors opened. I thought if I went to church enough and was good enough, I wouldn't have to worry about dying and "praying the Lord my soul to take." I listened to the hellfire and brimstone sermons and shook in fear.

At age nine, my preacher brother C. J. called me into the kitchen and talked to me about accepting Christ as my Savior. I don't remember much about this event, except he said a prayer, Mother cried, and everyone wondered why I still wanted to go to the movies on Sunday afternoon. I had witnessed many baptisms and decided I did not want to be "dunked in the water." The prospect of walking into a huge tub—dressed in my Sunday best—and being pushed under the water frightened me. I wondered why God would want anyone to go through such an ordeal. I do not remember my actual baptism, but it was the beginning of my life as an official member of God's Kingdom and the Southern Baptist Church.

When I was ten, Dad had a stroke that left him paralyzed and unable to walk. He was able to talk normally, but could no longer carry a tune. Overnight, I went from a carefree and happy child to an insecure and fearful one. Now I had to depend on relatives and friends for transportation, or I had to walk. "God's in his heaven; all's right with the world" no longer had meaning for me. I realize now that Dad's stroke had a profound effect on my vision of God. How could God, a loving Father, let such a thing happen? I remember taking the scissors and cutting the legs off my paper doll father. I became resentful because my parents weren't "normal." When I was away from home, I worried that the house might catch on fire or that some other dreadful thing might happen to them. Mother, who was crippled with arthritis, told me later that they had felt they couldn't take care of me properly so she had asked God to send a guardian angel to watch over me.

I communicated with God through singing. My piano teacher gave me free voice lessons when she learned how upset I was because I couldn't carry a tune. I know that God and my guardian angel put Mamie Hizer in my life because I needed to sing. I practiced at home, and Dad would nod his approval and cry.

At home I often sat in the mesquite tree in front of the house reading Nancy Drew mysteries and daydreaming. How I wished I had a car like hers and could help others with their problems. I read *The Lilac Lady* by Ruth Alberta Brown, and it opened my eyes to the feelings and struggles of others. Sometimes as I sat there, I sang the songs I loved so much and felt peaceful and secure.

Relatives on my mother's side of the family often visited us. When they were around, the house was filled with jokes, laughing, hugging, and fun. The Clecklers were mostly Methodists, and I wondered why Methodists seemed to have more fun than Baptists. They didn't talk about religion or God but just had fun and loved each other. Mother always told everyone she was Methodist-Baptist.

When I was in high school, I was involved in a church contro-
versy about allowing black children to participate in Vacation Bible
School commencement. The leaders had decided the four or five
black children involved should have their own program in the basement. I wrote a letter to the adults of the church and signed it
"The young people." I wrote, "You teach us 'red and yellow, black
and white, all are precious in His sight,' yet you won't allow the
black children in the church auditorium." Mother listened with
great interest. She did not make any comments but smiled her
acceptance. I don't remember specific reactions from the adults of
the church, but on commencement night in Roscoe, Texas in the
1950s, black and white marched down the aisle together.

After high school, I prayed for a miracle that God would provide the money for me to go to Hardin-Simmons University in
Abilene. My parents' income from a trailer park did not include
money for college. During that summer, Mr. and Mrs. A. C.
Donahue, of Odessa, passed through Roscoe and stopped at the
trailer park. While Mr. Donahue visited with Mother and Dad, he
learned that I wanted to go to H-SU. Mr. Donahue went to the car
and got his wife, saying to her, "God has sent us here." They explained that they had sent other young people to college and would
send me. Again, my guardian angel was working in my life.

While I was at H-SU, I wrote a diary to God. In it I expressed
my thoughts and struggles during those years. I told God about
everything that happened to me. "Dear God," I wrote at the end
of each day, "Help me to know what you want me to do." I told
Him about problems, friendships, hopes, and disappointments. I
asked His guidance with my studies. Almost daily I asked Him to
help me with my feelings of inferiority.

When I was a sophomore, I took a sociology course from J. D.
Osborne, and a light came on deep within. The direction I wanted
to go became as plain as day. I had never been so excited. I knew I
would be a counselor or social worker. My daydreaming in the
mesquite tree, my fantasizing about helping delinquents, my concern with the black children in Bible School suddenly made sense.
I summoned enough courage to talk to Mr. Osborne. He encouraged and supported me, assuring me that I could serve God as a
social worker or a counselor.

After college a gentleman from Georgia, who loved to sing gospel music, came along and captured my heart. After we married, my husband Gene and I attended the Baptist church, but I had begun to question Baptist doctrine, and we did not make the church our whole life. We went to dances and to wrestling matches. I could see nothing wrong with dancing, though I had heard many sermons against it.

Soon after the birth of our son Alan, we joined the Presbyterian church. I liked the positive preaching and did not want Alan to grow up scarred by hellfire and damnation sermons. We continued to attend the Presbyterian church for several years, but when we moved to another city, Alan began asking to stay home from church. Then a friend invited us to the Episcopal church. At that time in my life, the quiet worship and ritual filled a need. Alan liked it, and we all decided we wanted to become Episcopalians.

Somewhere along the way, though, we made less and less time for church. When we moved back to Texas, we had to drive to another town for services. Gene traveled a lot. Alan again lost interest. I still sang as a way to communicate with God, but then suddenly the music stopped. I quit singing aloud as everyday problems crowded my life. In the rush of living, I moved further and further from God. This was such a gradual process that I was unconscious of my spiritual alienation.

I became a chronic worrier, resentful and angry because things weren't going as I wanted them to. I thought if everybody around me would do as I wanted, I could be happy. Most of my hours were spent trying to fix somebody's problems or control their actions. One night I was at my lowest point. I went out on the patio, looked up at the stars and cried out to God, "Help me. I can't do anything alone." Immediately there came to me the words to the song "Fear thou not, I'll be with thee; I will still thy pilot be."

Several days later, a friend told me about her struggles living with an alcoholic and how a twelve-step program had helped her to find the God of her understanding. She explained that it was good for anyone needing spiritual guidance. I had friends with drinking problems, and I had once counseled alcoholics and their families, so I decided to try it.

At first I could not identify with the program. I had lost touch with who I was and had difficulty grasping new ideas. Soon, however, I realized I had already taken the first and second steps that night on the patio when I had called on God for help. I had admitted I was powerless and turned to God to restore my sanity. The third step—making a decision to turn my life and will over to the care of God as I understood Him—was difficult, as I had to find the God of my understanding instead of the God of the Baptists, Presbyterians, Episcopalians, my parents, and my forebears.

After several months of meetings, I suddenly realized I was worrying less and was becoming aware of my controlling and resentful attitudes. My dear friend Ann helped me stay with the program. Again, God and my guardian angel were putting significant people in my life.

After we moved to Lubbock, Texas, I could not find a job. For a short time, I worked for a man who guided me on my spiritual path by showing me how affirmations work, and by introducing me to the Mastermind prayer meetings of the Unity Church. As I look back, I see how the movements of my life have led me. I have the God of my understanding—a loving Father who is here with me and not above the clouds. When I think of God, I am also including Jesus and the Holy Spirit. The God of my understanding wants me to be good to myself, to love myself so I can love others.

Now when I have difficulty letting go of something or someone, I put the problem on a slip of paper in my God box, made from a square Kleenex box. Words and phrases such as "Peace," "A New Beginning," "Joy," "Just for Today," and "This Thing Called Prayer" are pasted on the box. A picture of a field of bluebonnets adds color. Putting problems in my God box helps me let go. I have come to realize that if I am worrying, God cannot work. Now, most of the time, I can allow others to make their own mistakes without my control or interference. I have let go of most of my resentments of childhood. I can attend a Baptist church and enjoy the music without feeling angry and resentful.

Today, I work with those suffering from the disease of addiction. As the Executive Director of the Lubbock Faith Center, Inc., a twenty-four hour residential treatment center, I am privileged to see lives changed each day through guidance from the God of their own understanding. Most of the clients come to us from inpatient treatment. Their goal is to learn how to live serene, sober lives, to move eventually into an independent setting. I see men and women finding fulfillment in old or new careers. Many return to college to finish what was halted by alcohol and drugs. Many regain healthy self-esteem, while others gain a feeling of self-worth for the first time in their lives. Husbands, wives, children, and families are reunited. Those who make progress do so by making wise choices with the guidance of the God of their own understanding. They live a chemical-free lifestyle, one day at a time.

Many come to the Faith Center with little laughter, taking themselves and others too seriously. What joy to see depression and isolation replaced with laughter and interaction with others! Humor is healing, and I think God likes us to have a sense of the ridiculous. We laugh a lot and tease playfully. One of the women calls me "the old lady," and I call her the "young lady." I told her I hoped I lived long enough to see her my age. She replied, "If you do, you will still be the old lady!" One man feels confident enough to laugh when he sees me in a loud outfit he calls my clown suit. Best of all, he can now laugh at himself.

I have a sign behind my desk which says, "God put me in this world to do a certain number of things, and at the rate I'm going, I will never die." A song is in my heart—"One day at a time, sweet Jesus, one day at a time."

SHIRLEY FAYE BOYKINS

The third child of three children born to Jay and Ester Boykins in rural East Texas, Shirley Faye Boykins grew up in the Baptist church. She graduated from Lon Morris College in Jacksonville, Texas, in 1990. She is a member of Sweet Union Baptist Church. The mother of two children, Shirley works for Stage Stores in the collections department.

HALFWAY DOWN THE PATH
by Shirley Faye Boykins

I was born in Cuney, Texas, and spent the summers there with my great aunt. As you enter Cuney going west, you see to the left a small, brick building among a group of badly worn gray ones. This is the Rock Hill Baptist Church.

The first thing I remember about Rock Hill Baptist Church was the day I was baptized. I was about five or six years old. It was a lazy Saturday afternoon, a while after the country folk of Cuney had returned from the nearby small towns of Jacksonville and Frankston with their week's purchases. Two older children and I were herded into the back seat of an automobile which was owned by one of the wealthier parishioners. During the ride to the community fishing pond, I was filled with goose bumps, anticipating the special event. I was still wrapped in a blanket of awe as we moved around the heavily weeded pond. When we finally found a suitable place for baptizing, I was chosen to go first. Being first was special for me because up to this time I had never been chosen to do anything. My childhood habits of thumb sucking, bed-wetting, and pulling my hair out by the roots caused people to make fun of me or to ignore me.

I stood listening to the preacher pound out the words: "I now baptize you, my sister, in the name of the Father, the Son, and the Holy Ghost." He suddenly held the back of my head, put his right palm over my face, and bent me backwards into the lukewarm water. As suddenly as he dipped me in, he lifted me out again. I was still kicking and struggling and coughing as I heard the ladies from the church singing "Take Me to the Water." After I had calmed down a little, I realized that by choosing to be a Christian I might be in for a struggle. At that time I did not know if I was jolted off the path of sin or onto the path of righteousness.

Not only did our religious lives begin in Rock Hill Baptist Church, but our social and recreational lives started there as well. It provided a place for special dinners, teas, quilting bees, young people's meetings and other occasions. It also served as a town hall: I remember a meeting in the church when people held up voter registration cards preparing to take a stand in the next election.

At Rock Hill Baptist Church everyone looked forward to what we called "The First Sunday in August." This gathering seemed about as important to us as Christmas. I remember how special the day was. The early morning air was filled with the aroma of chicken and dressing, and there was a big butter cake, which took twelve whole eggs to make, and smooth, orange potato pies. I would get dressed in a new dress and nylon underpants, with a tiny row of lace around the leg, which I showed off to my friends during frequent trips to the outhouse.

Neither long distances nor hot sun would prevent anyone from attending this special service, since it served as a marker of where you were in your life at the time, both spiritually and economically. All who could afford to buy new clothes used this opportunity to do so. This was a time when everyone could look and see how the Lord had blessed us and our friends and neighbors.

During a lengthy service everyone squirmed and fanned themselves and eyed every new dress and pair of shoes that came in the church door. After all the curls and puffs slid out of our bangs, after our new shoes pinched our toes unmercifully, after our new dresses had perspiration circles from our armpits to the middle of our ribs, only then did the preacher end his sermon. He panted and puffed and wiped his brow with a damp handkerchief, and finally announced the wonderful dinner-on-the-ground.

The congregation would eat and mill about, carrying on conversations about health, happiness, jobs and families, with the people they had not seen in a year, as well as the people they saw every day. This was a time to set aside daily tasks and to feast, pray, and sing in the name of the Lord.

The Black church often has gatherings of this sort. Such an occasion signifies our thankfulness for a happier time when we are no longer in bondage and can exhibit the fruits of our faith and prayers. We come to praise and thank God for a nice place to gather together and for plenty of food to eat, new clothes, and good jobs. The primary purpose of the worship service is to look back and see how far we have come since the days of slavery, and thus to confirm that the Holy Spirit has never left us. The predicament of slavery led us to God; then God gave us the Holy Spirit which in turn led us to the church, our own gathering place for worshiping God. We sing the mournful hymns that our forefathers sang during the days of slavery so we will not forget where we came from and how far we have traveled with the help of the Lord.

As I grew up, I lived in Jacksonville with my mother most of the year. She worked two jobs to provide for our family's needs. With her I attended the Church of God in Christ. My mother contributed to my spiritual life in many ways. She taught me to be grateful to God for all my blessings, and she instructed me about the vices of the world. She believed, for example, that if people started using things that did not belong to them without first asking to do so, they would eventually start stealing and end up in jail or prison.

Since all of my grandparents died before I was born, my great aunt in Cuney took their place in my life. She always made a fuss over me no matter how much I sucked my thumb, pulled my hair out, or wet my bed. When I stayed with her during the summers, she read to me from the Bible and tried to answer questions that I asked about heaven and hell. She recited the Ten Commandments and explained to me what they meant. She was the first person to instill in me a feeling of guilt for doing things that were wrong. I remember how she would sit on the porch, look up into the sky and sing "Swing Low, Sweet Chariot." She often explained to me that she was "going to leave this old world and go to a better place on the other side."

Early one hot August morning, when I was eight or nine years old, my aunt awoke before dawn feeling very ill. When I went to get help from a relative who lived nearby, that was the last time I saw my dear old aunt alive. At her funeral, even after I watched her casket lowered into the grave, I did not feel that she was gone forever, but that she was only gone away for a visit. At night, I could feel her presence on the right side of my tiny bed. I was not afraid but felt that she was hovering there to give me the reassurance that I was still her special girl, no matter how badly others treated me.

At the age of twelve or thirteen, I developed a love for reading. I was asked to teach the elementary class in Sunday School, and I would read the lessons over and over so I could tell the story to the younger students and help the older ones who could read only a little. I took a step further by teaching myself the books of the Bible. I remember going to Mrs. Brown's little store around the corner to buy two sticks of peppermint candy for a penny. I would then sip ice water and eat tiny bits of the candy while I learned the books of the Bible. I copied this idea from the character Francie, in the book *A Tree Grows in Brooklyn.*

By the time I was a senior in high school, I had the dual role of elementary Sunday School teacher and secretary of the whole Sunday School. I was old enough now to understand that the Lord had delivered me from the bondage of sin as well as slavery. I knew well that I was to confess my sins, pray and ask forgiveness, and, at the same time, I was supposed to take advantage of the doors that were now open to my people.

Following high school graduation, I moved to Dallas and worked for a large company. In a society of people with different personalities and backgrounds, I was exposed to a way of living that I had often heard ministers mention in their sermons. I could now see firsthand that the Christian path was not an easy one. My understanding of the Beatitudes became sharper with more opportunity to apply them. During this time, I often remembered how I sat in my little church at home and listened to the preacher explain the scriptures in a loud, punctuated voice. I thought then that the Beatitudes would never apply to me, but I could see now that I did not have to be doing wrong for people to persecute me. My refusal to follow the crowds by doing the "in" things brought a certain amount of persecution. But I knew I was there to fulfill my blessings, and I did not want to waste my deliverance. I did not want anyone to look at me and say, "We gave them equal opportunities and look what they did with them." I wanted to look back and see how far the Lord had brought me personally.

I can now understand why the minister said, "Humble is the way." I did as he said, and used humbleness, without friction, to cope with people and situations. I had to put into practice all the teachings that I had received in church. I gave credit to the Lord for watching over me and keeping me from falling prey to the vices that lay waiting for young people on their own away from home.

I lived and worked in Dallas for ten years, until my mother's health started failing and she asked me to move back to Jacksonville. There, I soon became a member of Sweet Union Baptist Church and joined the choir and the young adult Sunday School class. This Sunday School class contributed the most to my growth in Christian maturity. In this class, we were given research assignments that required a great deal of cross referencing, reading, and researching. I used the skills I learned to complete my associate of arts degree. After graduating, I decided to give back to my community, especially to the people who have been socio-economically deprived, as I was.

Eventually I came back to my first love and the thing that made me feel good about myself. I started working with children in the Head Start program. In my work, I try to meet the needs of each child, so I fulfill many roles: nurse, substitute mom, referee, bodyguard, and babysitter. I practice patience as I work with each child and wait for results. The greatest gift that comes to me is not on the day the wages are tallied and distributed, but on the day that one little child learns the concept that I have been trying to teach her.

As I look back over my life, I feel that I am about halfway down the path of Christian maturity. I can stand and look in one direction at the steps that brought me to this point, and I can turn and look in the other direction and see that I still have a long way to go. I pray that I will continue to grow in Christian stewardship and choose the paths in life that will fulfill my blessings.

DONNA LEE BRUNK SUTER

Donna Lee Brunk Suter has lived in Virginia since age nine and is a Mennonite Charismatic. She is the mother of four adult children and eight grandchildren. Donna, along with her husband of forty-three years, is involved in marriage-strengthening support groups. She currently is caring for her bedfast father and enjoys extended visits from her mother.

Donna says, "I am an ordinary lady serving a great God. I enjoy writing and investing love and encouragement into the lives of younger women and 'Tired Saints.'"

WINTERBOURNE
by Donna Lee Brunk Suter

I was two months conceived in the womb—this fact as yet unknown by my father. My parents drove in hostile, hurting silence. They were returning from seeing a California divorce lawyer. Suddenly, my mother burst into tears, blurting out, "I'm carrying your child. In seven months we'll become parents." My father was stunned, thoughtful. Later, after a heated discussion, they decided to remain together for the sake of their child—me. They endured it for three more miserable years.

Then Daddy left. Mother tried to support the two of us by doing laundry and working in a restaurant. Two years later, Daddy married a woman who very much wanted his little girl because she could not have children. They fought for custody of me and won. But because my stepmother had an alcohol problem, their marriage lasted only two years. I was left with deep emotional scars. Four different foster homes followed in the next two years. At age nine, I was bordering on a nervous breakdown. My father took me to live with his parents in Virginia. He was about to be married again, and this wife did not want to have to deal with an emotionally disturbed little girl.

From the beginning, my grandmother's love was unconditional. My coming must have felt like a tidal wave hitting a small, quiet, peaceful inland lake. My grandparents loved me and made room for me, but they did not know what to do with me. My grandfather washed his hands of my discipline at an early stage. My grandmother tried, but much of the time I treated her disrespectfully and made her weep. I didn't think she loved me; later I came to understand the full extent of her unconditional love.

I continued to show two sides. One was the tender, sensitive girl who loved beauty, books and music, who felt compassion for those who hurt. My other self was the hostile, moody, willful girl who often wished for death—who wanted to run away from pain and who carried a lasting sadness inside.

And then Nelson came into my life, Nelson with his incredible blue eyes. He was quiet and strong, from a stable Christian background. He felt like a rock to me, a rock to build my life upon. I came to love him. I was fifteen and he was almost nineteen. We dated two years and right after my high school graduation, we married. We bought a little trailer home, planted a garden, and filled a second-hand freezer with our own fruits and vegetables. Life should have been good for us. Nelson worked hard. He did not expect a lot from me. He was kind, quiet, and easily content. I, on the other hand, was a goal-setter and a planner. I preferred talking things over, exploring different ideas and possibilities. I looked to my young husband not only to be a tender lover and a breadwinner but also to be the big brother I never had, the father I had sorely missed. I also thought he would love me unconditionally as Grandma did, regardless of my unpredictable moods

The babies came quickly, three sons in two and a half years. Nothing had prepared me for the intense mothering responsibilities. Suddenly, my hours were filled with someone wet or wailing. There seemed to be no night at our house.

I struggled with a low energy level and weak stomach. Dirty diapers and upchucks made me turn inside out. And the endless squabbles that three little brothers can get into were overwhelming. When Nelson came home at night, I felt I had been on the battlefront all day and finally there would be some reinforcement. However, Nelson believed that it was his job to provide for the family financially and it was mine to care for our home and children. He didn't see anything wrong in leaving me alone each evening to do "my job." On weekends, he enjoyed going to the mountains with his buddies to relax after a hard week of work. I felt alone, hopeless—the years stretching out before me with miles of dirty diapers, crying babies, sleepless nights, and a house I could not keep clean.

I became discontented, contentious, irritable, full of self-pity. I began to overeat. I got hooked on afternoon soap operas. My life was undisciplined, unmanageable, out of control. I started taking diet pills. My already unstable emotional state swelled and ebbed in unpredictable mood swings. Almost every day, I was a good mother for part of the day—playing, reading, bathing, fixing nourishing meals, washing mountain-high laundry. By afternoon, I crashed physically and emotionally. I wanted to sleep, but that was impossible. So I would turn on the TV while snacking on sweets. By evening, the children were more feisty; the baby, colicky. I would try to have a hot supper ready when Nelson got home, but I was usually close to tears.

The resentment toward my spouse mounted when he would leave right after supper. But the times he did stay home, I would pour out all my unhappiness, frustration, and unmet expectations for our marriage and home. Nelson retreated into silence that sometimes lasted for days. He stayed away from home more and more, distancing himself from the world I felt trapped in.

Then gradually, I began to grow up. My coping became less frenzied, more stable. The Lord gave me two older women who were like spiritual mothers to me and a close friend my own age who shared Jesus' love with me in tangible ways. These three were good role models for me. I was changing, slowly, but markedly.

When Lisa, our lovely little daughter, was only three weeks old, our brown-eyed Brent, at four and a half years of age, was tragically electrocuted.

The grief process was long and hard. After Brent's death, I began to see that my husband needed more than a tired wife with a long list of complaints when he got home. I started meeting him at the door with a smile, to help build up the children's sense of anticipation of daddy's homecoming. Always I tried to have a hot meal waiting. But as I reached out, I found only a wall between us—a rock wall of silence. Except for the chatter of children and the nightly ritual of spilt milk, our evening meals were silent.

After supper, Nelson would get down on the floor and tussle with the little boys, then he would cuddle his blue-eyed baby daughter for a few minutes. Next came the dreaded words, "Well, I guess I'd better get back to work." One half-hour a day was about the most we ever saw the man of the house. We had become married singles, each living alone together.

"Who is this man I married?" I wondered. A sense of despair engulfed me. I realized that I was losing respect for my husband.

Two older women invited me to join them for a summer Bible study on the book of James. Their patience with my immaturity and their loving acceptance of my imperfections gave new meaning to life. It wasn't that either woman had extra time to invest in an unhappy, self-centered young woman. One had eight children; the other had nine. They helped me apply to my everyday life the scriptures we were studying—to be doers of the Word and not hearers only. Through them, the Lord prepared the soil of my heart for the next gift God had planned for my life.

Through the empowering of the Holy Spirit, Jesus took a new priority in my life. I became hungry for the Word of God and for fellowship. I became involved in Bible studies and prayer meetings and was always begging Nelson to go with me. One night, when I began sharing with him my picture of a Christian home and family, he suddenly said, "I think living a Christian life is the most boring thing in the whole world." And then he was silent. I was astounded. Again, I thought, "Who is this man I married?" We no longer shared the same values in life. I felt paralyzed, torn, much like when I was a child and my parents separated. Now it was Jesus and my husband pulling me in opposite directions. Jesus was my first choice. But I didn't know how to choose one without rejecting the other.

Our fifth child was born, a dark-haired, brown-eyed baby boy who looked much like Brent. We named him Brenden. But our marriage and family life worsened. My children rebelled, and my husband remained a stubborn rock.

I remember one ladies' night at Nelson's monthly Ruritan meeting, the local community service organization for men. I had dressed with care, wearing my prettiest, soft lavender dress. A babysitter came to watch the children. All day I had looked forward to this rare date with my husband. The car was heavy with our silence. "I really don't have time for this dinner tonight. There's so much to do at the shop." He looked toward the apartment where one of his secretaries lived as we drove by. The cold anger of rejection filled my heart, and I fought back tears. After we got home, I lay in bed thinking over the past fifteen years of our marriage. The hours ticked away as a heavy despondency settled over me. "Lord, we don't have a real marriage—I don't know this man I'm married to." I began to perceive that we had never had a real marriage and began to cry out to the Lord, "Lord, give me a real marriage. Teach me to be a real wife."

Then the Lord asked me a very hard question. "Am I sufficient for you? If your husband never comes to love you, if your children never come back from the enemy's camp, am I sufficient for you?" That was a life-changing question. I wrestled with it long and hard, through the night, until my strong will had been truly broken. Next morning I said, "Yes Lord, you are sufficient."

The wall of silence grew higher. My inner life was growing, but our home situation grew worse. Several more years passed. Our oldest son was exploring drugs and the occult. Our second son was locked within himself. Our daughter was in rebellion, and our youngest son was growing up like a wild weed, unattended. Nelson had thrown all his energies into his work and seemed content with his world, especially when he was away from home. But he was beginning to look old. At thirty-five, I felt old.

The Lord gave me several promises then. He said, "If you will learn to be a wife, I will cover your children until they can be covered by their father." At a fasting and prayer retreat a year later, the Lord gave me a precious promise for my family that I held onto for seven more years. "Daughter, I have had you on the potter's wheel. I have allowed you to be dropped and broken. I see the fragments as they lie at my feet. But daughter, think not that I cannot gather up the pieces and fashion a new vessel. And this time, it will be more usable and more lovely than the first. Daughter, I speak not of you alone; I speak of your whole family." That word of hope and encouragement told me that He did intend to heal our marriage and our family. But how? When?

Slowly, He began to change me. He took away my addiction to soap operas and gave me a deeper hunger for His Word. He taught me that a soft answer turneth away wrath. I began to look for ways to please Nelson. Little things like having a pitcher of cold tea always in the refrigerator, and big things, like trying harder to enjoy sex, the intimate part of our marriage. I had most longed for spiritual oneness and also for communication and sharing ideas and goals. I felt if we could experience intimacy in these two ways, I would find it so much easier to give of myself physically. I felt so unfulfilled and depleted in my relationship with Nelson that it was hard to be responsive. The Lord began to teach me in that area.

Two more years went by. At another time of fasting and prayer, God showed me a garden parched with dryness, great cracks in the earth. And He said, "You have been going to your family for water, but they have no water to give you. You have been going outside your home for water and greenness. You have sat at the feet of some of the best spiritual teachers. But I would have you stay at home and begin to draw water from Me. For I am the Living Water. Drink daily, hourly, from Me and begin to water your family, asking nothing in return. Beneath that cracked, dry soil are seeds of new life. I will make your family a well-watered garden. The greenness will be my doing, but I shall bring it forth as you are faithful to stay home and water your family."

Shortly after that, my uncle, whom Nelson always liked and respected, was scheduled to speak at our local Full Gospel Businessmen's Fellowship meeting, and we attended. He told this story: "After the accidental drowning of our two children, I came close to losing my wife as well. When she learned of my infidelity, her fragile emotional makeup almost cracked. But I saw a beauty of strength in her that amazed me. I recognized the Lord's hand on her life and it broke me, causing me to want to clean up my own wrecked life, to seek a relationship with Jesus Christ and His indwelling Holy Spirit which I saw reflected in my wife's willingness to forgive and love."

Nelson was somber as he drove home. "I never would have suspected all that was a part of your uncle's testimony."

I didn't respond; I just kept thinking, "How could she forgive him and be so supportive?"

For weeks afterwards, I kept asking the Lord to make the wall come down between us and to teach me to be a real wife. Again, the Lord began to say, "What are you willing to pay to have a real marriage? There is a cost for the wall to come down. Can I trust you with that cost? Would you be willing to face a confession of unfaithfulness?" At first I said, "No, Lord, I just can't face that. I'd rather die first. Please don't ask me to pay that price." Finally, one day I said, "Yes Lord, I'm willing to pay the price. I've counted the cost and nothing is too high for you to heal our marriage."

Following that relinquishment, the Lord gave Nelson and me a rare weekend away from home together. The first afternoon we were away, Nelson said, "Honey, I have to talk to you." He began to cry. I had never seen him cry except at Brent's death. He said, "I think I've just become a Christian. I don't think I ever really asked Jesus Christ into my life before and meant it. This time I mean it. Honey, the Lord has a lot of cleaning up to do in me. I have to tell you some things, and they will be hard for me to tell and for you to hear."

They were excruciatingly hard. Inside I was crying—screaming, wanting to run away, my hands over my ears. I sat very still and listened, praying, "Hold me steady, Lord. Let me respond as a real wife would." As the harsh, cutting truths came forth, I sat there and chose to forgive. The feeling of forgiveness was not there, but the choice was. Before my eyes, the wall began to crumble, and we were suddenly in each other's arms, tears mingling, the beginning of a unity we had never known.

The eyes of my understanding began to open. I saw how much I had contributed to our marriage vows being broken, how much I, too, had broken them. How little I had praised, affirmed, honored, and shown him respect. I realized how seldom I laughed, how unpleasant I was to come home to, to live with.

A few months later, Nelson asked for the baptism of the Holy Spirit at a small group meeting we began to attend. Strong men wept that evening. Shortly thereafter Nelson, who had scarcely spoken a word in church, stood before the whole congregation to share what God had done in his life and what He was doing for our family.

I stumbled over someone's feet as I responded to Nelson's request for me to come to stand with him. I remember thinking, "I'd climb over seven alligators if I had to, to go be at his side right now!" As I stood there, my arm around him, silently praying, Nelson spoke in his humble, faltering way, "Most of you know me as a shy, quiet fellow who never speaks much in public. But sometimes God touches your life with such a hammer blow and gives back a wife to a fellow who doesn't deserve it."

Again, men wept. And I thought, "This is what it means to be a real wife—to be needed, to be wanted, to be loved." And I stood tall beside Nelson in his hour of humility, proud of his tears, knowing we were beginning to rebuild our foundations, a man, a woman, and Jesus Christ.

Several years have now passed. God's faithful promises are coming to pass: "And I will restore the wasted years the cankerworm hath destroyed." (Joel 2)

Our youngest son is married. Our courageous son-in-law battles a life-threatening disease. Our four children and their spouses walk with the Lord. Our seven grandchildren fill our home and hearts with creative energy and joy. Our comfort zone keeps being stretched beyond our own adequacies as we invest ourselves in others' lives.

Nelson and I share in a support group for couples who have gone through the devastation of broken vows and now are rebuilding. Ginger's and Ben's faces radiate a special joy tonight. They hand us an envelope. Nelson and I open it and read:

Dear Nelson and Donna,

> The purpose of this letter is to invite you to a special service of renewing the marriage vows Ginger and I made almost twenty years ago. By the miraculous grace of God, we are experiencing repentance, renewal, and restoration in our relationship. Though it has been an extremely painful process, especially for Ginger, we have seen God's healing love rebuild our marriage and home. It is our desire that we renew our vows in the presence of our dear friends and family members as a testimony of God's grace and as a witness that God can restore a marriage the world would say is broken beyond repair. We have been blessed and encouraged by your personal sharing with us of your own pilgrimage. It has helped to give us the courage to face our own pain and failure and has helped us establish the desire to rebuild.

Nelson and I embrace these two who have become precious to us over the last two years. In their marriage and in our own, we realize God's promise to create for us a winterbourne: a stream of fresh water which breaks through the ice and snow of winter, causing greenness and new life to spring forth.

BEFORE THE PEOPLE

BEFORE THE PEOPLE

A mong Christians, the practice of testimony dates
to Biblical times. Believers are called on to be ready at
all times and in all places to give a testimony of their faith. The
earliest extant spiritual autobiography in English is such a docu-
ment. Margery Kempe in fifteenth-century England traveled over
the countryside weeping and praying, telling everyone she met of
her faith and defending it often before ecclesiastical and secular
authority. To preserve her testimony, she dictated to two male
scribes the record of her experiences.

Many spiritual autobiographies by women written in the centuries since Kempe have this same rhetorical purpose: to tell of
the author's spiritual experiences so that children or friends or
other readers will understand the faith to which she testifies. Anne
Bradstreet wrote for her children, titling her short autobiography
"To My Dear Children." Elizabeth Ashbridge, a Quaker, wrote, "I
most earnestly desire, that whoever reads the following lines may
take warning and shun the evils that through the deceitfulness of
Satan I have been drawn into." Jarena Lee, the first black female
autobiographer in America, wrote hoping that the record of God's
work in her life would help lead others to Christ. Dorothy Day in
The Long Loneliness describes the testimony of a life committed to
peace, nonviolence, and social justice.

Through the years, when Southern women did not speak in
church for any other reason, they rose to give their testimony. In
Protestant churches where the individual is at the center of the
process of salvation, every convert is expected to be able to testify
to the particulars of her experience. As she stands before the people
and tells what the Lord has done in her life, she edifies the church

and kindles its evangelistic spirit. In this collection, church women Mary Lou Santillán Baert, Betty Thrall, and Ann Baker testify to their personal experience of a life controlled by God's grace. Lee Merrill Byrd pictures the intrusion of God's painful grace, to which she is compelled to give testimony.

Not surprisingly, the women whose stories describe their involvement in twelve-step programs also choose testimony as their mode of sharing their story. By immersing themselves in storytelling and story-listening, twelve-step participants begin to see where they have been and where they want to go. Kelly Hunt Lyon follows this classic twelve-step formula as she describes the void out of which she has risen and the goals she sets for herself.

Testimony is becoming increasingly important as a source of truth. Bookstore shelves are filled with personal accounts of well-known and not-so-well-known people, each wanting to share his or her own truth. Patricia LaVigne and Catherine Chapman, Catholics who have struggled with the source of truth, tell their stories, describing their struggles and the understandings they have reached. Florence Birmingham, a Jewish woman, and Ruth Powell, a Quaker, offer persuasive, but non-traditional, "testimonies," indicating the spiritual diversity emerging in the South.

LEE MERRILL BYRD

Lee Merrill Byrd was born and raised in New Jersey but has spent most of her life in the Southwest. With her husband, poet Bobby Byrd, and her daughter and son-in-law, she runs Cinco Puntos Press; they publish fiction, non-fiction, poetry and children's literature of the American Southwest, the U.S./Mexico border region, and Mexico. Lee and Bobby have three children and live in El Paso.

Lee's collection of short stories, *My Sister Disappears,* was published by Southern Methodist University Press in 1993.

IN A NEW COUNTRY

by Lee Merrill Byrd

It was the day of my daughter Susie's tenth birthday party: February 22, 1981, a sultry spring Sunday after a dry winter. The telephone rang just as her team was about to beat Laurie Miller's in a relay race. I cursed and let it ring. I didn't want to be bothered right then.

But it kept on. I went inside, annoyed, to pick it up. "Yeah?" I said.

The unfamiliar voice on the other end wanted to know if there was someone named Bert there. Wrong number! I started to slam the phone down, but a sudden instinct made me bring it to my ear once more.

"Do you mean Byrd?" I asked.

There was talking in the background, the sound muffled by the hand of the caller, and then another voice, a man.

"Byrd," he said, in confirmation. "Is this Mrs. Byrd?"

"Yes."

"Mrs. Byrd," he said slowly. "I'm the fire marshal. You have two sons, John and Andrew?"

Yes, of course I have two sons. But they were over in another part of town visiting a friend while Susie had her party. Weren't they? "What's wrong?" I shouted at him.

"They've been in a serious accident, ma'am," I heard him reply. "They've been burned."

They were burned indeed, caught inside a palm-branch fort they'd made, thoughtlessly set on fire by their playmate. They had been rushed immediately to Sun Towers Burn Unit in our home town of El Paso, Texas.

The doctor's first assessment brought frightening news: John, age seven, was burned on the left side of his face, on both hands, on the back of his head, in two places on his legs. These were second and third degree burns, the latter involving the complete destruction of the top two layers of skin and penetrating into the fatty tissue beneath. Taken altogether, the burns constituted thirty-five percent of his body. For Andy, our four year old, things were even more serious. Sixty-three percent of his skin was gone-from his chest, from his back, from his left arm and hand, from his face. Half the hair on his head was gone.

Within fourteen hours my husband Bob, the two boys, and I had been flown by private jet from Sun Towers to the Shriners Burns Institute in Galveston, Texas, almost a thousand miles away. Between us we had one suitcase, stuffed with unmatched clothes. We had no idea where we were going, no understanding at all of the world we were about to enter.

I remember many things about the three months we spent in Galveston, but two stand out particularly.

We didn't know if Andy would live. He lay wrapped in white gauze on a high bed, in isolation, and did not talk. A fungus stalked his bloodstream; the antibiotic they gave him to counteract it made him vomit. They had a tube in his nose that led to his stomach so they could keep milk in him, an IV in his arm, machines on both sides of his bed to monitor his heart and lungs. It was a month before we knew for certain which way he would go. During that time the infection took an ear and three fingers.

When Andy recovered, there was a second thing to deal with, in its own way just as hard. During the last five or six weeks of our stay there, we struggled with the ever-more-apparent fact that John and Andy would be permanently scarred.

We were devastated by the fire. We were undone by our children's suffering, by the fact that our two handsome boys were bald and earless, had lost fingers, and had faces that were not "normal."

Everyone said that this sort of thing was tragic. I agreed. Yet, even so, there was some part of me that refused to see it that way.

It leapt to the fire, elated by it, as if I had waited all my life for just this moment, as if that fire had raged hot and bright these thirty-five years waiting for my life to intersect it. Though with my mouth I would have told you there was no God, a part of me knew that through the fire He was going to make Himself apparent to me.

The long stay in the hospital, so far from all that was familiar, made a strong impression on me. It was another world, strange and foreign; the kids there its unearthly citizens. Their faces and bodies startled me every time I saw them, reminding me again and again that I had to push past what I could see, that I had to trust my heart, not my eye. And what my heart told me was that these were remarkable children.

The Shriners Burns Institute at that time was a thirty-bed hospital—fifteen beds for the acutely burned and fifteen for kids undergoing reconstruction. They only took the major burn cases: there was always a child burned over ninety percent of his body, always a case where a sister or brother or parent had died in the same fire. There were always children whose smoke inhalation had caused severe internal injuries, brain damage, comas.

There were kids burned years before who had come back for reconstruction work. Some had noses, some didn't. Others had no hands or legs. Just when my eye thought it had seen all it could bear, I would open a door on a child who had no face at all, two holes for a nose, a line for a mouth. Just when I thought I had heard the worst stories I would ever have to hear, I met a young girl who was half bald, whose nose and lip were distorted, who got burned when a drunk driver rammed into the back of her mother's car, whose brother died in the same fire. And she'd take out a picture of herself before any of this happened, a picture of herself on the school playground with her books in her arms, as pretty a girl as you'd ever seen.

These children. They were an uncomely bunch: hard to look at, often frightening, marked for life, misshapen. Most of them seemed undaunted, especially here in the hospital. When I sat among them in the playroom, listening to them laugh, watching them horse around, it felt good. What I could see of them was burned, but what remained unseen was no more misshapen than a rod of iron. What remained unseen—that remarkable tenacity and courage—blossomed and flowered despite their scars.

These faces, these strange odd faces, were like signs to me, like omens. But of what? I used to stare out the window, stand in the hallway, look in the rooms, trying to see it, trying to catch it. What was it I didn't understand?

The hospital was a remarkable place, a strange and foreign country. I didn't know it then, but it was giving me a longing for and a taste of the new country of the spirit that I was only beginning to suspect existed.

At the end of three months, we left Galveston and returned home to El Paso. We had begun to adjust to the way the boys had changed. We had seen them right after the fire, screaming and crying, the skin coming off their bodies in stinking yellow strips. We had seen their heads swollen with edema, so bloated that their eyes and mouths wouldn't open. We had seen Andy so sick he couldn't even talk, lying on his high bed, hallucinating. We had seen them recover, laugh, begin to get well.

For three months our eyes had been assaulted by the sight of burned children, many of them so much worse than John and Andy. The more we looked at the two of them—despite their scars—the better they looked. They looked, in fact, really good.

But other people could not see what we saw. All they could do was stare, astounded by the change. As the months passed, it only got worse; it seemed to me that the better the boys looked, the more people stared at them. They were terribly rude. "What happened to your face?" strangers would blurt out. Or worse, "Were you two little boys playing with matches?"

Those who weren't rude, often acted ignorant. Because their own children's faces were unscarred, perfect, they acted like what we had been through could never happen to them. It made me angry. I was raw and edgy, just waiting for a fight, and coming slowly and surely to the end of myself.

Oddly enough, the weight of my anger fell on my neighbor, Ginny Baker. People told me that I should be angry at the boy who started the fire, but I didn't feel angry with him. It was Ginny who really upset me. I had known her for three or four years. Because she was younger than I was, I liked to imagine that I could advise her about things: about raising children, about marriage and then, too, about some spiritual matters that I felt I knew a lot about— my conclusions about God and life.

It seemed to me that during the last year or so something strange had happened to Ginny. For one thing, she started going to church. For another thing, she started talking about Jesus, putting Bible verses all over her kitchen cabinets. But much worse than that, she didn't seem interested in my advice anymore. That really made me mad. After all, hadn't I just been through this fire? Didn't I know plenty?

One afternoon in February, a year after the fire, I went over to talk to Ginny, determined to save her from her church and set her straight about Jesus. She was in her kitchen, ironing. I sat at her kitchen table and I began by explaining to her the logic of certain ideas I had about karma. But she kept asking me stupid questions. Like: Where had I gotten that idea? How did I know that it was true? Her questions surprised me. I had imagined that she would immediately see that what I was telling her was true. Maybe it was her reaction, but suddenly I couldn't seem to make sense out of karma either.

Ginny kept on ironing. I stared at her. I felt as if my life depended on convincing her that I was right, but my tongue felt heavy and powerless. Ginny stopped talking, too. It was as if we both had been emptied of words and thoughts, as if this struggle took place in some other arena and was being fought and won while we stood by mute and helpless.

"I better go home," I said finally, but just sat there, dazed and stupid. Right then Ginny leaned across her ironing board and blurted out, "Don't you know that Jesus died to save you?"

Suddenly I woke up. That was the limit! Of course I knew that Jesus died to save me. Hadn't I heard it a million times? But I knew something that Ginny obviously didn't know, and I was exultant, thinking that at last I'd won the argument. I knew that Christ was an idea and that his dying was a symbol. Couldn't she see that? Maybe he had lived, maybe he had been a good man, but his dying couldn't do anything for me. Could she possibly believe that it had? I was horrified. Only stupid people believe that—only stupid people and religious freaks.

And I let Ginny know how I felt. The argument ended at her front doorstep.

I went home feeling terribly depressed. I lay on my bed thinking that I had lost everything. The boys were burned, I didn't have anyone who listened to me, I didn't even have this one friend that I had wanted so desperately to have. It was impossible for me to be friends with her, knowing what she believed. All night I wrestled with the words of our argument, trying—in my imagination at least—to get her to agree to what I knew was true. But even in my imagination, I couldn't turn her around. Once you start believing in Jesus, you're lost. You're a goner.

The next day was a Saturday. It was our family's habit to take a long walk on Saturday, usually in the desert near our house. As I walked beside Bob and the kids, I kept going over and over my argument with Ginny, still trying to persuade her to see things from my point of view.

We stopped to rest by a dry stream bed. It was there that the argument resolved itself. I saw something, not with my eyes, not in my imagination, but in my heart, the way I discovered much later God's Spirit allows us to see. I saw Ginny's life laid out like a long golden thread. It lay in two parts, one part empty, and the other part full. And the part that was full was filled with gold.

I had no idea what that gold was or how I knew so certainly that the long thread was Ginny's life. But suddenly, it seemed as if the answer to the problem that I struggled with was given to me. It was so obvious it made me laugh: I would believe whatever Ginny believed. It was that simple.

I began to go to Bible studies with Ginny. Even though I was determined to get at the heart of what she knew, I didn't want these church ladies telling me what to think. Of course I offered my opinions—all of them!

At one study, the group leader quoted from the Bible a verse that grabbed hold of me; for the first time I felt the power of God's word. She said, "For by grace are ye saved through faith, and that not of yourself: it is the gift of God: not of works, lest any man should boast." (Ephesians 2: 8,9)

I didn't understand much about that verse, but all week I kept hearing that word "works." God did not look at works. This stuck in my mind: nothing I could do would save me. I am certain that I didn't know what I had to be saved from or why I should be saved or even that I was lost. I only knew one thing: I was miserable.

The night before the next Bible study I had a dream. I was stuck inside a long pipe, trapped; all night I struggled to get out. The next day, I told the women about my dream. I told them that I often had dreams about dying and that these dreams frightened me.

"Do you know what will happen to you when you die?" one of them asked.

No, I didn't, even with all the ideas I had in my head about God.

"Do you think you'll be with God?" she asked again.

"I don't know," was my weary answer.

She began to talk to me about eternal life and about Jesus. I listened, not understanding, but wanting to know. She promised me that she would call me later that afternoon and explain more. But I couldn't wait and I knew it.

"Can't you tell me everything right now?" I asked her. The other women helped. Together they told me about Jesus, that He had died to save me, that He had given His life to bring me to God. They helped me to pray, and on that day I asked Jesus to be my savior.

I had no idea then what had happened to me or if, indeed, anything at all had happened. But as time passed, I began to feel Jesus' love for me and be aware of the way He had been working all through my life.

I remember waking up one morning and feeling that my heart was absolutely clean, absolutely empty of hatred and despair, of malice. It would not always be that way, but that day it was, and I knew Jesus had given me that gift. I knew that there had been only one goal in my whole life and that goal, whatever else happened, was to come to Jesus.

The fire that nearly took the lives of our two sons was a tragedy. But God, as the Bible says, works all things together for good to them that love Him—even our most tragic things, even our most foolish mistakes, even our darkest intentions. So much good has come from the fire, and there is so much that we have to be thankful for.

The most wonderful thing is that our boys are alive. Their scars grow less apparent as they grow older. You should see how handsome they are! And they are wonderful, remarkable young men, strong and tender and courageous.

And Susie, too, that young girl who led her brothers resolutely past all those critical staring faces, has become a young woman who is filled with compassion and energy for other people. The fire brought us closer together as a family. And God took from all of us the desire to blame anyone for the fire, kept us free from bitterness.

Why did God use this fire to bring me to Himself? I don't know. I do know, however, that one day He will show me why. And I know this, too—the fire brought me to the end of myself in a way nothing else ever did. It made me listen. It made me turn to God and take, finally, the gift He has always offered me: His son and His new life.

ANN BOYD BAKER

Ann Boyd Baker, retired court reporter in Harris County, lives in Houston with her husband, Alick. She says that her husband; her two daughters, Rev. Janis Smith (Presbyterian) and Terry Smith Hedrick; and a grandson, Otto Smith-Goeke are "an essential part of God's blessing" in her life. Ann is the youngest of six children born to the Rev. James Cleveland Boyd (Baptist) and Isla May Splawn Boyd. She says, "Preceding me as most fortunate offspring were J.C. Boyd, Jr., Jennie Boyd Bull(deceased), Elizabeth Boyd Carr, Ruth Boyd Brown, and Isla Lucile Boyd."

Who's in Charge?

by Ann Boyd Baker

As the smallest and the noisiest at our dinner table, I loudly demanded of my parents, four sisters, and one brother, "Why do I have to eat something I don't like?" After briefly explaining that, whether I liked it or not, my body needed good food to grow properly, my dad said, "When you clean your plate, you may leave the table." An hour later, deserted by my parents and siblings, I finally gulped down the cold spinach and ran outside to play. Scenes like this were repeated often in my early childhood. I threw temper tantrums, endured spankings, was sent to my room, apologized, promised never to do it again, repeatedly tested limits, and seldom got by with breaking the rules.

Today, as I approach my seventieth year, I realize how God's Spirit has used unlikely and sometimes negative experiences to change a self-centered child to an adult who is eager to follow His will. Throughout the years, God's Spirit has gotten my attention through encounters with reality in this imperfect world.

I was a P.K., a Baptist preacher's kid, indulged by my mother, disciplined by my father, and loved by both. Thoroughly spoiled with attention as the baby in the family, I was strong willed, self important, stubborn, and intent on having my way.

My training in things spiritual was inextricably tied up with the church. In the city of Fort Worth and in each of the three Texas towns where dad served as pastor during my youth, our family lived in the parsonage adjacent to the Baptist Church. The church building was my second home. I played in the church yard, up and down the banisters, and even down in the church basement when my parents were busy elsewhere. At least three times a week, we went to church services. Without questioning, I participated in it all—sometimes disruptive, but mainly conforming—in an effort to please and to gain the approval of my parents.

Our family prospered through the 1920s but experienced hard times in the economic depression of the '30s. Dad left his position as pastor of the North Fort Worth Baptist Church to serve as Superintendent of the Baptist Hospital in Fort Worth in 1929 and 1930.

Economic conditions, which were grim all over America, affected this hospital. When a group of doctors bought it from Texas Baptists, Dad was out of a job. After a period of unemployment and uncertainty, Dad was called to pastor the First Baptist Church in the small town of Grandview, Texas. We moved from the large, two-story home in Fort Worth to the parsonage next to this church. Our faith that God would provide was tested by the reality of weekly church collections which were insufficient to take care of the financial needs of the church and the pastor's family.

Because the church members in this farming community had little money, they had a unique way of supporting us. Every fall, when our family returned home from a Sunday night service, we found the parsonage overflowing with church members of all ages shouting, "Surprise, surprise!"

What a wonderful surprise it was. We had been "pounded," the term used to describe gifts of a pound of sugar, a pound of butter, and generous donations of other foods: canned vegetables, sacks of potatoes, loaves of homemade bread, jars of delicious homemade preserves, smoked ham and bacon. Mother found storage space under our beds for the surplus food, which lasted many weeks.

God provided again when we were allowed to pick corn, peaches, pecans, peas, etc. on the nearby farms at harvest time. We enjoyed fresh eggs and fried chicken from the feathered occupants of our chicken pen. Dad milked our two cows, and we females strained the milk, made butter and cottage cheese, and delivered the extra milk to neighbors.

We never went hungry, and we even had enough to share with the hoboes who stopped periodically at our back door. All of my clothes were hand-me-downs, home-sewn, or donated by church members. I remember putting two layers of cardboard in my shoes to keep my feet dry when I walked to school. For years I believed that everyone used safety pins to make undergarments fit.

My faith and trust in God was growing as our physical needs were met. God, our church, my loving family, and the sharing community were somehow all responsible for my sense of well being in spite of material poverty.

Living through the Depression shattered any illusion of self-sufficiency. We willingly shared our goods and energies to meet common needs. As an adult, I have identified with the poor because I have been there. The poor were and are my brothers and sisters.

Almost every Baptist church service ended with an invitation for those present to take Jesus Christ as their Savior and to join the church. At age thirteen, I affirmatively and intentionally gave my heart to God, joined the College Avenue Baptist Church of Fort Worth, and was baptized by my father. This was not the result of some outstanding revelation, but my response to years of Bible study and the positive teachings and influence of Sunday School teachers and ministers. I wanted to surrender my life to this creative, all-powerful, all-knowing God.

There was no radical change following this conversion experience. I just became more willing to do what I knew was right and felt more guilty when I did not follow my inner compass and Biblical truths. I felt a greater sense of love and wholeness when I asked for and received forgiveness.

At that time I felt that Christians in general, and Baptists in particular, had a monopoly on compassion and acts of kindness. I first questioned my Baptist upbringing when I was a junior at Texas State College for Women in Denton. There I met a middle-aged professor, whom I will call Dr. Jones, who believed in the teachings of John Dewey, a philosophy professor at the University of Chicago.

In my previous years of schooling, the conventional teacher delivered unquestioned knowledge to passive students, who just accepted and swallowed whole what was offered. Dr. Jones challenged her students to question, to search for knowledge on their own, and to think independently.

As I became Dr. Jones's friend, I learned that she was a humanist who did not believe in the existence of God. She was convinced that men and women, using only their own capabilities, could solve the deeper problems of our world by working toward the right goals and using the right methods. No higher power or spiritual dimension was available or necessary.

I not only learned about Dr. Jones's beliefs, but I also watched her actions. Dr. Jones had a Negro maid named Clara, whom she had grown to love and appreciate. When Clara became ill, Dr. Jones went to Clara's home, cooked for her, and even weeded her small garden to save the vegetables.

This impressed me very much because I had grown up in a completely segregated society. In Grandview, the Blacks "stayed in their place," which meant that during daylight hours, they came over to the more affluent homes and the surrounding farms to work as maids, servants, and field workers. At night, they returned to their section of town. Blacks and whites lived in very different and unequal worlds in Grandview, and yet this arrangement was not questioned by anyone I knew.

I had seen many examples of love and kindness toward individual black persons in Grandview, but I could not imagine any of the ladies who attended the First Baptist Church lowering themselves to actually work in a black person's home or garden. They might give money or take food, but it was always charity from a higher social level to a lower social level.

By her actions, Dr. Jones exemplified the teachings and example of Jesus, but she did not believe in Him or the God of the Bible. This humanist was living out Baptist teachings better than the Baptists, including me. I wrote to my father about my doubts. Dad wrote back that God had revealed Himself to the children of Israel progressively, as they were able to understand. God's greatest revelation was through Jesus, to show us what He is like, ready to forgive and, through His grace and our cooperation, to enable us to grow more Christ-like. God would reveal Himself to me and guide me as I opened more of myself to His control. Dad, essentially, directed me back to my personal responsibility to God.

After much thought, I concluded that there are situations in life that I cannot understand, that I cannot be sure about. I am not God, and I am not to judge. From my observations of Dr. Jones's actions in the early '40s and my observations of the actions of other unselfish and caring persons over the years, I know that God's goodness is not limited to organized religious channels. It flows through any person who is kind and helpful to others.

In the summer of '42, against the wishes of my parents, I married Joe E. Smith, my high school sweetheart. Joe left three months later to serve in the U.S. Army in North Africa, Italy, and the Philippines. The anxiety I felt during those thirty-eight months of separation compelled me to draw closer to God in prayer. I attended church prayer meetings, receiving support from other Christians who had family members involved in that tragic war.

I asked for help often during busy days as I finished college, worked as a legal secretary, taught science in Angleton High School, and served as a laboratory technician for Dow Chemical Company in Freeport. My prayers were still mostly self-centered: "Please end this terrible war. Please bring Joe home safely. Please help me pass this exam, get this job, acquire this new skill, work out my finances."

In the postwar years, Joe completed his bachelor's degree; a first daughter, Janis, was born in 1947; and we adopted our second daughter, Terry Jo, in 1955. Joe and I enjoyed about ten happy, productive years, actively assuming responsibilities in the First Baptist Church and in community organizations in Woodville. Throughout this period, I mostly used my prayer time to thank God for my blessings and to ask for the strength and energy needed to keep up with home duties and all of our activities. For the next nine years of our marriage, I was increasingly dependent on God because our marriage was in trouble. We were on different paths, with changing priorities and preferred activities. My prayers were mainly pleas for help: "How can this marriage be saved? What can I do?" I needed help in handling my anger, frustration, depression, and anxiety about the future. If God's Spirit hadn't been close, I do not know how I could have survived those years and the grief that followed our divorce in 1961.

My moves to Beaumont and then to Houston a year later were traumatic for my daughters—Janis, age fifteen, and Terry, age seven. My new career as a court reporter kept me working nights and weekends. With the help of a dear friend, Martha F. Mathes, who lived with our family for several years, our lives stabilized. Martha's loving heart and generous spirit blessed our family as she shared expenses, often cooked special meals, and took time to listen to Janis and Terry as they matured.

Things began to go well financially. The girls seemed happy and were doing well in school, and I began to run on my own battery, assuming that I had it all together and could figure out the answers for any problems. As stress decreased, my prayers became routine and less frequent. Instead of staying close to my Loving Source, I drifted away, arrogantly assuming I was capable of functioning on my own.

A watershed experience occurred as I interacted with a loved one who had a drinking problem. In my ignorance of how addiction works, I thought I could straighten out this difficulty by giving practical advice. Nothing I did or said helped. My frustration led me to attend an Al-Anon group to learn how to help this person stop drinking.

Over a period of months, the message I received from contact with this twelve-step program was essentially the same as the one I had received from my father when I raised questions about Dr. Jones. My number one priority should be to straighten up my own personal relationship with God. Who was running the show? Who was guiding my decision-making? Whose life was mine, anyway? In following the same twelve steps that alcoholics take, I rededicated my life, giving it over to the care of God as I understood Him from biblical teachings. Step five directed that I admit to God, to myself, and to another human being the exact nature of my wrongs. I took this step, admitting my pride and other sins, and my willingness to be changed. I asked God to help me conform to His will. I apologized directly and by letters to several persons for occasions when I had taken advantage or been unkind and un-Christian.

As a result, God's forgiveness, which is always available, became real, and I no longer carried those inner spiritual blockages from the past. I determined not to let guilt and the sin of unforgiveness accumulate in the future. Since then, I have tried to keep current on my accountability to God and to others.

What a freeing-up experience! It is ironic that it took the influence of an Al-Anon group and, later, an Emotions Anonymous group to motivate me to do what I had been taught from childhood: to put God first, to confess sins, to forgive and to accept forgiveness, and to seek His guidance one day at a time. Through these channels, God's spirit taught me that I would never know it all, particularly in relation to others.

After giving God permission to take charge of my will and my life, I expected radical change as the result. Although I was open to whatever plans God's Spirit had in mind for me, I received no drastic revelation.

How was I to know God's will?

Two authors, Hannah Whitall Smith and Catherine Marshall, helped me understand how to "hear" God's Spirit in the routine of my daily life. In *The Christian's Secret of a Happy Life*, Smith suggested four guidelines: to follow the clear teachings of the Bible, to use common sense, to consider outer circumstances (opportunities and obstacles), and to be aware of recurring inward impressions. Marshall added a fifth guideline in *Beyond Ourselves*: to seek advice from someone who knows and loves you.

I decided that until I received "the biggie call," I would volunteer to serve in small ways as needs were presented in my church. The congregation of South Main Baptist Church, which I joined in 1974, was and still is moderate, innovative, inclusive, and ministering. Over the years, I felt led by inner impressions to visit cancer patients and their families at M. D. Anderson Hospital, to assist adult Bible study groups, and to join other South-Mainers in leading our congregation in 1984 to join the newly-formed inner-city Emergency Aid Coalition.

The Coalition began with a food pantry and expanded its ministry to the homeless, the poor, and the underprivileged, as fourteen downtown interfaith congregations pooled their resources and volunteers. While working with these salt-of-the earth volunteers, I was led by God's Spirit to help establish the E.A.C. Main Street Clothing Center and to enlarge the Aid to Families ministry.

As I relaxed and sought God's guidance, God's Spirit became closer to me than any person. I felt and continue to feel His love, peace, serenity, and joy, even in difficult situations.

In my later years my gratitude to God has mushroomed because of this closeness and because of outer circumstances: the blessings of a happy home life with Alick H. Baker, a kind, gentle man with a sense of humor, whom I married in 1980; the joy of a grandson, Otto, now fifteen; and the satisfaction of seeing Janis, Terry, and Terry's husband, Chris Hedrick, leading positive, productive lives.

As a child, I was more interested in the gifts than the Giver. As an older adult, I know that experiencing God's love directly is the greatest gift, the source of all my good—good that I can share.

KELLY HUNT LYON

An Arkansas native, Kelly Hunt Lyon lives in Little Rock with her husband Martin Lyon. A graduate of Lyon College in Batesville, Arkansas, Kelly has worked in public service for the past seven years in the offices of the Lieutenant Governor, Governor, and now the Arkansas Science and Technology Authority. She is a member St. James United Methodist Church and active in church and civic activities.

"Writing my spiritual autobiography has reinforced my belief that God is an active participant in my daily life. This project has given me a much-needed spiritual focus and marked a special time in my spiritual journey."

OUT OF THE VOID
by Kelly Hunt Lyon

My grandfather could make himself so still and quiet that birds, squirrels, raccoons, and deer would come up and eat out of his hand. I often thought they sensed his gentle, kindred spirit. He was part Cherokee Indian; nature was a part of his being. He was wise, gentle, giving much of himself to his family, his church, his community.

I came to live with him and my grandmother on their farm when my father was killed suddenly and tragically in Vietnam. I loved my grandfather as my second father. He was the only constant, steadying force throughout my uncertain childhood and anxious teen years.

Below his gentle spirit lay a strong will. I could sometimes sense the two qualities conflicting inside him. He wanted me to be independent, self sufficient, educated—and religious. He taught me never to accept another man's truth blindly; he expected me to think for myself. Unfortunately that teaching applied to everything *except* my grandfather's religion. When I questioned his vision of the truth and rejected parts of it, a rift opened between us, although we continued to reach out to one another with love.

Sometime during my sophomore year of college, I became acquainted with a woman on campus. She had seen many college students experience a period of confusion, called disequilibrium, after the excitement of their first year at college subsided.

When we met, I was a confused, frightened young woman. Our visits became islands of tranquility in my turbulent and ever-changing young life. She helped me sift through the rubble that was my soul and find a few precious pieces which would later become the building blocks of my spiritual foundation.

I especially remember our winter visits. We would sit by the fire, drink spice tea, and venture down one spiritual path, then another. We declared no specific path right or wrong, just possible. I remember telling her one time, "My insides feel like a jumble of puzzle pieces. A few fit together. But most don't, and some are missing. I just *know* there is one piece that will fit perfectly and solve the puzzle."

Sometimes she would mention a particular book or author I might investigate. And often on my own I turned up books about how to meditate, how to pray, how to lead a spiritual life. I searched for a belief system, whole and intact, that I could adopt to end the incessant questions that kept bubbling up from deep inside me. I felt that if I could find the right author or the right book, I might understand what was happening inside me.

My life seemed like a paperweight with water and plastic snow bottled up inside. Some unseen force (God?) had picked me up, shaken me to make everything fly around, and then set me back down to watch where the pieces settled. Looking back, I now realize my feeling of being shaken apart coincides with the beginning of my spiritual journey in earnest—and my grandfather's death.

Suffering a heart attack, Granddaddy died quietly and quickly beside his wife of forty-seven years. He died in the same woods in which he had grown up, the same woods where I grew to womanhood. He had taught me many precious and valuable lessons there. In his lessons about trees and birds and flowers and all living things were couched all he knew of nature and life and God.

The night Granddaddy died I returned to my childhood home, only to find it filled with people and flooded with light. Every possible light burned brightly, as if to announce my family's loss to the world. Someone gave me a turkey sandwich and a glass of milk. The turkey tasted like cardboard and the milk like chalk. I was numb. I was tired. My inner self began drawing away from the people in the house. I felt as if a glass wall closed down between me and the other people. I could see them but could not hear them talking. I hung in limbo, suspended between shock and grief.

Then I heard a faint, distant voice. Slowly it became clearer and more audible. It echoed within my being, yet it was not of me. Instead of registering in my brain, the message spoken by this voice settled deep in my core. And from this core radiated a knowledge which defies description. With this knowledge also came a physical sensation of a warm, comforting embrace. It could have lasted five seconds or five minutes. When it was gone, I knew my grandfather had died in the manner he had always wished for, because God was merciful.

After my grandfather's death, I embarked on a reading frenzy. The subject matter varied—New Age, Christian meditation, textbooks on world religions, Native American stories, self-help literature—anything that might answer how I should live. My foundation had crumbled, leaving me without a firm foothold. For two years I asked my friend, asked an unknown god, asked myself unceasing questions. These nagging queries kept bubbling up from inside in one form or another. Later, I realized every question was simply a variation of one three-part question: Who, what, and where are you God?

Although I felt God did exist, I did not know where or how to find him. I clung to the voice I heard at my grandfather's death, and it took on a "burning bush" quality. As a result, I spent much time seeking dramatic, larger-than-life encounters with God, only to be disappointed. I began to see in my mind's eye where I wanted to be spiritually: connected to God's Spirit and secure in my faith that he was guiding my life. Unfortunately, a deep chasm, devoid of light, loomed between me and my goal. I despaired of ever being able to cross this void. Frightened and confused, I searched futilely for a passageway. Not finding one, I gave it up. I attempted to turn my attention to other pursuits. I launched into a challenging physical journey. I left behind my turbulent campus life and set off for Europe, having been admitted to the Institute for European Studies in Vienna, Austria.

There, the one place where all the beauty, culture, and emotion of Vienna converged on me was the Votivekirche, or Church of Light. Its twin spires, ornately decorated, reached heavenward. Inside, walls of brilliantly-hued stained glass depicted persons and symbols of Christianity. The striking blues, reds, greens, yellows, and purples depicted clear, clean, and precise scenes which especially moved me. They embodied exactly the spiritual qualities I longed for. The windows contained no blurred or murky areas. As I gazed, awe-struck, at these works of beauty, my spiritual dilemma surfaced again.

Stunning as they were, the windows remained only a small part of my fascination with the Votivekirche. One afternoon, as I sat there thinking, I heard something which sounded like an organ, a choir, and an orchestra combined. Turning, I saw a man seated at a synthesizer. His music filled the sanctuary with haunting and beautiful sounds. The surroundings and music drew my spirit into contemplation. Here was a man who could compose and play beautiful music reflecting his life experience. What could I do? What did God intend me to do?

Over and over again, the Votivekirche drew me into its cool shelter. After setting out for a different destination, I would repeatedly find myself standing inside the church, staring at the windows. I also became acquainted with the man who played the synthesizer: Romayne Wheeler. We talked about music, poetry, inner journeys.

Wheeler staunchly believed that people who never embark on a spiritual journey simply exist instead of living life fully. Contrary to my belief that I should somehow already know the answers to my questions, and therefore had failed in some way, Wheeler felt his inner journey complimented and enhanced his outer journey. He believed that real living demands a continuous, individual, inner spiritual journey with no map, no absolute path, no destination—just the journey.

Had I at last found a foothold? Or even a crossing? Perhaps it was no longer imperative that I have all the answers. Perhaps I might never have answers to all my questions, but some would surely come in time. Perhaps there was no absolute right or wrong road to travel. Could I chart my own path? Perhaps more than one bridge spanned the chasm between me and my goal.

After I completed my studies in Austria, I returned to the small liberal arts college I had been attending. But my renewed spirit soon shriveled. Once again turbulence threatened to overwhelm me. I questioned what I should do. Perhaps I should embark on another journey. Should I join the Peace Corps? Or maybe I would volunteer to work on an Indian reservation in the Badlands of South Dakota. Or I could return to Europe. I wanted to go somewhere, anywhere, where I could pretend I was happy.

I resumed my visits with my friend. She noticed a difference in me but did not pry. However, the Dean of Students did. He called me aside one day and shared some of his observations with me. Having known me for over three years, he knew that my current behavior and companions were drastically different from those of my early college years. My academic work and personal life were now characterized by erratic highs and lows.

A sense of doom crept over me. If the dean could see things were not right, then anyone could. Anyone who cared to take a close look could see that what I was using as the glue to hold my life together was no longer working. My life was beginning to come apart. In Vienna, I felt sure the answers I found in the Votivekirche would sustain me. Sadly, they only broke my fall for a time. Without hope, I finally slid over the edge—into my deep, dark chasm.

As a child I had depended upon my grandfather for order and stability. As a young college student, alcohol seemed like the glue necessary to hold my life together. When I drank alcohol, I thought it enabled me to do things I felt inadequate to do otherwise. I was shy; alcohol made me bold. I was afraid; alcohol made me fearless. I was alone; alcohol was my friend. I had many questions; alcohol had all the answers.

My life had flown out of control. My efforts to live my life spiritually had failed. I reached the turning point, yet I did not have the faintest inkling what to do. There was no hope for me. I had done my best and still felt miserable. At age twenty-two I reached a point of complete surrender. I was wholly and utterly defeated. I needed more than self-will to live, and live happily. However, I had no idea what I needed—God, religion, or a how-to manual for life. I could no longer deny I needed something greater. Crying out to an unknown, unseen God, I begged for help.

Ironically, in admitting my defeat, I unwittingly found the bridge I had been so desperately searching for. I had looked for God in books, in buildings, in people, in experiences. I had also looked inside myself numerous times. But not knowing exactly what I was looking for, I repeatedly overlooked the most important part of my being.

This has been a vitally important lesson for me. When I am seriously and earnestly searching for God, I become entangled in the exterior process, and my search and my link with him weakens. All the energy I pour into the search for him seems to act like a dense cloud or heavy smoke screen. It obscures my vision. I cannot see what is just in front of me, or rather just inside me.

When I turned to a Twelve-Step recovery program for help, God was the last thing I expected to find. I had no idea that this program was to become my spiritual bridge. But as the years passed and I attended Twelve Step meetings with real commitment, God began to speak to me.

Recently, I stood up in our meeting room, located in the basement of a small church, and took my place beside the table at the center. I looked around at forty friends. Some of their faces showed inner peace and serenity, results of the efforts of the daily struggles outside that room. Other faces revealed hesitancy in removing protective masks, and still others wore resentment at having to be there at all. Some faces registered understanding and acceptance of our need to share with each other. At this moment I was elated, yet scared, both proud and humble for I had just passed a mark— five years of sobriety.

I identified myself and started to speak. Almost immediately my voice quivered, not from nervousness but from overwhelming joy and gratitude. I told how much I loved them for nurturing me and allowing me to put down roots here. I fought back tears as I thanked them for allowing me to remove my masks at a snail-like pace. I praised them for accepting and loving me unconditionally when I could not accept nor love myself. Unable to hold my tears longer, I told them they were my family of choice.

I don't remember everything I said that night. Old-timers tell me that's good, because God was speaking to others through me. I need these people to remind me of God's presence. Their faces reflect his presence in my life. I only trust that, sometimes, my face, my words, and my actions also reflect his presence in my life.

When I concentrate on living life on its own terms, I am more aware of God's presence. I become aware of him in the ease with which my life flows, and the smooth, effortless way everything fits together. My life is woven together by an unseen hand to form a unique and beautiful tapestry. But I must remember that I am not the hand; I am the fiber.

Today, some of God's Spirit lives within me. Unlike my grandfather, I have not yet developed the capacity to lead both a religious and a spiritual life. It is much easier for me to find God's Spirit in a flower than in a building. I see signs of his existence every day—in nature, in kind words from a stranger, in shared experiences with loved ones. For me, leading a spiritual life is the process of accepting God's will and molding my will to his. Self-will defeated me once. It can do so again.

When I speak of God's will, I do not mean God speaks to me and gives me a detailed account of what he wants me to do. Instead, I am presented with a series of choices each day. One choice affects the next, and they are all intertwined. When confronted with a choice, I inventory my feelings and motives, become quiet enough to hear that soft, still voice deep inside my being, and find signs of God's will. If I make the choice based on what I feel God's will might be, the process is easy and effortless. Things I could not do alone are simply done for me. Options and opportunities present themselves.

I try to remember that God is only a prayer or thought away. Too often I succumb to selfish desires and distance myself from his spirit. Usually during these times, I have a lesson to learn or a direction in which to grow. My life is a series of these cycles, each molding me into a more spiritual person. Often, choices or problems keep presenting themselves until I have learned the lesson. Each time I work through a situation, I gain a deeper awareness of God's presence in my everyday life.

Of course there are times when I feel I am going to fall back into a spiritual void. But as surely as God showed mercy at the time of my grandfather's death, so he shows grace to me daily. When I am fearful, he reminds me of his presence in all areas of my life—in work, at home, with friends and loved ones, with strangers. Nothing is too great or too small for God's grace.

I have finally found a bridge across my spiritual void. Yet, like most humans, I am short-sighted. I assumed I would reach a final spiritual destination once I found the bridge and crossed it. Now I know there is no spiritual destination for me. I spent years looking for God's Spirit in the outer world. His spirit is not something I must find outside myself and bring inside. It is already there, residing in the place deep inside where questions once arose. My goal is no longer a place, but a state of mind and heart and spirit. I must simply wake each day with a willingness to go where God wills me, learn what he wants to teach me, and grow.

Patricia LaVigne

Patricia LaVigne has lived in the South with her husband and two children since 1978. She teaches third grade in the Jacksonville, Texas, public schools. As a past member of Our Lady of Sorrows Catholic Church, Patricia lectured and led congregational singing during the Sunday mass. She and her family have also provided musical entertainment at the local nursing and retirement homes on occasion. Presently, Patricia and her family are members of the Cathedral of the Immaculate Conception in Tyler, Texas.

"I think part of my destiny is to grow in the understanding that humanity is both strong and feeble. I am both, but in my weakness, the Holy Spirit gives me strength."

Vows

by Patricia LaVigne

I have always loved my religion and could never understand why Catholics would give it up. The church's doctrine of the resurrection of Jesus gives me hope for happiness in eternity. And yet, over the years I learned that circumstances affect us all, turning some from God, causing some to seek Him in other faiths, and moving me from one field of Christian devotion and service into another.

As a child I felt secure in the Roman Catholic Church's teachings. Things were either right or wrong, good or bad, black or white, distinctions which became very clear when I attended the second grade at St. Patrick's School in my hometown of Seneca Falls, New York. We had spent the entire year memorizing the catechism and learning the commandments in preparation for receiving our First Holy Communion. The Sisters made sure we attended Mass every Sunday. They also taught us to obey our parents and never tell a lie. My young mind became a sponge which soaked up the doctrinal knowledge that prepared me for the ultimate—receiving the body and blood of Jesus Christ in the Eucharist.

In those days, we had to go to confession prior to receiving First Communion. We practiced with Sister, who played the role of the priest. She sat in the confessional, and we took turns going in and confessing "pretend" sins. We were taught how to go the rail, kneel down, fold our hands, and stick out our tongues to receive the sacred Host. We were to receive our First Communion in mid-May, the month dedicated to the Virgin Mary. Before this special occasion, my mother and I went by train to Syracuse to purchase a traditional white dress. The one we chose was organdy with small sparkling rhinestones scattered over it. My veil, with its ruffled crown, draped to my elbows. Mother bought me a pearl rosary and a leather-bound prayer book with gold embossed printing on the cover.

I did not eat any breakfast before Mass that Sunday, for the Church forbade taking any nourishment after midnight as spiritual preparation. Sunday turned out to be a beautiful day. At church, when the organ began to play, we walked solemnly up the middle aisle. My eyes focused on the tips of my folded hands, for the Sisters had told us not to look around, but I was still aware of the candles on the altar burning brightly and the rays of sunlight passing through the stained glass windows making a kaleidoscope of colors across the gray stone floor. The pungent aroma of incense permeated the church. Finally, it was time. The richness of the day was only a moment in time, but forever in memory.

I kept the prayer book and rosary for many years. I recall how I used to embrace the rosary crucifix and try to pull the nails from our Lord's hands and feet because I had been taught that our sins were the reason for his death—a simple expression of my love for him.

In 1954, when I graduated from high school in Glen Burnie, Maryland, I found a position as a switchboard operator with the local telephone company. One evening, during a severe storm, I made my way to work, wading through puddles of water. I had just crossed an intersection when I heard a deafening crack behind me. I jerked around in time to see a live wire spitting sparks on the very spot from which I had just stepped. Transfixed, I thanked God that He had miraculously saved me from death. But for what purpose?

As I walked on to work through the rain, I suddenly realized that although I had been baptized in infancy, I had yet to willingly commit myself to Christ. I had assumed that my godparents had spoken my choice for me and that nothing else was necessary. I began to attend daily Mass and felt a real communion with God in the solitude of the old stone church, yet I continued to wonder about my life purpose.

About a year later, life grew more complex—my mother began to complain of feeling very tired. Her doctor's diagnosis was anemia. A blood test revealed other results, and she was sent to Johns Hopkins for further tests. I learned later that Mother had been diagnosed with leukemia and the doctor expected her to live only three or four years. The doctor and my father decided not to tell her, as they feared that an adverse emotional reaction might cause her health to decline more rapidly. Consequently, she knew she didn't feel well, but didn't know why. She and my father began to argue; my brother's work at school declined, and I grew unhappy. I sought consolation through the daily Mass, searching for an answer.

At times throughout my childhood, my mother had talked to me about becoming a nun. Her suggestions took root, and that summer I contacted a friend, Father Hebert. I told him I desired to enter a religious order but didn't know where to start. He mentioned that the principal of our parish school was looking for lay teachers to work with the Sisters and suggested that working with them in a classroom setting might help me make a decision about entering religious life.

That September, I took charge of a second grade. At year's end, I decided to enter the novitiate at Ilchester, Maryland. I felt this was indeed my purpose, where God wanted me to spend my life. My parents shared my happiness. By now I had been told of my mother's illness, although she still did not know how seriously ill she was. I wanted her to make peace with God, and felt that by turning my own life into one of intense prayer and sacrifice, I could be an instrument for her.

The glory of those days was short-lived. Six months later, I returned home. I had liked the simple life of prayer and meditation, but the academic regimen at the convent overwhelmed me. I grew confused and thought I had made the wrong decision. Although my father indicated more that once he was glad I was home, my mother felt embarrassed because of what others might think. Most people, however, seemed to think my coming home was due to her illness, and at the time I did not say otherwise.

That September I returned to teach second grade at Holy Trinity School. My renewed association with the Sisters there brought me even closer to them. Gradually, I began to see more clearly their compatibility, their stability, and the structured periods of prayer within which they moved. I began to desire religious life again, but I moved more cautiously this time. In fact, because of my previous experience, I tried to convince myself that this foolish notion would pass. I did not want to embarrass myself or my parents again. The inward struggle lasted for several months, but I finally decided. The following August, I once again entered Notre Dame Novitiate with my parents' blessing.

Two and a half years later, twenty-one novices and I professed our vows of poverty, chastity, and obedience. Over the next five years, we would repeat these vows before we could make a final commitment to the religious life.

My mother continued to be treated as an outpatient at Johns Hopkins Hospital. One day when she visited me at Ilchester, she told me she had accidentally learned about her leukemia. From that day on, she seemed to overcome her agoraphobia, a condition she had suffered for many years. She began to attend daily Mass. She planted an abundance of flowers. For the last year of her life, Mother was a new person, although her health continued to decline. In May she was hospitalized. My superior and I visited her one day, and I was permitted to spend one hour with her. She was very thin and had dark circles under her eyes. Her arms were purple from the many intravenous injections. At the end of the hour, my superior came to get me. I rose to leave, although I wanted very badly to stay longer.

As I walked down the hall, I heard Mother sobbing the words, "I'll never see her again." My heart tore apart. I wanted to go back and stay by her bedside, comfort her, hold her, but I had made a vow to obey my superior. Why was I afraid to risk my superior's disapproval of doing what, in spirit, I felt was the better thing? I continued down the hall, hoping my mother's words were wrong. But they weren't. It was the last time I saw her alive.

About this time Vatican II began to look at the role of the contemporary Church and "open the windows" to other religions in a spirit of ecumenism. The changes governing religious community life designed to enhance some areas took their toll in others. The Sisters of Notre Dame de Namur had always maintained a strict rule concerning silence, prayer, and the association of Sisters among themselves. After Vatican II, Sisters were freer to attend functions outside the convent. The change was difficult for some, and friction among community members sometimes resulted. The "black and white" answers so long a part of Church history suddenly became areas of gray.

The Church mandated some universal changes—the vernacular would replace Latin in the liturgy, and congregational singing would be a part of the Mass. The Church also told Catholics they could now eat meat on Friday. These mandates shocked many Catholics—often to the point of asking, "What makes us different from other religions?" At the convent, these and other changes resulted in greater individual freedom and more interaction with the outside world. I liked the changes in the liturgy, but my dissatisfaction with some of the local decisions grew stronger. My superior hinted that this was a tool of the devil used to discourage a spiritual commitment. "Pray harder for the grace to see this through," she encouraged. So, in 1965 I made my final, perpetual vows to God, vows that included a life of devotion and service under the leadership of my Superiors in the convent.

Within three years, I grew discontented and spiritually dry. When I searched for reasons, I concluded that as community life grew more relaxed, I saw how very human even a religious community can be. I continued to struggle inwardly with my feelings, trying to cope with the difficulties. I talked with some very understanding Sisters, but nothing helped. After much prayer, I approached the Provincial Superior to request a dispensation from my vows. She voiced her disappointment, but knew I was very unhappy.

In January, 1969, I signed the necessary documents in the presence of Bishop T. Austin Murphy. I never regretted the decision, but often wondered how I could best continue a life of service and devotion to God outside the convent.

Four years later, I renewed my friendship with a friend from a former parish, Father Anthony Sauerwein. Through him I met Pierre LaVigne, a former television weathercaster whom I had often seen and thought to be quite handsome and personable. Never would I have imagined that a priest, a mutual friend, would arrange a blind date for us. Father Sauerwein took us to dinner and I grew even more impressed with Pierre. Six months later, we stood before Bishop Murphy and Father Sauerwein to promise each other love and help for the rest of our lives. I felt the Divine Blessing in those moments before the altar. As I took the sacramental marriage vows to honor, love and obey my husband, I felt they opened a new world where I could better serve and devote my heart to God.

After twenty years, I still feel blessed. Pierre and I became partners and chose the traditional roles of husband and wife, committed to help each other. Two children were born to us and we brought God to them; we taught them religion at home and helped them prepare for their First Communion. Weekly attendance at church was always important to us. We taught the children how our faith and Christian values can be lived daily.

And I depended upon God to give us help when things went wrong. Pierre's widowed and invalid mother, Helen, who lived with us, continued to decline in health over the years. One day she confided to me that her worst fear was that she might be moved to a nursing home. I promised her that as long as Pierre and I could take care of her, she need not fear.

When she could no longer get out of bed, we began a regimen of turning her every two hours to avoid bedsores and pneumonia, taking care of her elimination accidents, and feeding her. We watched her slowly degenerate into a non-responsive state. I cannot count the times I cried in total frustration, "Why, Lord? Why don't you take her? You take babies from their parents; you allow young people to be crippled for life; you leave children orphaned. Where is your justice?" I could not understand why God allowed Mom to suffer when she was so ready to go.

When Mom passed away in September 1990, at age ninety-seven, I was simultaneously sorry and relieved about her death—relieved that Mom was no longer bound by her incapacitated body but sorry that although I had put the situation in the Lord's hands, I had not allowed enough of Christ's grace to work in me as I questioned his reasons. I consoled myself that at least I was able to keep my promise to care for her at home.

I believe we are all born with a destiny to achieve eternal happiness, whether we fulfill it or not. I also believe that humanity as a whole is both strong and feeble. I have found I am both, whether serving God through my work in the classroom or at home with my family.

One of the saints we honor in the Church is Therese of Lisieux, France. Convinced that very few people are asked to perform great and heroic actions, she felt sanctity was achieved by performing the ordinary daily tasks in an extraordinary way. Most of the time, I try to do the simple things, the little things I am asked to do to the best of my ability. Whether I achieve sanctity in this way is solely the judgment of God. But my faith tells me that my struggles with temptation, great or small, are His challenges for me to grow strong in His love. My hope is that I will never lose sight of the destiny to which He daily calls me.

BETTY THRALL

Betty Thrall is a native Texan living in Jacksonville, Texas. A member of Central Baptist Church, she is a former youth director and teacher. Betty is a homemaker with one grown daughter who is single and teaching Spanish at Wayland Baptist University after completing her doctorate at the University of Texas. Betty and her husband, Gordon, a senior partner in a local law firm, are active in their church and community.

GOING STILL
by Betty Thrall

I met Jesus as my personal savior as a child and never had cause to doubt the reality of the experience, largely because of the wise counsel of my mom at the time. Only today, when I see so many shattered and torn homes, do I realize how fortunate I was to grow up in a happy, Christian home.

Money was never in abundance, but our parents gave us the confidence that we could do anything we attempted as long as we let God do the leading. That sounds a good bit simpler than it was. For instance, college was financially out of the question for me, but since my folks had always wanted me to go, I knew we would find a way. A quick business course, a year as a secretary, and I was ready for school. I worked part-time during my college years, as well as serving in local and state leadership for the Baptist Student Union, all of which gave me a sense of the importance of each minute. I worked hard and played hard—and I still do!

During my first year as a school teacher, I met and later married James Shamburger. My crisis came when he died two years after the wedding. This didn't fit in with my philosophy: trust God, do your best to give Him priority, and everything will work for you. My husband's death threw my carefully-laid plans in a heap. I had meant to teach school only temporarily until my home was filled with loving kids and a happy husband.

Even as I asked God "Why?" I knew in my heart that God was still in control. His answer came through loud and clear to me, "Where were you when I created the world? You don't have to know why."

During this time the value of each moment intensified for me. One day while I sat in a restaurant drinking a cup of coffee, the boy serving me said, "You don't remember me, I guess. You taught me in school. You taught me not to say 'git.' You ain't never gonna catch me saying 'git' 'cause you taught me not to say it." And I thought, "Oh Lord, please, there is more to life than teaching that boy not to say 'git.'" I wanted my time to be invested in eternal values.

In a few months I felt strongly that God was calling me to a special vocation in the church. When I went to the school superintendent to take out the money set aside for my future retirement he said, "Betty, this is just a reaction to your husband's death. Don't take your money out."

I said, "I want that money. I'm going to buy some good-looking clothes and then live on pennies, because I am returning to school." I was very sure of what I was doing. I did not want to go to seminary, where I had seen the girls wearing dowdy clothes. But if that was what I had to do, I would do it. However, I wouldn't wear dowdy clothes while I was there.

I approached a church vocation with fear and trembling because I had always been a behind-the-scenes organizer, not an extrovert. The youth leaders I had known were vivacious, talented extroverts. For me to feel that I was talented in that way seemed downright egotistical; but God opened doors, and I walked through with confidence.

Just before I was to register for seminary, the personnel committee from a leading Baptist church in Dallas called, asking me to come over for an interview. They had known me through my BSU work and hired me immediately. "We wanted someone with seminary training, but we feel that you have the equivalent." To me that was very strong evidence of God's hand directing my life. I did, however, attend seminary part-time and eventually received my degree at Southwestern Baptist Seminary.

For the next fourteen years I built youth programs in Baptist churches, and the Lord blessed those years. My knack seemed to be in building youth programs, and I was asked by the convention to go many places. I traveled to at least twelve states to lead conferences on how to build youth programs. On many occasions I was amazed at the hand of God in this work. Perhaps the most unusual phase of this period was the two years I spent in Hawaii as teacher and counselor in our Baptist academy. This was my first close touch with other nationalities, and I was completely fascinated. My work was with high school and college students whose Buddhist parents sacrificed to send them to our Christian school. What a delightful atmosphere in which to plant and nourish seeds of eternal truths.

In retrospect, I feel I was probably better at youth work because I did not have stunning talents of my own. It was easier for me to seek out and develop the talents of others. I knew the Lord was my shepherd during those fruitful, happy years. Yet I never gave up a tiny hope that "Mr. Right" would surface. When he did, it was swift and sure!

Gordon and I met in July and married in September. How could a lawyer that had used a week of his own vacation time to take teens from his church to camp be anything but Mr. Right! Since we were older, we didn't need a long courtship; we knew what we wanted.

My marriage and my fortieth birthday came in the same month. I discussed with my doctor the possibility of having a child, and he said physically all was well, but he would not advise it because the child would be a teenager when I was a mid-lifer, and psychologically it would be tough. The only words I heard were: "Physically all is well."

Jenifer came along two years later, and she has been the icing on our cake. Gordon and I agree that she has the best of each of us in her, plus a special gift or two that neither of us can claim. When she was small, it was fun to introduce her to the wonderful world, making the exploration a daily adventure. It was also fun when she shared the good and bad news of her days at school.

Gordon and I worked with the "early teens" in our church for eight years, the eighth year being Jeni's last year in middle school. I had asked God for the capacity to stay with this group until our own daughter came through it, thinking we would then be ready to "set-a-spell." That same year a Spanish mission opened in our area. We went over to visit and introduced ourselves to the pastor, "We don't speak Spanish, but can you use us? Gordon plays the piano, and I can work with kids." The pastor was delighted to have us.

We thought we would just go for Sunday School, and that is what we did at first. I taught the children; Gordon played the piano. Eventually our involvement increased. We would be called when someone had run out of gas miles from home or when a husband had come home and was beating up the kids. Eventually the mission became our church home.

One day an eight-year-old boy said, "I don't understand why God loves Anglos better than He does us. Look at this dump we're in. Just look up there—I can see rats running through the rafters." Soon we were drawing up plans for the new building. Everyone was excited, and all brought their pennies for the construction project. Still, the eight-year-old boy prayed, "Lord, is this just another thing that's not going to work out right? Are we really going to get that building?" (This same little boy went with his mother once a month to see his daddy in prison—a recurring situation in his life.)

Getting the new church built was by no means easy. When we started in this work, the attitude of many in the community toward our work was very negative. They were scared of people they didn't know anything about and of the idea of having a church full of illegal "wetbacks." We did not have enough money for many years. In fact, we barely got by. Today we all take pride in the lovely building and beautiful families who worship at Primera Iglesia Bautista.

During the twelve-year period we have worked with the children of these undocumented immigrants, we have not taken a political stand on their right to be here. We are just trying to share God's love. We think that whether they stay or return to their homeland, we will all be better off if they know how to love God. To briefly summarize this period doesn't seem fair because the trauma, heartache, and joys of this work have gone beyond anything we expected when we dropped in to visit that first day. We wondered at the time if we were smothering Jeni by doing this work, because the problems of the children and their parents became such a daily part of our lives. But Jeni has received a world vision that is more valuable than what she may have missed in the "us-four-and-no-more" culture of many of her peers. Once during church, when Jeni wore a leg cast, we placed a chair in front of her on which to prop her leg. Three-year-old Ricardo Alvarez moved a chair beside her for himself, and another chair in front to prop his own extended leg during the entire service. What an apt picture of the love we all shared.

Because of Jeni's cross-cultural awareness, she has spent a year teaching in the home of medical missionaries in Mexico, has participated in mission trips to Brazil as a Portuguese interpreter, and continues to find her Christian walk exciting. Today she is preparing for her doctoral dissertation and is teaching Spanish in the University of Texas at Austin.

When Jenifer was three, I had a retina detachment, a problem which took me through seven eye surgeries, and the threat of blindness at any time. I had thought prayer would be the one thing I could do while incapacitated. Not so. A person can feel so bad that the mind refuses to pray. Yet, I knew all the while that God had not forsaken me. I knew that He was there even though I could not reach out to Him. The last surgery was many years ago, but the reality of God's assurance is still mine.

To watch a child suffer is yet another matter. Four times Jeni had major knee surgery, the first time as a nine-year-old. Each surgery involved weeks of casts and months of rehabilitation. Watching her having to handle the pain was far worse than contemplating the possibility of my own blindness. During my eye problems, a friend said, "God has given you the stewardship of suffering." I never wanted such a gift and surely didn't want it for my child. But I have to admit that the knee problems may have given Jeni a compassion for others beyond her years.

The Bible teaches that we should thank God for all things. This is not always easy for me. I do want to praise God for His constant presence, which touches even the difficult days with deep and abiding peace.

I have always worked hard and played hard. This is as true at age sixty-eight as it was in my youth. I started learning Spanish in my early sixties and began snorkeling in my late sixties. No matter how heavy the work load, the time to play has always filled a comfortable niche in my life. Maybe this is because I know a joyless life has little impact on others. Maybe it's because I just plain enjoy living. I don't want to look back on any one part of my life as the richest or the most meaningful. Each day is full and has eternal value. To me, the important thing is that I will keep going!

CATHERINE CHAPMAN

Continuing her spiritual journey, Catherine Chapman felt called to leave the Dominican Sisters in March of 1995. She has continued her spiritual growth through the mystical experiences of energy work. She has a doctorate in Body/Mind Psychology from the Union Institute and has developed a method of psychotherapy known as Spiritual Energetic Psychotherapy integrating spirituality, energy work, altered state work and psychotherapy. She lives in Houston, Texas.

BECOMING
by Catherine Chapman

Being born and raised a Catholic, going to Catholic school for ten years, and learning the tenets of the Catholic faith did not introduce me to a personal God. When I was eight and nine years old, my mother would take my brother and me to Confession on Saturdays. We would leave the noise of the outside world and enter the imposing, silent, white structure of St. Anne Catholic Church. Somewhat fearfully, I would advance to the closet-like confessional hiding the priest. Kneeling before the small black square of translucent material, I would wait. Suddenly the hidden door would slide open, and I would begin, "Bless me, Father, for I have sinned. . . ." So I went to Mass every Sunday, didn't eat meat on Friday, and did everything possible to avoid chewing the host, which would bring a stiff reprimand if caught. I did think about God fairly often and had questions about Him. What did He look like? Would He really give me anything I wanted if I asked? Could I be good enough for Him to love me?

In high school, if someone had told me I could know God in an intimate manner, that God could be a true friend, I would have thought that person was deluded. My first year of college changed that.

My mother had become involved in the Charismatic Renewal. As any mother, she wanted to share with me the joy and peace she now had. Although I was reluctant to become involved, I listened to what Mom said about feeling close to God, about God loving me in a special way, and about God answering our prayers. "Ask and you shall receive," she said. I listened, but I was dubious.

The end of my first semester of college, I was frantically studying for my biology final. I vividly remember standing in the shower, very stressed, asking God to help me study. Into my head, clear as spoken words, came the thought, "Memorize the Krebs cycle (how citric acid is manufactured) and the stages of photosynthesis." I don't remember how many steps are in each of these processes, but possibly as many as sixty all together. At that point I had already studied a number of hours and had about six chapters left to review. Throwing my usual caution to the wind, I decided to spend the rest of my time memorizing those two processes and ignore the remaining material. It turned out that more than two-thirds of the answers for the test were contained in two questions: list the steps of photosynthesis; list the steps in the Krebs cycle.

After that love gift from God, I asked to be "prayed over" for the Baptism of the Holy Spirit. My sister Anna and I knelt across from each other on opposite sides of a coffee table. We held hands while a group of people, including Mom, placed their hands upon us and prayed that we be filled with the Holy Spirit. I could feel the love and energy in the room. I had a sense of expectancy of God's power as they prayed for us in both English and in tongues. Their voices joined in an unusual harmony when they sang in tongues. But after the prayer was over, I was very disappointed. I didn't *feel* anything. My sense of disappointment was heightened as my sister spoke of the peace that filled her and moved her to tears. She excitedly described how she felt an energy, like electricity, go from my hands into hers. I remained silent, feeling nothing but disappointment.

The next week, I was returning from the last class of that particular summer day. A few clouds dotted the blue sky as I walked the three blocks to the dorm. Unexpectedly and instantaneously I was overtaken by indescribable joy. I was so full jubilation that my chest felt like it would burst. Suddenly I had a tremendous desire to read all the psalms of praise. I literally ran to my room, breathlessly grabbed my Bible, plopped on my bed, and began with Psalm 1. I read any psalm that contained joy, praise, and happiness. I skipped any psalm or any part of a psalm that was not joyful. As joy continued to fill me, I experienced a deep realization that I was loved by God.

As a result of the Charismatic Renewal, my prayer style changed. No longer did I repeat only memorized words. As I became more aware of the personal presence of God, I would talk to Him. "Hi!

God, what a beautiful day. Thanks." "Hi! God, I'm really confused right now. Please help." I would tell God things in a conversational tone just as if a friend of mine were sitting beside me. My prayers at this time almost always began with "Hi! God."

I also was gifted with the ability to pray in tongues or pray in the Spirit. This was a gift I really wanted because it was, to me, a sign that I was in God's favor. When I received this gift, the strange words just escaped from my lips. I could stop and start the words even though I had never heard those particular sounds before. Now I am familiar with the sounds of my "prayer language" and am struck when I am temporarily given a new language. Many times when I pray in the Spirit, I do not know the exact meaning of the words, but I do know what or who I am praying for. Rarely do I use this gift aloud. When I am with others, I pray in the Spirit silently. I do not begin to understand this unusual gift, but I do know it is from God and often feel great peace when using it.

For four years I attended prayer meetings, was a member of a retreat team, and grew spiritually. My awareness of God's love for me continued to grow, I attended graduate school at Stephen F. Austin State University in Nacogdoches, Texas, and worked on my master's degree in psychology. After ending an engagement to be married, I began to ask God, "What do you want me to do?" The word "convent" kept coming to my mind. I responded with my lips, "No." I continued to ask the same question and continued to receive the same answer. God was relentless in urging me to the convent. To get God off my back, I compromised. I told God I would try the Houston Dominicans for six months. I entered in December 1975.

Shortly after taking my initial vows of poverty, chastity, and obedience, I was on retreat at our Motherhouse. Several other women were praying quietly in the large room. As I was lying on a couch praying, a beautiful image appeared in my mind's eye. A woman with eyes so deep I could fall into them looked straight at me. Her eyes were bottomless pools of love. She began to dance around the world. As she danced, she touched each person she came to. She touched the starving child in Africa. She touched the criminal in another land. She touched the victim of that crime. She touched the unbeliever in another country. The entire time she literally danced around the world and gracefully and lovingly touched each and every person. She loved them all, totally and completely, no matter who they were, what they had done, or what they had failed to do.

Whenever I recall this experience, I can see her eyes and get lost in them. I know to the depth of my being that what was revealed to me that day was God's own feminine nature. I am still filled with peace every time I remember Her love of every person, no matter what my opinion of them. This image of God calls me to strive to love others as She loves.

My striving to love as She loves pervades my work as a psychotherapist, which I began as a member of the Houston Dominicans. I had become aware of my gift of healing through the Charismatic Renewal, although I do not believe an individual has to be Charismatic to have this gift. I have heard of and witnessed many physical healings, ranging from the healing of minor infections to the miraculous disappearance of a brain tumor, but physical healing is not my gift. My talent is for helping with inner, emotional healing. Through inner healing, God can take our wounds from abuse, abandonment, rejection, depression, and despair and fill them with love to make us whole again. A woman with sexual difficulties resulting from incest can be healed and made whole, as if the incest never happened. A man physically abused as a child and now unable to form intimate relationships can be healed of those wounds and freed to love.

Being able to talk to God, my friend and lover, and receiving the gift of healing have enhanced and complemented my skills as a psychotherapist. I have discovered that those who are willing to pray with me allow God to enter into them and become well more quickly. At times God heals instantly, but usually God heals by degrees.

I have also worked with women who are in emotional turmoil over previous abortions. This type of prayer I call "healing the unborn." Before working with these women, I had little compassion for those who had made this choice. As I began to use imaging prayer in trying to help them heal, I discovered that God loves and cares deeply for these women and their children. Watching the pain and anguish, listening to the moving descriptions of the prayer experiences of these women broke the hardness of my own heart. I became more aware of God's unconditional love. I experienced healing as I witnessed God's healing of the emotional scars of others, and I became less hardened, more vulnerable to others' pain.

Being a companion to people on their road to recovery has made me aware of how our inhumanity to one another results in terrible wounds. This awareness, coupled with my life with the Houston Dominicans, has moved me to work to end the situations which wound. Most often I write letters to protest what I see as an injustice. When I see the pain of women who are abused, I recall the Biblical passages where Jesus healed women, and I am moved to write letters to congressional representatives or to newspapers. When I hear of children who are unwanted and abused, I recall how Jesus called the children to him. I ask Jesus to protect those children, and I write another letter. Amnesty International sends a communication about someone unjustly imprisoned. I remember that Jesus came to free the captives. As an Amnesty International Freedom Writer, I write a letter asking that this particular captive be freed.

In this activity I stay rooted in God through personal and community prayer. Privately, I pray quietly with the scriptures. At times I sit in my prayer corner before my lighted oil lamp and attempt to be still and know that God is present. Whenever our Dominican Sisters gather together, we lift our voices in prayer, song, and ritual. We gather strength from one another before we go our separate ways to teach, minister, and preach.

I would not be who I am today if God had not entered my life so gently and insistently when I was nineteen. Neither would I be who I am now if I did not have my Houston Dominican community. My spiritual life at present is an interplay between the quiet solitude of my prayer life, the active work for social justice, and the facilitation of inner healing through therapy. Daily I connect with God in the deep stillness within me. Only by drinking from the well of God do I have the energy and courage to be an instrument of God's healing love.

FLORENCE RICHINGS BIRMINGHAM

Florence ("Fran") Richings Birmingham lives in a rural area of East Texas with her husband, two daughters, and son. She has worked in the fields of graphic arts and journalism and, for a time, operated a catering service out of her home.

"When asked to identify myself," Fran says, "several titles come to mind—in order of importance: wife/mother/homemaker, Jewish woman, maintainer of my heritage, creative person, and lover of people, nature, and peace. Each of these characteristics is influenced by my spiritual self which, in turn, is nurtured by my loves and interests."

FLOWERS IN THE DESERT
by Florence Richings Birmingham

It's Friday night, our two beautiful preteen daughters giggle for a moment before gathering in the light, covering their eyes with their hands, and reciting the blessing over the Sabbath candles. My husband breaks the special Sabbath bread I baked today. We say another blessing and settle into our weekly Sabbath meal. Our seven-month-old son sits on my knee wearing a homemade yarmulke to match his daddy's.

It is a special time for us—to sit down and enjoy a meal as a family, to feel the reassuring comfort of tradition and culture, and to be so warmly reminded of the laws and guidelines that help us in our quest to be good people. Tomorrow morning, we'll drive an hour to the only conservative synagogue within a hundred-mile radius to attend Saturday morning services.

If anyone had told me fourteen years ago that I would live this far from town and synagogue, on a dirt road, on a farm, next door to my in-laws, married to a man who prefers talking directly to God while sitting under a pine tree, I would have called that person crazy. Yet I am here, happy with my family and my place. Granted, raising my children so isolated from other Jewish people is an ongoing concern, but a problem that can be overcome. It is no accident that I, who did not have the ideal Jewish childhood, rely on my faith as a source of strength and guidance.

My dad married my mom, who was always known to me as Mamsie, in 1954 in Morocco, Africa, her birthplace. Although intermarriage has always been forbidden, my Jewish grandparents, shocked by the horrors of the Holocaust and the hardships of living through World War II, consented to give away Mamsie to the young American Episcopal sailor with nice manners and a serious disposition.

It was my Episcopalian dad who first exposed me to organized religion. I went to a Palm Sunday service with him, and although I don't remember what happened there, I do recall coming home proudly waving a palm branch in my little gloved hand. That was the last time he ever took me to church. He didn't go himself, for that matter, until many years later. Yet, as he took my younger brother and me fishing or pear picking or flower gathering, he taught us what was important to him—to be considerate of life, be it human, animal or vegetable. He told us to behave, not to take the Lord's name in vain, to treat our mother with respect.

One day when I was six, I ran in from school, ecstatic with my beautiful Easter basket full of candies and cookies given me by our classroom mothers. To my horror, my mother, who was on her hands and knees scrubbing the floor, promptly tossed it all out the back door. She dried my tears, took me on her lap, and explained what "cleaning for Passover" means. That was the first time anyone told me specifically that I was Jewish and kept different observances and traditions than the Christians around me.

Mamsie became more involved in my spiritual upbringing after the Easter basket incident. I gladly spent more and more time at her side in the kitchen learning about my Moroccan-Jewish heritage. We didn't read the scriptures or discuss religious issues, and we seldom went to synagogue services until I was twelve. But Mamsie told me stories of "home" as we prepared festive holiday meals and the Sabbath and festival bread.

In each place the Navy sent us, Mamsie found something to remind her of Morocco. In Boston was the large Jewish community and kindly Mr. Kessel, the kosher butcher who befriended our family. In Maryland and Florida, Mamsie could eat giant fresh fish to her heart's content. In Rhode Island, her sister and nieces moved near us while they waited for their husband and father to return from Vietnam. But twenty-five years ago when my dad, whom we now call Zado (a form of the Yiddish word "Zayda," meaning Grandpa), retired from the Navy and we landed in Waco, Texas, everything fell in place. The climate was almost identical to "home," and the Jewish community—large, established, and welcoming—was unlike all the temporary synagogues of our Navy days.

To my brother and me, this was a problem initially. Without much previous religious background, we found ourselves forced to attend a weekly three-hour service in an unfamiliar language. In spite of this, something wonderful happened. This synagogue "family" adopted us. It was as if all of a sudden we had dozens of cousins, aunts, uncles, and grandparents. An elderly congregant took my brother under his wing. With genuine kindness and consideration, he helped Chuck through the complicated prayers and hymns as he prepared for his bar mitzvah, following a basic Jewish precept that encourages bettering the lives of others, be they friend or stranger, Jewish or not.

Even while the Jewish community was welcoming us, we became increasingly aware that we had moved not only to Texas, but to the Bible Belt. Living on Navy bases and attending Navy schools, even though they were mostly in the South, we were used to everyone being pretty much equal, thrown into the same stew pot, so to speak. Although I was no stranger to the hatred and cruelty of anti-Semitism, now, the summer before my freshman year of high school, I began to realize how protected life in the Navy had been.

The moving van was still in the driveway when the girl across the street invited me to the neighborhood pool. I gladly accepted, but as I talked to her in the water, I felt like an alien. She asked me if I had a "church home." I said, "A what?" She explained, and I told her I was Jewish. Then she stared at my forehead. I felt at the same time a little silly and embarrassed. What could she be staring at? She informed me that she had never seen a Jew before. Her Baptist preacher had told her they were terrible people, in thick with the devil to the point of having their own personal horns. Telling her I didn't believe in the devil must not have impressed her. She spent the rest of the day staring at my forehead. Yet we became friends, not best friends, but close enough that we were always kind to one another. It impressed me greatly that this girl, a devout Southern Baptist, had the personal strength to relate to me as an individual on my own merit, rather than blindly following the ideas of her pastor.

For a period during high school, I began to wish I were a Christian, but for all the wrong reasons. My brother and I, the only Jewish students in the district, were separated from our synagogue peers who attended school fifteen miles away. As I began to feel friendless and isolated, the girl from the pool invited me to her church youth group Christmas party. For whatever reason, Mamsie said I could go! Anticipation and excitement set in. It was my first social event since moving. All the popular girls and cute boys I saw every day at school were at the party, and for a moment I felt I was part of the group. I was whisked around town in a pick-up truck full of giddy teenagers on a scavenger hunt, then I played a hysterical game of charades and was kissed under the mistletoe. I wanted that night and that feeling to last forever. But it didn't. The kids I had enjoyed so much at the party treated me with the same indifference at school the next week.

I turned to the synagogue as an anchor. The weekly visits drew me closer to the traditions, laws, and customs of Judaism. The continuity of celebrating familiar holy days in a new and unfamiliar place helped immensely. My passion became helping Mamsie and the synagogue ladies in the kitchen to prepare for holy days, bar mitzvahs, and social events. I loved listening to them discuss and compare family traditions, children, recipes, and social issues.

Like Mamsie, I never set out to marry a non-Jewish man, but it happened. A good person is a good person, no matter what his religion. At the time we met, my husband-to-be claimed no formal religion, but I knew he was a good man and he seemed to find the idea of Judaism very agreeable.

I told him how important my faith was to me, how I wanted to be like Mamsie, strong and active in the synagogue, in the observance of custom and ritual. Tim agreed to support my wishes, and we were married. Soon we had two little girls and were firmly planted on the farm.

Like many young families, our first years together were a little rocky as we learned to grow with one another. Even though Tim was eager to participate in Judaism, Mamsie rejected him thoroughly. She actually liked him quite a lot, but not as the husband of her only daughter. As a result, Tim refused to return to the synagogue or to let the girls go. We celebrated the Sabbath and holy days at home, but I missed the constant guidance, reinforcement, and extended family of the synagogue.

Then, when our oldest daughter was in the third grade, Mamsie passed away. I was so devastated that the only comfort I could find was in going to the synagogue once a week to say the mourner's prayer in her memory. When I finally made it clear that the girls were to go with me, Tim joined us. I don't think he was prepared for the welcoming kindness he received or the comfort and guidance he found in the services.

Through these years, Tim's Catholic/Southern Baptist parents, our next-door neighbors, were loving, supportive, and open-minded toward me and my Jewishness. To me, Tim's mother embodies the traditional Southern woman. Her small mobile home with two added rooms is one of the warmest, most welcoming places I have ever been. The girls love wintertime power failures because we "have" to go to Grandma's house to cuddle in front of her fireplace on her clean wood floor and stay warm until the lights come back on. Now that Mamsie is gone, it is "Mom" that I look to as my role model. During the "Mamsie and Tim wars" in the early part of our marriage, Mom never found fault with anyone. She was always there for me, encouraging me to hang in there and "take care of those little girls."

Judaism's underlying strength, for me, is its emphasis on religious, moral, physical and social goodness. It is a positive religion; there is no disdain for those not like us. The overall idea is to be good and right for the sake of being good and right.

An Israeli friend once observed that being a Jew in Israel is somewhat like celebrating Christmas in the United States. The atmosphere is so intensely concentrated around you that you don't have to do a thing to be a part of it. She went on to point out that she felt more Jewish in East Texas because she had to work so hard to make the traditions, customs, and celebrations come to life for her family. She lived a few blocks from the synagogue. Out here in the woods, I feel I have to make an even greater effort.

I want to establish a sense of history, a sense of security, and a sense of belonging in my children. I want them to know that, no matter where we are or what happens, we can depend on our faith to help us through. I want them to have a warm, inviting home where they can feel good about their Jewishness, can feel that the synagogue is not too far away.

My daughters are the only Jewish children in their school district. They attend the school Christmas parties, sharing information about Hanukkah and having fun with their friends. They know, if the school Easter party coincides with Passover, to ask the teacher to save their treats until Passover is through.

Children born in Israel are called Sabras after a particularly beautiful and strong flower that blooms in the desert. I feel that we are Sabras, too, in a different kind of desert. Yet as long as we nourish ourselves deeply on knowledge and our traditions, our roots will never die.

Ruth Powell

Ruth Powell, the daughter of a native Southerner, lived five years in the South as a child. As an adult, she has chosen the South as home. She loves being out-of-doors, especially in the woods.

She has been happily married for twenty-one years to a very supportive man. They share a commitment to religious search and spiritual journeying.

She is an educator who works with young children and understands her vocation as integral to her spirituality.

PROPELLED INTO THE UNEXPECTED
by Ruth Powell

The first week of my freshman year in college, I had the shattering crisis of losing my religion. I was in a Quaker college and had attended an evening sing-along of religious folk music. As I left the event I found myself asking, "How was this different from a secular folk-sing for me?" My mind answered, "It wasn't." Though this seems utterly irrational, it precipitated a monumental crisis for me. From that moment I lost touch with anything spiritual.

I had grown up liberal Methodist and Lutheran and took my religion very seriously, but in this crisis I no longer sensed any experiential content to words such as "worship," "fellowship," or "faith." One by one I examined such words and put them out of my life until they developed some content. For two agonizing years I was driven by the pain of my loss and by a great need I could not fully define. I described myself as "one who does not know," meaning "one who does not know about God and religion." I soon learned not to tell those around me of my driving need.

At the end of my sophomore year of college, out of curiosity I signed up for the campus Quakerism course. The first thing the professor had us do was to read excerpts from the spiritual journals of the early Friends. As I read these three-hundred-year-old attempts to describe the encounter with God, I understood for the first time what would fill the need that had been driving me. I needed to encounter and experience God in my soul. To me these journals seemed like the cicada shells left on trees in the spring. They were indications of where life had been. All I had to do was to find the life reflected in these journals. This experience defined the persistent need of my life and relieved my agony. It also prepared me for my eventual commitment to Quakerism.

At the beginning of my junior year, despite a two-year habit of silent suffering, I blurted out to my friend Jeannine the need that had been driving me. She did not act surprised or leery. She smiled and said, "Let's have a Bible study." During the school year, Jeannine and I met weekly for an hour of prayer and Bible study. In those times, I felt a powerful sense of the presence of God, as though the prayer had a life of its own, moving us to unknown depths and leaving us fed. Another friend invited me to have weekly sessions with her as well, to explore what she called "going on in Christ." She taught me to seek the depths of private prayer and to listen for God's answers inside myself. I became convinced that prayer is no simple thing. It is an ocean of infinite depths, each layer with its own "character."

I remember one evening going to an isolated spot on campus to pray about something I knew I must do but wished not to do. My emotions were in turmoil. I found myself fervently praying words that were not my words, words that were actually requesting the task I was seeking to avoid. Something much greater than I was sweeping over me. With tremendous exhilaration I prayed on and on, the words pouring through me. None were words I had chosen to say but seemed to come from beyond me, through me. When it was over, I found myself transformed. I had already embraced my task and was filled with joy and peace.

On another occasion I sought out an empty classroom in an empty building for private prayer. Early in the prayer I envisioned myself as a long hallway with many rooms on both sides. I kept the doors safely locked but held in my hands the ring of keys that opened them. I knew that my task for the evening was to be able to hand that key ring to God. Doing that would give God the freedom and right to enter any room of my being, hand me a mop, and tell me to clean up my garbage. I knew I would not be choosing what parts of my life I was willing to change once I did that. I would be giving up control. I knew I would stay in that classroom until I was able to give up the key ring. Daylight turned to deep night and still I struggled with the prayer. I did not want to do this thing. I did not even want to want to do it! At the moment I defined the situation in this way, I was given grace. Grace came in the form of inspiration to pray, "God, help me want to want to do this thing." Twenty years later I am still convinced that is the most transformative prayer I know. God answered with the grace to want to want. That was all I needed. I gave God the key ring.

Over the years I have had a tendency to snatch back the key ring without even realizing I have done so. The prayer of returning it to God has invariably been an immense struggle. Most people believe that the spiritual life is supposed to be a life of joy, but I have learned the truth in one of the verses of the song "It's a Long Road to Freedom": "I walked one morning with my King and all my winters turned to spring, yet every moment had its sting." The sting—a controlling chain that binds—is as much an integral part of the spiritual life as the joy. Giving up the key ring is risky business.

Outwardly, I find myself called to walk into things I want to stay away from, motivated by the knowledge that the intimacy of my prayer life will suffer if I do not, that my disobedience will cut me off from the joy that feeds me. Inwardly, God's demands are even harder. Old attitudes are comfortable and painful to change. Yet I cannot turn back, not because I am being forced, but because no other path has real meaning in comparison.

The last three months of my junior year in college were a time of great grace. I lived what Quakers call the centered life—when all of life, moment by moment, is lived from that deep center within our being where our soul meets the Spirit of God. With one exception, this is the only time I have succeeded in living a centered life for a prolonged period. It seems odd to spend a lifetime working my way back to that condition where I started, but with a bit more maturity.

Two years later I returned to Texas where I have lived the last twenty years. I sought out Quakers and began to attend meetings for worship. From the first, I was jolted to discover that in this particular meeting I was worshiping with a number of people who considered themselves Jewish, Buddhist, or Moslem instead of Christian. As I listened to them speak of their spiritual lives, I became convinced that they knew God. I came to understand that God is most interested in the state of our hearts and in whether our spirits recognize His Spirit when we meet Him in our souls. During these years my vocabulary began to shift away from the male "God/He" to the genderless "the Divine/It." This was not because my own concept of the Divine had changed but because I wished to be able to speak to all the different kinds of Quakers without creating verbal barriers.

Within two years I married one of those non-Christian Quakers. I delayed accepting his proposal for a year and a half because we did not communicate well on spiritual topics. For a long time our attempts to discuss anything spiritual led to arguments. When we each fully accepted that the other was not going to adopt our deepest beliefs, we were able to talk freely about spiritual matters.

Over the first ten years of our marriage we learned to draw closer and closer together in our spiritual lives despite the theological gap that remained. My husband learned to respect my intimate prayer life which came out of my Christian walk. Although his concept of the Divine did not include personal intimacy, he learned to hear and respect spiritual experience in Christian terms. I learned from him some Zen Buddhist concepts that have remained to this day part of my ideas about reality, spirituality, and the Divine. Although I had previously learned to respect that the Divine worked in people through paths other than Christianity, my own personal walk had drawn only from Christianity. Now I began to understand that Zen Buddhism (and therefore possibly other religions) had concepts that could aid me in my spiritual journey.

About eight years into our marriage, I entered a spiritual dryness. I felt adrift with no sense of the presence of the Divine. That summer a Quaker friend and I took a trip into the desert mountains of southwest Texas. Several times we stopped along the roadside and climbed over the edge of a mountain to hold worship. We felt we were straining to hear something important to our souls, something beyond our ability to hear.

One morning as we were worshiping under the cliff of a desert mountain, I heard the message. It formed itself as a question, "How long will you have to sit still and wait for a wild turkey or javelina to walk out of the desert bush?" There was no answer to that question because it was a wait without time limits. Yet the wait was well worth it. Then again the question: "How long do you have to wait to sense the Divine Spirit in the desert times of your life?" There was no answer. It was like waiting for the wild javelina.

I had been running in circles, waving my arms and shouting my frustration for a year. But the desert was now teaching me. It was full of life, small, inconspicuous, hidden life. I had to learn to look in a new and different way than I looked in the lusher woodlands of home. The desert times of life were an invitation to me, an invitation to a deeper way of relating to the Divine. I understood that the old way of experiencing the Divine was removed so that I could move to a deeper level, a quieter level, a less conspicuous level.

Later, during a three-month retreat, I had another experience filled with grace. For the first two months of that retreat, I spent nine hours a day sitting in silent Quaker worship. Quaker worship is a silencing of the mind as well as the body to listen for the touch of the Divine Spirit. I found myself drawn into contemplation quite unexpectedly. I had planned to read spiritual texts, but I found I could not. Nothing satisfied me except sitting hour after hour in private worship.

A week or so into the retreat I had a powerful dream. I was visiting a church. We had finished with Sunday School and worship and were in the kitchen preparing a covered dish fellowship meal. Suddenly a tall woman appeared and grabbed the end of my skirt, throwing me into a sitting position on the floor. Pulling on the lower edge of my skirt, she dragged me across the floor the whole length of the kitchen and out onto a back porch. Then she picked me up and threw me over the porch rail. I landed in knee-high grass in the same sitting position she had thrown me into. The woman turned into a mink and jumped down beside me. Suddenly I knew I had to touch the mink, even though it might bite me. As soon as my hand came in contact with the fur, I was overwhelmed by awe and joy greater than anything I had ever experienced before. Intuitively, I knew the powerful woman-mink was a surprising and unfamiliar personification—a manifestation of the Divine as female.

In my dream the mink then changed into a huge male lion like Aslan, the Christ-figure in C.S. Lewis' Narnia books. The lion bent over me and breathed on me as Aslan breathed on people he blessed. I awoke at that point. The awe and joy I felt in the dream did not fade. Since that time, I have never again met the Divine as Father, Son, or Holy Spirit. The lion was my last experience of masculine Divinity, and I am grateful that it was in the form of a blessing.

In spite of a desperate desire to cling to Father, Son, Holy Spirit, and a terror of the statements made by Old Testament prophets against goddess worship, the old images no longer worked. I could not connect with Father, Son or Holy Spirit. At the same time the intuitive sense of the Mother's presence grew strong and intimate. After much struggle, I concluded that if I wished to go deeper with the Divine, I could not control how the Divine came to me. Once I accepted this, I entered more deeply into the inner communion I was experiencing.

The remaining months of retreat were intense, joyful days as I spent my time, moment by moment, with the Mother. I was drawn outside and began to spend my prayer and worship time walking or sitting against a tree instead of in my room. I seemed to sense the Mother especially in nature and came to understand Her as Earth Mother. Sometimes I had a sense of "seeing" Her in a rounded hillside. One time when I was walking through the retreat center kitchen and someone was kneading bread, I saw Her in the curve of the bread dough.

Yet, anxiety over the visitation of the Mother resurfaced. What I was experiencing did not seem to exist in my religious training. Christianity is a religion focused on the person and mission of Jesus, with no teachings about an Earth Mother. I had held to and depended upon the Christian story, its beliefs and theology. But my encounter with the Mother was vivid and on-going. How could this be? I lost the whole structure of my reality.

Then a visual image presented itself to me, a vision which helped me understand my mounting confusion. I saw myself living in a comfortable, safe house. Suddenly a wind knocked all the walls down—straight outward. I was left standing in open space and staring out to infinity in all directions. That infinity was so bright that nothing was visible in the brightness. I realized that the fallen walls represented the structure of my reality. I was so blinded by the outside light that I could not see anything; I could not begin to structure a new concept of reality. I had no idea what to expect of my new world.

Long after I came out of retreat, I was able to identify core beliefs I still held. I understood I had something that had not been swept away. My world is upheld by Truth and Love. And I am convinced that the material world is a carrier of the Divine. The Divine permeates the material. Over the years as I have walked with the Mother, I have been receiving a feel for the world in which I find myself, adding features to the landscape of my life. I understand that the Mother is an incomplete experience of the Divine, just as the Father is. I want to move away from this duality but my mind is incapable of encompassing the fullness of Divinity. Perhaps the Zen Buddhists are the only people on the globe who even attempt to reach an image of Divinity that surpasses limitations—the Great Void that is mysteriously full. I believe this Divine Void wishes contact with us and so takes on manifestations our minds can grasp. Presently, the Divine is manifesting herself as Mother; whether this is permanent or temporary I do not know.

Now, instead of a structure of beliefs and doctrine, I am building a structure of hypotheses, ideas that seem to explain the world as I grope within it. I no longer feel I am totally blinded by bright infinity. Yet, having lost a two-thousand-year-old system that had solidarity, I need to stay aware that whatever new structure I build can fall as easily. Perhaps someday the walls of my new house will have to be blown down, and I will need to face the sting of that bright infinity again.

Mary Lou Santillán Baert

Mary Lou Santillán Baert is a Mexican American clergy member of the Rio Grande Annual Conference of The United Methodist Church. When she retired in 1996, she was appointed to El Divino Salvador United Methodist Church in Sherman, Texas, on a part-time basis. During her years of service, she was a teacher, an accountant, a missionary in Mexico, an editor, ministerial supervisor, and a pastor. Her ministry also included serving three Methodist churches in the United Kingdom.

Mary Lou is married to Simon Baert. They have two adult sons: Timothy Gerard and Reimund Nathanael. In November, 1997, they accepted the responsibility of raising a one-and-a-half month old grandnephew.

I SHALL NOT WANT

by Mary Lou Santillán Baert

"Jehová es mi pastor y nada me faltará."
"Yahweh is my shepherd and I shall lack nothing," that is, "The Lord is my shepherd, I shall not want." These words—which I memorized as a young girl—have carried me forward in life, especially when I have walked through the darkest valley.

I have believed them all my life, but in 1984 when I had to conduct my father's funeral and preach, I struggled and I anguished in my grief. My father, my mentor, my friend, was dead. How could I truly say that I lacked for nothing? How could I tell my mother that she had no need after sixty years of marriage? How could I convey to my brothers and sisters the faith witness proclaimed in thought and deed by the one who had given all of us life and love? I certainly could not consider his death a loss, because the word that becomes flesh does not perish. And he embodied the written word of God which he believed, lived by, and trusted. God was everything to him.

When I graduated from Southern Methodist University with a bachelor's degree, I informed my father that I was going to find a good-paying job so that I could help him with the education of my younger brothers and sisters, nine of whom were still at home.

Then I was invited to teach at one of our Methodist schools, Holding Institute, in Laredo, Texas. The salary offered was only ninety dollars a month, plus room and board, but I wanted to teach. I asked my father, "What should I do?" His response was, "The time has come for you to make your own decisions."

And so for the first time in my life, I left home with my parents' blessing, fearful of being on my own. Yet I had made a promise to my father, and I managed to send home at least half my salary. He never made any claims on my words, and I never heard him complain about hard times or financial needs.

Then when I decided to go to Mexico as a missionary a few years later, I had to confess to my father that I would not make any great fortune. He looked at me, smiled, and spoke, "Don't worry about money so much. God has always provided. And God will do so again. I would rather have you be a good example to your brothers and sisters than offer me a lot of money."

I grew up in Dallas, Texas. My parents originally came from Mexico, where my father was a government worker. My parents were strict and loving. They spoke the same language of discipline and expectations. My father was always available; he made an opportunity for each of us during the day or night to be in dialogue with him. My mother's time was occupied with babies and household duties, but she was a praying woman. She always had time to sit in the kitchen, read her Bible and *The Upper Room*. Many a night I also saw her kneeling beside her bed praying.

My early awareness of God came through the living example of my parents. Faith glowed in their faces, love manifested itself in daily living, hope was kept alive through the realization of dreams. I do not remember when we first began attending Sunday School and church. But by the time I was ten years old, I know I thrilled at hearing Bible stories and singing hymns, even in English.

We were first drawn to the church in our Spanish-speaking community through the Wesley Community Center, a project of the Women's Division of the Methodist church. There, all the activities and programs were in English, so I first learned the words of many hymns and Bible verses in English. However, we attended a church where everything was in Spanish, and so I learned the same hymns and Bible verses in Spanish. I did not mind the double dose.

Many families in our community took their children out of school because they did not have enough financial resources. They went to wherever the crops were so that all the family could work and stay alive, returning to Dallas at the end of the harvest season. Many of the children had a hard time in school trying to catch up or pick up where they had left off.

Our family stayed. How my father managed to keep us in school—elementary, high school, and college—year after year with only his salary still amazes me. God indeed provided, not with a tight fist, but with open hands, for God blessed us with good health also.

I cannot pinpoint a time, occasion, or place when I first knew God was calling me into service. I do remember that during my junior year in college I was offered a part-time job at the Wesley Community Center where I had gone as a young girl. I was to be the secretary, translator/interpreter, and club assistant. I began to see the great plight of my people at a closer range. How difficult it was for those who were poor, spoke no English, had no jobs or education, and had lost all hope. Here I was on my way to getting a degree and could envision a bright future. What I saw every day made an impact on me, more so when I heard and sang the hymn, "The Voice of God Is Calling." Through these words, I saw my people suffering, and I could not run away. I had come out of that community and somehow it seemed only right that I should return to it.

The idea of servanthood was not too attractive to me, especially since I knew several of the men and women in my community who worked as servants in the homes of the wealthy. They slaved long and hard and got so little. That did not seem right. Even though this idea of being a servant did not appeal to me, I never minded doing a clean-up task when asked or even volunteering for it.

Later in life another incident helped me understand the call to servanthood. While we were living in Germany where my husband was stationed, I became involved with the Protestant Women of the Chapel. A few months after arriving, I was elected vice-president of the local unit. The following year I became president of the local unit; and the following year I was elected president of the district. The year after that I was elected to the European Council. Just before the installation service, I went into the ladies' lounge at the General Walker Hotel in Berchtesgaden, Germany, to make sure everything was in proper order. My hair was neatly combed, my slip was not showing, and I had a smile on my face. I left and headed for the hall where the service was going to take place. Walking down the hall, I noticed people looked at me, then turned sideways and snickered. Here I was, very proud of my accomplishments, a Mexican American in a high position. What could possibly be wrong with me? I had checked everything, and everything was in place. I did not dare stop or look at myself with so many people around. I waited until I was going down the stairs, and when I saw no one, I looked at myself. I saw that one of my high heels had caught a square of toilet paper attached to a roll. I had been dragging it behind me down the hall and stairs.

"Oh God," I voiced, "why are you doing this to me? You are making fun of me. You are ridiculing me. Me, in this high position!" But as I calmed myself, it seemed to me that God was saying, "Mary Lou, I called you to be a servant. It was I who put you in this high position." I interrupted God, protesting, "No, God, not a servant. All my life I have seen how hard my people have worked as servants, harvesting someone else's crops, unable to buy them for their own table; building swimming pools and being denied entrance because of their ethnicity; getting the lowest wage and no benefits; being abused and having no advocate. I don't want that kind of life. Let me enjoy being here at the top."

Yet as I stood there being installed, I knew God was right. God had always been right. If I were on top, it had not been my doing, because in the human eyes, a Mexican American was nothing, but in the sight of God I had potential and God could use me. In my heart I thanked God for opening my eyes.

When I married in 1965, I thought my life of service was over. I dedicated my life to my husband and children. God kept opening doors, but I was blind. I had opportunities and encouragement to go to seminary, but I did not see that as an option because of my traditional cultural upbringing; later I excused myself as being too old. Eventually I did get my license to preach. When my husband was about to retire from the Air Force, we did not know what the future held for us. The children were still in middle school, and my husband worried because he did not have any job waiting for him. I went to annual conference, and one of the District Superintendents approached me and asked if I would like to take an appointment. Since Simon, my husband, did not have a job; and since I had my license to preach already, I said yes without even consulting my spouse. God had indeed opened another door and wasn't taking no for an answer any longer. I served for a year and then went to seminary full time. My husband still did not have a job, only his pension. God had provided for one year, and I knew that God would continue to provide.

Up to this time my ministry had been with Hispanics. But when I was in seminary, I had the opportunity in 1981 to take my family with me to Jersey, Channel Islands, Great Britain, for one year where I pastored three churches—in English! This assignment enabled us to be close to Holland, my husband's ancestral home, where his family still lives.

The churches in Jersey gave us a tremendous welcome. They had never had a person of another ethnic group or a woman as a pastor. They wondered whether they would be able to understand me, especially since the summer before I arrived they had had problems understanding an exchange pastor from Georgia, whose first language was English. I learned to listen carefully how words were used after my first Sunday there. In my first sermon with a new congregation, I usually say a few things about myself, my family, my life. There in Jersey I shared that in winter I had begun to wear pants, which my parents never allowed me to wear when I was growing up. After the service, the circuit steward took me aside and quietly said, "Rev. Baert, please use the word 'trousers' rather than 'pants.' Pants are undergarments."

My ministry went well. We shared Dutch and Hispanic Christmas traditions with the three congregations. Simon made a piñata for the children, and I made a Mexican dinner for the churches. Holy Week came. On Saturday night, I was reviewing my notes for the Easter proclamation and Simon was watching the late news. Shortly before midnight the telephone rang. It was my youngest sister calling to say that our father had been rushed to the hospital and was not expected to live. Here I was on an island across the ocean. It would shortly be Easter Sunday. There would be no air service, and Monday would also be a holiday. I felt stranded and helpless. I questioned myself, "How can I preach on the resurrection when my father is dying? Do I believe what I have preached all these years?" My husband noticed my anxiety. Gently he asked, "Do you remember what your father said when he took us to the airport in Dallas to catch the plane to England?" I shook my head. He waited a few seconds and then he continued, "He said, 'I do not know what will happen during this year while we are absent one from the other. But this I do know, that whether we live or whether we die, we belong to the Lord.'" Indeed! My father had always trusted God. God would surely be with him in death if God so chose to take him. And I knew that my father was at peace, that he would not worry. I would be ready on Sunday morning with a message of life and hope. After the church service, I called my sister, who told me my father had made it through the night and that the doctor had given them hope for recovery.

There in Great Britain I often found myself with too many activities and too many sick people in the hospital. One particular week, Wednesday came and I still had not begun my sermon preparation. My husband and I paused in early afternoon to grab a bite to eat. While eating, I turned on the radio to listen to classical music. I needed something to ease the tension building within me. As I listened, all of a sudden I heard a melody that caught my attention. It was the melody that a boy in elementary school used to sing to me every time he chased me. He went around singing near my ear, "Mary Lou, I love you. Mary Lou, I love you." Here was God again assuring me that I was not alone, that together we would finish out the week in God's good time.

Every morning when I wake up, I feel God giving me another opportunity, another taste of grace, another Easter morning of coming to life again. I find excitement in waiting for God's surprises. They happen again and again. The Lord has indeed been my shepherd and I have lacked nothing. Thanks be to God!

ACROSS THE TABLE

ACROSS THE TABLE

After the supper dishes are cleared from the table, the children have run out in the yard, and the menfolk are lounging in the living room, the women linger to talk around the table. Cicadas hum through the open window as the women talk about gardens, canning and freezing, recipes. Their conversation deepens. They speak of ailing uncles and aunts, and finally of their problems—with children, in-laws and husbands. As they sip iced tea, they look directly into each others' eyes.

When Southern women find themselves in an urban or small town setting far away from mothers, sisters, and cousins, they re-create this same scene with a friend or two. Over a cup of coffee, the dialogue quickly deepens as they question each other—how can I deal lovingly with this problem? How is God speaking to me in this circumstance of my life? What is this dream saying to me? They would like answers, but as important, they want space and listening ears. They need to hear themselves say their questions and know their friend cares enough to listen.

For many of us dialogue is the heart of spiritual discovery. In the process of speaking we come to know what we know. We acknowledge our doubts and verbalize the changing form of our faith. Spiritual friendships have shown us who we are, have directed our footsteps through the years as we walked beside a friend for a time.

When we began to collect the stories of Southern women, we realized that some of them should come in the form of interviews. Some women tell their stories best in an interactive setting, and some readers find interviews appealing and instructive. Telling one's story under the searching questions of an interviewer often opens up the spiritual dimensions of a person's life. The popularity of media interviews is an indication of a growing interest in autobiography as truth.

Valerie Sayers, a novelist, does not write autobiography as such; but her reflections on her writing indicate her kind of spiritual quest and expression. Gerry Harrison and Dottie Fitchett are busy ministers whose stories emerge in graphic detail under the questioning of an interviewer. Barbara Lee, Susan Purtle, and Sarah Hays are professional women whose stories demonstrate the diversity of expressions of spirituality emerging from traditional Southern roots.

The interviews were taken by the editors in 1992-94, usually in the home of the interviewee. They have been edited and the transcript as printed here approved by the interviewee.

VALERIE SAYERS

Raised in South Carolina, Valerie Sayers calls the South home. A Roman Catholic and novelist (*Due East, How I Got Him Back, Who Do You Love?, The Distance Between Us* and *Brain Fever*), Valerie is married and the mother of two sons, ages 15 and 20.

In the fall of 1993, Valerie moved from New York to South Bend, Indiana, where she is Professor of English at the University of Notre Dame.

MOMENTS OF POSSIBILITY
by Valerie Sayers

Tell us about your early life.

I was raised as the middle child of seven in an Irish Catholic family which moved South just before I was born. I still see myself as a southerner, although I have now spent more of my life in the North than in the South. I think of my childhood as a very happy, in some ways idealistic time, very close to nature. We lived in a little tract house by the marsh—so crowded that we had to spend a lot of time outdoors, and I think that was a great experience for a child. I had the run of the town, Beaufort, South Carolina, which is a beautiful place next to the ocean. I have often felt that my early religious faith was completely intertwined with growing up in that place; living so close to nature, it did not occur to me to doubt. Later on I had plenty of doubts about the nature of God and the ways in which (and here comes the pronoun) He reveals Himself, but never about His existence. That pronoun has been part of my upbringing and, since it falls from my tongue very easily, I'll probably be more consistent if I use it. I have been thinking a lot about the use of that pronoun.

My family is devout Catholic, but of two different strains, I would say. My mother is a very conservative, dogmatic, fundamentalist Catholic. My father, who got his doctorate during my childhood, was liberal.

You spoke of doubts about the nature of God. How did you resolve those?

I have resolved some of the most childlike and fearful doubts, but other doubts will never be resolved. I will live through them, I suppose, and try to do so with faith. In my early adulthood I was profoundly affected by Camus, who could not reconcile a loving God with the world's evil. There's a question we must all work through. The freedom God gives us sometimes seems unbearable, and it is difficult, in witnessing suffering, to see how He is revealing Himself.

How did you decide to become a writer?

I started writing as a pleasure when I was a child. I was always writing or reading this or that, and my parents were wildly enthusiastic. They were incredibly supportive parents. They took tremendous pride in each child for something different, and for me it was academics and writing. They were delighted by my writing talent, my mother especially. She always saw it in a more positive light than anyone else and was convinced that I was going to be a writer. Ironically, I rebelled against that. I was terrified of a writing life, and I really struggled through my college years in New York. I went so far as to declare myself a social science major. I had enough courses to be an English major, but I just walked right past that door. I even threatened to go to law school, but that lasted about a week. I also went to New York to become an actress, which I thought was so much more glamorous than being an author.

So being a writer was something I ran away from, but—and this was very important—I went back south to decide what to do. When I finished college, I retreated to South Carolina and taught there for a year and wrote a lot at night. It was a very intense period of my life. Then my husband-to-be came down to fetch me. We considered living in South Carolina together after our marriage, but he is a Chilean and never felt comfortable in the South. So we went back to New York together, and I made the decision to become a writer.

Do you think of yourself as a Christian writer?

Absolutely. I feel that my vision is guided by my beliefs. The difficulty for me is to separate how a Christian states her beliefs in rational terms and how she states them in artistic terms. And I think they are very different. Christian readers often call on the artist to become dogmatic within the work, to make the work do something that really should be done by another medium, an essay, for instance. We need art because we need a different way of seeing things. We can't just keep restating things and moving a statement into an artistic image—because it chokes off the artistic urge, which is quite unruly and irrational.

A number of reviewers have seen that my themes are Christian. An especially good review of my first book appeared in *Commonweal,* and I am aware of a couple of academics who are interested in the Catholic element in my work. What amazes me is how often the Christian themes are completely ignored (or missed, or both).

Do you see your writing, your creativity, as connected to your spirituality?

Yes, but how is a mystery to me. Creativity and spirituality both involve a different level of consciousness than the worldly. Of course, we are always *of* the world, so I'm interested in the attempt to integrate the heightened level of consciousness that comes when we try to create something or when we try to reach God with our worldly level of consciousness. I'm especially interested in the integration of all three kinds of consciousness—worldly, creative, and spiritual—in my work.

I had particular difficulty with this issue when I was writing my second novel, *How I Got Him Back,* because much of that book portrays the institutional Church with all its foibles. I was terribly concerned about how my own snappish look at the Church—my worldly look at it—would connect to my spiritual life while I was writing. I decided it was a time for humility, and anyone who knows me will tell you what a stretch *that* was. I ended up praying a lot to Mary, because her statue is in one of the first images in the book. It was very important to me not to take that lightly.

Your novels portray women of all ages and their relationships. How did this emphasis develop?

It seems quite natural to me. In that sense it is not a consideration before I begin. I have never said before I sit down, "I think I should write about women, and they should be of a certain age." The stories develop quite naturally. I am very close to my five sisters; I have only one brother. So it seems to me completely natural that I would be writing about women a lot. But it has never consciously occurred to me that I must write this novel about a woman.

I am also a feminist, without apology, but I have never thought my job as a fiction writer is to tell "women stories." I have never tried to impose my feminist beliefs on my fiction, although I think they inform the stories. In fact the only one I have really struggled with is this new story I am starting, which is narrated by a man.

My characters often come to me. I'm sure, looking back on it, that my own pregnancies had a tremendous impact on my first book, *Due East*. The central character is a pregnant teenager, Mary Faith. She is trying to avoid an abortion, and although she has no philosophical difficulty with abortion for others, for herself she must have this child. Her dilemma is to affirm life without affirming God, since she is an adamant atheist, at least up until the moment when she gives birth and calls on Christ. She is, in some sense, functioning in an irrational way. Her rational self says there is no God, and yet her impulse to create life, to affirm life, is her only way of affirming meaning. It is a necessity to her own existence, this affirmation. In a story something happens, and so love is very visible rather than abstract. Love is the gist of Christianity. Christ in the flesh is love in the real world, and I think that is why fiction is so appealing.

Mary Faith is so profoundly changed by childbirth that she calls out in a way that she never has before. And then, at the end of the novel, she experiences a love for her father that she has not previously experienced. The last scene in the kitchen is very physical. The same meal that was so sad at the beginning of the book is just infused with the possibility of the father and daughter loving each other, being at peace with one another.

Sex and religion are predominant themes in your novels. What do you see as the relationship between sexuality and spirituality?

Well, I don't see them as necessarily dichotomized. Sexuality is just one aspect of our lives. What is interesting to me, particularly about Catholic characters, is how the sexual dimensions are sometimes denied or skewed. Sexuality often takes on more importance, having been denied, than it naturally would. It becomes a matter of obsession. It is for Dolores, the mother in *Who Do You*

Love? As a little girl, she was deserted by her father, and, if not technically abused, at least taken advantage of by an older cousin who should have been her protector. She holds herself responsible for both. And because the first act she committed in response to her father's abandonment was a sexual act, sex has taken on a skewed meaning in her life. In the final moment of the book, after having committed a sin that I think she could finally perceive was even worse than her father's, she is, for a moment, able to forgive him his sin and so perhaps forgive herself. There is a moment of possibility.

For me as a writer, it is very important not to resolve my character's lives. To do that seems unrealistic. We are not stuck in time. We come to moments of possibility. In the upheaval my characters have been through, in the moral crises they have faced, they have had a moment to see themselves in a different way. And for me as a writer, that is resolution enough. It is a moment of such hope, such joy when that moment evolves—and it doesn't evolve easily out of the plot— I don't want to go on and manipulate a happy ending beyond that. For me that little moment implies happiness, because it implies such possibilities.

Can we return briefly to the question about sexuality and spirituality? Do you see the sexual union as a sacramental experience?

Sometimes I think it is. And sometimes it is not. It has the potential. The novel I am just completing is about a girl who has a promiscuous past, not wildly promiscuous, but as a teenager she slept with a lot of boys with great pleasure, great joy. She just likes it. And she comes to sacramental sex in a sense that she comes to fall in love with someone and to marry him and to find a kind of pleasure which can be for both their good.

I use my old catechism definition: a sacrament is an outward sign instituted by Christ that gives grace. The marriage itself is the sacrament, but every time these two characters engage in loving sex they renew the promise of the sacrament. The sensation of sexual joy can be closely connected to the sensation of spiritual joy: both involve abandon and trust.

How do you understand prayer?

I really stumble at this issue because the habit of prayer was very, very strong in my childhood. We prayed formally so often in our family. We said the Rosary every night at 8:45, a fifteen minute ritual which caused a struggle within the family. The children used to say, "Couldn't we just make it 8:30 so we won't have to turn the show off in the middle?" Anyway, that aside, formal prayer was so much a part of my life, and such solace, that the habit has continued into adulthood. Formal family prayer before supper is my family's ritual. It is a very lovely moment. The littlest one always does it. Still, I often think, at other moments of the day, that in my childhood these would have been occasions to pray. And I have tried to bring that back into my life.

I mentioned Mary's importance to me as a child. In my girlhood, I kept up a running conversation with Mary, one which often operated without benefit of logic. I trusted her to fill in the gaps in my wandering thoughts, and I never doubted that this was prayer—that Mary would be able to interpret me and present my petitions to God in a tidier fashion. And that is something that has re-entered my life recently, a connection to Mary which was absent for many years.

I find this hard to put into words. The Catholic church, of course, has this formal prayer, the Rosary. My sisters and I have often laughed about this. One sister always says when she feels her life is threatened—if she is on a ski lift or something is wobbling—that is when that Rosary comes out. The Catholic version of Mary as intermediary to God is very interesting. And so I feel some ambivalence about my relationship to Mary. I sometimes think, "I am praying to Mary so much, do I ever pray to God?"

Often when I am concerned about our family, I also direct prayers to Saint Joseph. It is funny because you might expect a mother to pray to a mother. My image of Saint Joseph from childhood is such a positive one. I feel blessed in that regard. I think so many girls have such an ambivalent relationship to their fathers. But my father was an honorable and decent and loving man. So I think that is why that prayer to Saint Joseph comes through.

How does your spiritual autobiography impact your fiction?

That is a very complicated question which I try not to think about while I am writing. I have found the most productive way for me to continue work is not to agonize over what the relationship is between a character and me, but instead to lose myself in the character. I have not tried to recount the experiences of my life in my fiction. On the other hand, it has been very important to me to recreate the place where I was born and raised and to recreate a sense of the people without actually trying to reproduce people I knew. In the same way, I certainly must be exploring elements of family happiness and unhappiness as it appeared in my past and appears in my present. But psychoanalyzing myself in relation to my characters is not particularly fruitful for me.

I think spiritual autobiographies are useful, moving documents. Not everyone is called upon to write one, but I have been tremendously moved by reading them. I think about Thomas Merton's *Seven Storey Mountain,* which continues to have quite an impact on my life. But I don't work in the field of spiritual autobiography; I work in the field of fiction. And once I create a character, my obligation is to be true to that character's spiritual life, not to my own. In exploring that character, that otherness, I am able to observe other people and see myself more clearly.

DOTTIE FITCHETT

Born in Virginia, Dottie Fitchett continues to live in the South by choice. In her story, Dottie shares her commitment as director of HIS House in Tyler, Texas, a residential care facility for men and women who are HIV positive. Due to increasing health concerns, Dottie is no longer able to continue in this ministry. For her commitment and service, she has been awarded the Crystal Golden Flame by JCPenny and Company and was a finalist in their national Golden Rule Award for 1993.

"As you review the story told here, don't forget to focus on the enabler and the enabled, of which I am but one of many. Be enriched by the courage and faith of those we serve."

Redeeming the Pain
by Dottie Fitchett

I know that your childhood was a painful one. Would you tell us about it?

I grew up in Norfolk, Virginia, and lived in my own home until I was fifteen years old. But from the time I was five years old until I was fifteen, I was sexually abused by a relative and forced to have sexual relations with both men and women as well as animals. As a young child, I didn't understand what was happening; I thought that I was just somehow special. Obviously, when I got a little older I knew that something was drastically wrong. When I tried to get help, I was accused of making up terrible tales and suffered severe punishment as a result. Needless to say, I didn't try to tell anyone after that for quite some time. My only recourse was to go along, to cooperate, so that I wouldn't get hurt any more.

One day I discovered that my sister was in danger of being abused. I was terribly frightened for her and didn't want anyone else to have to live like I did. The next day, I managed to steal a few of the many slides that had been taken when I was forced to have sexual relations. I gave the slides to my sister and told her to take them to the police, and she did.

That afternoon when I came home from school, the police were in front of my home. I could understand why they would arrest the adults who had been involved, but they arrested me, too. I thought that by saving my sister I was probably saving myself; but at the time, that wasn't true at all. I was sent to a detention home for my own good, for my "protection." But the detention home was full, and because I was fifteen years old, the oldest one there, they moved me to what was called the bull pen in the city jail. It was a terrifying experience.

The next morning, the police officers took me into a room with a slide projector and hundreds of slides which had been taken over a ten year period. I can't imagine how many—just tray after tray of slides. Two male officers and I were sitting in that room, and they were trying to make me date those slides because they couldn't get a conviction unless they had the dates when those things occurred. I was sitting there, bawling. I was terribly upset because, in spite of not having a Christian background, I had a strong honesty background. Since my father had been very keen on our telling the truth, I kept saying, "I don't know. I can't tell you, I don't know."

Fortunately, some of the slides had holiday themes related to them, so we could pick up on that, or I could remember when a particular dog died that was involved in the slide. Finally, the officers got dates on six out of those hundreds of slides. But for weeks, all I did was go in every day, sit in that room and look at the slides with those two officers. And I thought, "This is hell."

After that, I lost contact with my whole family and was sent to a state mental hospital where I stayed until I was eighteen.

What happened when you came out of the mental hospital?

I had been sent there as a "totally mentally disabled juvenile." When I was released from Eastern State Mental Hospital in Virginia, they sent me to my hometown, Norfolk. I was on nineteen tranquilizers a day and was seeing a psychiatrist once a week. That was how I lived, and no one expected anymore than that out of me. They thought that because of what had happened, I would always be just a vegetable.

But when I got back to Norfolk, I decided I wanted to find my brothers and sisters. I wanted something, somebody, anything to feel a part of. In fact, I think I probably would even have welcomed an abusive situation again. I understand why people live with abuse, because if you don't have *anything,* something is better than nothing. Anyway, I started looking for my brothers and sisters. Somebody told me I had a sister attending the Salvation Army, which I knew absolutely nothing about. I asked where it was, and when I arrived there, I saw a big sign out front that said they were having Spring Campaign meetings at seven o'clock nightly for a week. I came back that evening at seven o'clock. That was in the mid-fifties, and people were wearing mini-skirts and fishnet hose and wide brimmed hats and red lipstick up to your nose. And that is exactly the way I looked. I went into the Salvation Army looking for my sister in the midst of those very plain-clad, navy-blue-uniformed people. I really stood out. My sister was there and was playing in the band. I sat through the meeting, and when the service was over, I went up to tell her who I was. She told me to get out of there, that she never wanted to see me again, that I was a tramp. She was planning to marry a young man who was an officer in the Salvation Army, and she didn't want them to know me or anything about our family. She just wanted me to go. I got really angry and hurt and disappointed because I had counted on finding somebody that I could be a part of. They were having meetings every night that week, and I decided I was coming back. So I went back every night and sat on the very front row. The fourth night that I was there, I answered an altar call. I went to the altar again, and again, and again. I certainly didn't get a quick fix. I had a very hard time believing that God loved me. One of the things that was tremendously helpful, though, was that the officers there were very patient and understanding. They didn't know the answers, and they didn't try to pretend that they did. They just loved me in spite of it, providing a model for me to believe that God loved me in spite of my horrible guilt and shame. It was so important for me to realize that God didn't look on me and see all that filth and guilt, but that He looked on me and saw someone for whom His Son died. God saw the intrinsic value of His own creation.

And their love led you to decide to work in the Salvation Army?

That is exactly right. They were very, very patient. In fact, my first job in the Salvation Army was picking up the bulletins after church and sweeping out between the pews. That's about all I was capable of. I was so drugged—legally drugged on tranquilizers—that I really wasn't capable of much more. I had only gone to the ninth grade in school, and I had no skills of any kind. But the Salvation Army officers took me where I was. That first job they gave me—clearing out the chapel after church—was something I could do, and I did it.

I eventually went to seminary, although it took a long time to get there because of my psychological profile, my background. I also had to get a GED. But the Lord just opened doors for me, one after another. Literally, it was the Lord opening them. Nobody anticipated that it would happen. When I said I wanted to be an officer, nearly everyone thought I had already become all that I would be able to become.

I went to Baltimore, Maryland, to fill an opening in the Public Relations department there. I didn't know anything about PR, but when they asked me to go, I said I would be glad to. I got through my first year working and going to seminary that way, and every successive year worked out so that I was able to get scholarships and work to complete my seminary training. I became an ordained minister and a commissioned officer and served in the Salvation Army for eighteen years.

How did you get into your work with AIDS patients?

I was a chaplain at the University of Texas Health Center, working with patients with HIV and AIDS. I had sought work at the hospital after reading a newspaper article about people with HIV being disposable people. That pulled some heartstrings, so I wanted to work with AIDS patients. While I was working there, they decided to cut back the chaplains' force. I had three months to decide what I was going to do and where I would go. One morning, I went into the chaplain's office and said, "I think I am going to look for a house in North Tyler, and I am going to do AIDS education." Nobody could believe what I said. But I said, "Well, I have a lot of background now, several years of experience, and I think I need to do AIDS education and counseling."

That decision led to HIS house?

Yes, within the week, a problem situation occurred at the hospital: a forty-four year old black male patient, who had been in our hospital for eighteen months, needed a place to go. I was on the treatment team for him as the chaplain, and we could find no place for him. We couldn't even get him into a nursing home. He was HIV positive, had full-blown AIDS, his family wouldn't take him, and he was scared to death. He had lived alone in the same neighborhood all his life, and he had nowhere to go. We saw him get sick and get well and get sick and get well. With his compromised immune system, he caught everything coming and going in the hospital. I decided within the next week that not only was I going to open a house to do education and counseling, but I was going to let him live there with me. That is really how it started.

Someone asked me the other day how I started HIS House, and I said, "I opened the front door." That is literally what happened. My intention was to do educational presentations and counseling with people who were HIV positive and just let the one AIDS patient live there. We were to have an open house on December 1, which is World AIDS Day, but on November 28, 1989, a young man was delivered to our front door by ambulance. He was nineteen years old and had nowhere to go. When I asked why he was being brought here, they just said, "Well, we read about HIS House," and so I had my second person within two weeks of moving over here.

I have since discovered that the need for a home for people who are HIV positive is much greater than the need for education and counseling. Many people are doing education and counseling. I still enjoy doing that and want to continue. However, I do it from a unique perspective because I have lived with thirty-five people who have had this disease. From my perspective, I can fairly adequately say that a person is not going to get this disease by casual contact and therefore doesn't have to be afraid to hug a loved one or to share a bathroom or to share the same linens or dishes. These are questions that are very important to families, especially adult parents who have adult children coming home to die.

One of the things that is really gratifying is to bring someone into our home, work with that person for a month or two, and then have the patient's family come in just to be with their loved one. They watch me and our four volunteers work with that patient, and through watching us, they become keenly aware that we are not doing anything they can't do, so they take their loved one home, enabling the patient to die at home rather than with us. That is a special gift. That doesn't always happen, but it has happened a few times. When it does, it is very gratifying.

***I know that you told me that you had to come to terms with your
understanding of homosexuality during this period.***

Yes, I did. I had a unique opportunity to do that. While I was
taking my first course for certification in working with AIDS patients, I determined that I needed to figure out what I thought
about homosexuality and actually come to grips with how I felt
about these people. I knew what the scripture said. I knew what I
thought theologically, but I wasn't sure how I felt personally about
people who engaged in this particular lifestyle. It made me very
uncomfortable to even consider thinking about it. The nice thing
to do—what I had done as a pastor for eighteen years as a Salvation Army officer—was to put it on a shelf and not worry about it.
But suddenly it was a face-to-face issue. Suddenly it was something I did need to be concerned with; I needed to figure out where
I stood with it.

After finishing the course, I was invited to go out to the Hospital Christian Fellowship in California and speak to AIDS patients
about the disease and the ministry from the vantage point of what
I did for people with HIV. In the course of doing that, I was able to
go to different places in California and actually be confronted with
a primarily homosexual disease. We know now that this is not a
homosexual disease, but then we certainly thought it was.

As a result, I went to the AIDS ward at San Francisco General
Hospital and spent a week there working as a volunteer. That in
itself was extremely confrontational for me because there were no
heterosexuals and no women. The fact that there were only gay
males on the wards was astounding to me and at first reinforced
the idea that this was God's judgment on homosexuality. I questioned and grappled with that. I went to the Names Project where
they do the quilt pieces and worked for three days with a young
man who actually made his own memorial quilt piece. I will never
forget that, and in working with him, I began to clarify my own
thinking about homosexuality. I now understand that judgment
is God's business. I believe that sin is sin, and if we are going to
preach against it or say that we are not going to allow homosexu-
als into our churches, then we need to be looking at the rest of
that list of sinners, which includes liars, adulterers, fornicators and
all the rest of that portion of scripture that we take bits and pieces
from.

I reached that conclusion while having lunch with a friend. I had not known that she had two sons who had died of AIDS. My friend was a nursing supervisor at a hospital, and she came to spend part of her vacation with me in California. In the Castro District in San Francisco, which is predominately gay, we were sitting in a sandwich shop surrounded by gay males. Suddenly she looked terribly distressed. She just looked at me and said, "These people killed my son." At first I didn't know what to think or say or do, and then the answer came to me. I said "No, your son made some choices and his choices led him in a path that led him to a disease that took his life. But no, no one killed your son. And these people, but for the grace of God, have done no more or no less than any of the rest of us have done, and we need to remember that God's grace is what this is about." And that is what HIS House is about, I hope. It is about God's grace and redemptive power.

Tell us how you understand prayer.

I think that living our life can be a prayer. Although I am careful to guard my quiet time and to keep a prayer journal and to keep up with the needs of other people that I want to pray for, I also feel—probably because of the work I do with people who are terminally ill and have a devastating disease—that every avenue I enter into with these folks is an avenue of prayer. It is unchartered water, so I don't dare try to do it without being conscious that it is an offering. We are living prayers. The scripture talks about praying in utterances we don't understand or know. I think even a sigh is a prayer. There are times when I'm just absolutely lost; I have no sense of knowing what to do or say next. And just that sigh is like the releasing of the channel, opening the channel, releasing myself and allowing the Spirit to come in and fill me and to actually lead me into the next step. That certainly is a prayer. And just the silence of staying with some of our folks is prayer. In our society, we are trained to be "human doings" instead of "human beings," and the hardest thing I have had to learn is to sit quietly with someone who is afraid to go to sleep for fear of not waking up. That is a prayer; that takes all of the prayer energy I have because I am very much geared to being active and wanting to fix it, wanting to do something. But I've learned to sit quietly beside somebody so that he can just sleep.

You say you learned about God through suffering humanity. Explain that.

A verse in the scripture talks about entering into the sufferings of Christ, to be counted worthy to be a part of His suffering. Through my own suffering, I certainly can relate to the sufferings of Christ and have come closer to the Lord because of that; I call it redeeming the pain. Then through that, by continuing to be in touch with my own pain, I have been able to learn about the Lord through the sufferings of others. Sometimes we think that—because of the divinity of Christ—His suffering wasn't real. I have discovered that not only was His suffering very real, but so is the suffering of humanity. He identifies with our suffering and He comes, not to alleviate it—which is what we would like Him to do—but to become a party to it. He comes to be in fellowship with us in suffering and for us to be in fellowship in suffering with Him. We tend to think that we should cure our suffering and then come to Christ. That is not what I read in scripture or what I see now in my own spiritual walk. What I see now is that in redeeming the pain and being a party to the suffering, I see more of Christ than I have ever seen before. Every person I have come into contact with who is reaching a terminal phase of life and is experiencing a devastating illness begins to have some serious questions about God, about the reality of God and about the life to come, about eternal life. Suffering brings you into focus in those questions; and when you are trying to answer them for someone else, you certainly need to be evaluating and finding some of your own answers and reevaluating all the time. And that is what I mean by growing and suffering.

You are still in therapy yourself—for what reason?

When I claimed salvation, I claimed total healing, and for a long time, I labored under the idea that my wounds were not important to God. Now, when I say that, the first picture I have is of Jesus in heaven with His wounds. He is not there without them, according to scripture.

So you feel that salvation did not heal your wounds? You have had to continue to work at that?

Oh yes. They told me that God was interested in me part and parcel with my wounds, that He loved me with them, that I didn't have to heal them to be able to be loved by God, and I am of no less value because of those wounds. In fact, I may be of more value because of them. I have had a psychiatrist tell me on several occasions that part of the problem is that I have no ego. That is interesting, because that is not true. I do have an ego, whether it is stomped on or not. It is a part of me and it is there. Esteem is something else, and I see so many problems with that today with the people I work with, too. We seem to pick up our esteem from what we do or who we are married to or where we grew up or anything outside of ourselves. But the scripture talks about who we are in Christ Jesus. If we want to know something about true esteem, we should look first at the creation process, the fact that we are—all of us—created in His image. How much more esteemed could we be than to be created in the image of the Creator? And then we mar that image. Coming into the world, living in the world, dealing with the hurtful things that come to us scars us and sometimes even destroys that image. But Jesus Christ sees us for who we are in His creation. He doesn't look on the sin; He looks on the sinner, and what separates us from being all that we can be in Him is our sin. But it doesn't separate His love from us.

How do you help people with self-esteem problems?

We transcend the self-esteem problem because their identity for me is not found in their illness; it is not found in their history. Their identity is not wrapped up in what they have done in the past. It is not wrapped up in their families or their lack of family. Their identity for me is that they are God's creation. They are created in His image and He loves them beyond anything I can possibly comprehend.

GERRY BODE HARRISON

Gerry Bode Harrison was born and reared in Texas, completed her undergraduate studies in Tennessee, and worked in Georgia before moving to Wisconsin. After completing studies at Garrett Evangelical Seminary, she served a variety of United Methodist congregations as pastor, then as District Superintendent of the Eastern District. She returned to parish ministry (where her heart is) and now serves a congregation in the Metro-South District of the Wisconsin Annual Conference. She currently serves as chairperson of the conference Spiritual Formation Committee and as a member of the Cross Cultural Appointment committee.

Like a Fire in My Bones
by Gerry Bode Harrison

"My call into the ordained ministry, my commitment to the church, to renewal of the church, and to social justice burns like a fire in my bones."

Where did that commitment, that fire, begin?

I grew up in a family that connected deeply with the life of the church. Religiously, my mother was a strong person, with a strong German piety. She was orphaned as a child, reared by an extended family, and separated from her only brother. To survive, she found that she needed to strengthen some of her faith resources. She passed those resources on to me. When I was young, I remember in the middle of a thunderstorm, she taught me a prayer that she had learned as a child. My dad, on the other hand, didn't talk a great deal about his faith. He was quiet, solid, dependable, and involved in the life of the church and community. My parents were people who lived their faith.

I developed a strong sense that there was much to be done in the world and that as a Christian, I should respond to those needs. Along with this realization came a solid sense of social justice. My mother gave me, not just tolerance, but appreciation, of persons who are different or who have different opinions. My family was involved in Democratic politics in the South. They had little tolerance for bigotry and racism.

The community in which I was reared was exceptional. Its leaders seemed to know that community survival depended upon their ability to work and live together in some kind of harmony. They were dealing with the same kinds of difficulties between Blacks and Anglos as was the rest of the South, but our community seemed to deal with a even larger mixture of races and religions—a balance of Anglos, Hispanics, Blacks, Jews, Protestants, and Roman Catholics.

When did you first hear your call and how did you know what it was?

There was no blinding flash that said, "This is it; go into the ministry." It was very much like a nudging. My earliest call was simply to be a Christian. That was to be my vocation, regardless of how I made my living. I knew very early that my baptism was important to me and that living it out through Christian vocation was the only option which allowed consistency between my job, my values, and my need to share the gospel message, in deeds.

By the time I was a sophomore in high school, many people sensed that I would enter a church-related field. I certainly did not feel called into ordained ministry at first, probably because I had never seen a woman in the ordained ministry, and so had no role model.

However, I was very strongly influenced by the mission activities of my church. Our congregation invited me, as a young person, to serve on the mission committee. I saw it was possible for a woman to be a missionary. Within my congregation there were strong women in mission through the United Methodist Women (known as WSCS at that time). My mother's associations through that group introduced me to women who had been missionaries, who became role models for me.

I attended a Methodist junior college in East Texas where I studied the writings of Buber, Bonhoeffer, Tillich, and others. There my vocational call was nourished. I then learned about Scarritt College, a small Methodist college in Nashville. While I was a student at Scarritt, I began to hone that calling a little bit more and realized that foreign missions was not where I needed to be. I looked instead at Christian education. I wanted the young people growing up in the church to have the same kind of experience I had. I sensed that the church should be a training ground for them, and I became even more excited about church renewal and social change.

How did your time at Scarritt fuel your fire of commitment?

Being at Scarritt in the midst of that wonderfully diverse community of international and American students was really important for me. The civil rights movement was very prominent in Nashville and throughout the world at that time. Before I went to Nashville, I saw an NBC White Paper about what was happening there and felt some strange sense of being beckoned to that place. John Lewis was interviewed on that program, and I later got to know him when he was chair of the Student Non-Violent Coordinating Committee. I became a part of a small cadre of Scarritt, Fisk, Peabody, ABT, and Vanderbilt students who felt themselves being called into the civil rights movement. We were concerned about social justice issues, about integrating the community, and about the need for cooperation between the races. Some of us established a group that became a campus-based movement in the South.

When friends in the movement in Nashville asked me how I got to be such a radical, I was surprised by the question. I thought of my actions as merely responding to what the gospel says. This is the way we have to live—to love and respect each other, cooperate, and stand up for what is right. I wasn't involved because I was liberal, but because, as a Christian, I didn't feel that I could *not* be involved. It was something I felt called to do. My group in Nashville bonded spiritually, similar to my Methodist Youth Fellowship group of younger days. We prayed and sang together and supported one another as we worked for a common goal. These friendships have continued to be a strong influence through the years. I saw our involvement as a sign and foretaste of the Kingdom of God.

After your time at Scarritt, you became a Christian Education Director. How did you finally choose the pastoral ministry?

While I was on the staff in Georgia as Christian Education Director, I began to do things that went beyond Christian education in its strictest sense. Through ministering to families in their grief and through hospital visitation, I began to realize that I could serve in the pastoral ministry. It felt fulfilling for me to be with people in the midst of their experiences. I also continued to feel a call to involvement in positive change in society, and to helping the church change.

call to involvement in positive change in society, and to helping the church change.

Early on I recognized that I would not let race be a factor in preventing my involvement with people—in friendships or intimate relationships. While I was living in Georgia, I met and fell deeply in love with an African American man whose family roots were in the South. We married even though there was a stigma against interracial marriages in most of the South, and it was even against the law in some places.

Even though my family had little tolerance for bigotry and racism, they had a real struggle with my interracial marriage. My mom seemed more able to deal with that decision than my father. It took him a number of years, during which time I had little part in the family life. Rather than hurt my family, I stayed away until they could find some way to resolve it within themselves. It was very painful for me not to be a part of that family circle for those years even though I understood their attitude. However, the experience bonded my spouse and me even more deeply, and my family eventually came to accept my marriage.

After a couple of years, I left Georgia the summer of the marriage and joined the staff at an urban church in a changing neighborhood. I was a student intern in a cross-racial appointment. Through the Student Interracial Ministry, white seminarians were placed in black churches and black seminarians in white congregations. I planned to go into seminary after this experience.

The experience was not what I hoped for. The white senior pastor I worked with was not able to deal with my aggressive ideas for involvement in the community, such as voter registration. In addition, he was already shell-shocked when I arrived. He had had one black member join the church shortly before I arrived, and the entire white congregation voted to move to the suburbs in response. Since I had been given the impression that the church in the North was open and liberal, I was disappointed. I had been told that the North was the "promised land for Blacks. It just wasn't so, and I felt the door was closed. I left that position after just three months and focused my attention on my relationship with my husband, whom I had married earlier in the summer.

Your pull toward the ordained ministry lessened for a time. What contributed to this?

At the end of the summer experience with the inner city church, I began work on the staff of the University of Wisconsin-Milwaukee campus, where my spouse was enrolled. My intention was to quickly put my husband through college, go to seminary, and possibly return to the South. Unfortunately, his health soon became a serious issue, and within a year his employment situation became rocky as well. He dropped out of school, and I became the primary bread winner. It became evident that part of my husband's trouble was alcoholism and that his health would not return sufficiently for him to support us. During those years I worked on a graduate degree in early childhood education. My love for children and desire for a family was somewhat satisfied by this interest. After being on the university staff in Milwaukee and Waukesha for twelve years and teaching a short time at an inner-city day care center, however, I again felt called into the ministry.

How did the rekindled call speak to you?

My husband's health improved somewhat, and he returned to school. We bought a house when I finally became pregnant, but shortly thereafter I had a miscarriage. This was a major disappointment for me. Although my husband was not able to support me emotionally, others were there for me. Until I went through that experience, I had not had a sense of how important it is to have somebody to stand beside you in a time of personal need. I began to realize I wanted to be present for others, as they had been for me in my crisis. I sensed that I could do that in parish ministry.

Another turning point for me was at a jurisdictional school of Christian mission which I attended in Illinois. There I heard Bishop Muzorewa speak, a man I had known as a student at Scarritt before he returned to Africa. I agreed to transcribe all of his addresses, which made the week a very powerful experience for me. I had a sense that I was being drawn into social justice ministries again. This, combined with my bonding with the people who supported me during the time of my miscarriage, made it hard for me to ignore my calling any longer. My spouse began to sense the importance of that call for me and was supportive of my being in ministry for the first time.

I was still the primary bread winner, however, so I could not give up work and go to school full time. I began seminary part-time and commuted for a number of years. My spouse was dealing with his own issues during this time, particularly his "lover's quarrel" with the church. My somewhat naive assumption was that he might find a way to resolve his conflict with the institutional church if I were serving a Black congregation. I had been serving on the staff of a large suburban congregation, so I moved to an inner-city church with a predominantly Black congregation and a large program. My spouse eventually joined the staff there after his graduation from college, which gave him an opportunity to resolve some of his difficulties with the church. But it was not a good experience for me because I never felt I was able to use the talents I had or grow in the ways I wanted. However, I learned again how important the local parish is to me and how complex the issues are among people with basic differences.

When I finished seminary at the end of that year, I moved to a rural appointment with two congregations. My husband remained in our home in the suburbs and commuted to the city to work. After a few months, his alcoholism became active again. When he refused treatment, I realized that I could not live through another episode like the previous one; the relationship had been damaged too much to salvage. So three years out of seminary I was divorced, with fear and trembling. Amazed, I found that the congregations I served were understanding and supportive. During the process of the divorce, I also suffered a ruptured disk and found them again supportive and understanding. I learned how to receive care as well as give it, a major learning experience and a time of grace.

While my husband's health problems had delayed my education and move into the ordained ministry, learning about his illness helped me understand my own co-dependency, although nobody used that language in those days. Before the miscarriage, I sponsored an Alateen group and began to see how important the twelve-step programs can be as an important spiritual resource and support base.

After the period of my own healing, I found ways to integrate some of the twelve-step principles into the ministry of the local church. I continue to have a strong commitment to providing recovery resources to addicted persons and affected family members and have had additional CPE in that field.

How did you know that God wanted you to continue throughout all these difficult times?

I never had the sense I was going the wrong direction, even though I think there were times when I wondered if God might not use a different instrument more effectively, and I wondered why God was calling me.

I always had the sense that I would be able to respond to the call, that somehow all of these experiences would make me stronger and be useful in helping others. All of those challenges re-enforced where I felt I needed to be. My husband's not seeing the same vision that I saw called me to question deeply, but I was reaffirmed every time.

Thinking back about how the struggles affected my spiritual life, I think they were opportunities for me to deepen my spiritual roots—to sink them deeper, acknowledging that those gifts were there for me and that I needed to claim them. So I think that some of the difficulties I faced made me stronger.

I couldn't get away from my call. Even now in my position as a District Superintendent, I am finding new ways to live it out. I have new opportunities to encourage growth and a broader, more inclusive vision of the church. I can see that some people are victimized by the church or its members, that people have a hard time being faithful. I also see that many times the church gets bogged down with petty stuff, has difficulty changing, is unfocused, and operates like a dysfunctional family. Ironically, that realization has strengthened my belief that the church is of God—otherwise it couldn't have lasted.

What is your spiritual life like now?

I have often identified with St. Theresa, who reportedly fell into a ditch on her way to found one of her convents. She shook her fist at God in the midst of that muddy scene, saying, "If this is the way you treat your friends, it's no wonder you have so few." A number of times I have had to work on my anger at God, and I'm glad we have worked through that.

I have been meeting with a group of women for about seven or eight years who are an important support system for me. We do a one-day retreat every six weeks or so to reflect on our journeys and where God is moving us and the church. They have been an incredibly supportive group through the divorce and other struggles, including taking this new responsibility as a District Superintendent.

Through the years, I have adopted a number of spiritual disciplines. Early in my seminary work, I took a course on the theology of prayer, believing that I wanted my ministry and my life to be grounded in prayer. Since that time, I have journaled on a fairly regular basis. Journaling has offered me opportunity to reflect on the grace of each day, on God's presence and sustaining grace throughout a variety of difficult experiences.

I can't say that my story is a "happily ever after" story. I think it will continue to be a story of ups and downs, of grace-felt experiences, and days when things really feel "like the pits." I have no idea where my personal struggles may take me or what opportunities I may have in the future. I will try to be faithful and hope to be visionary. I am content with the realization that the journey is my home.

BARBARA LEE

A young single woman with strong family ties, Barbara Lee is a native Texan presently living in Jacksonville, Texas. Her small Baptist church and choir activities continue to tie her to her roots. As she struggles financially to find ways to complete her college education, Barbara has recently gone back to school. She has a strong interest in writing and hopes someday to write a book.

She says, "I accept what life has given me and treasure the strength I have gained from my experiences."

Becoming an Amen Sister
by Barbara Lee

Tell us about your early life.

M y childhood was not the best situation to grow up in; I grew up without a father, and even now, I find myself wondering how I made it as far as I have without the guidance of a father. My mother worked hard to give us the things that we needed, not necessarily what we wanted. But we were never hungry, and whenever we needed medical attention, we got it.

I was born in Dallas but have been here in East Texas since I was about four or five years old. After we moved in with our grandparents in New Summerfield—and they were and are very religious people—Sunday School became important in our lives. It was a cardinal rule: Sunday School every Sunday morning. After a while, it became routine. Earl's Chapel Baptist Church, two to three miles from New Summerfield, is a part of my life. It is a typical, small congregational church: about fifty people, one or two deacons, the secretary, the minister, the "Amen Sisters" or missionary sisters, and a few kids.

Tell us about the "Amen Sisters."

The "Amen Sisters" encourage the preacher when he gets up to preach. When I was growing up, there was a section of the church where these women sat. They were usually the older women. When the preacher started preaching, you could always count on them to give extra support. I learned that it really helps a preacher out. He depends on that kind of background encouragement of "amens." It encourages not only the preacher but the whole congregation. And pretty soon you have "amens" coming from all around the room. The "Amen Sisters" are more vocal; they don't

mind getting up; they don't mind standing up before the congregation and speaking. If no one else stands up, the "Amen
Sisters" will.

You learn early that the sisters in the church keep things on a
high spiritual level. The deacons handle the business end of the
church, but as far as the spiritual things, the women have a very
large part in that. They are the ones who go out into the communities and check on the sick, for instance, and then report back to
the church. If there is a tragedy in the community such as a death
in the family or a disaster, the women pull together. There is a
great bonding. It is not something that the women are told to do.

My mother was the church secretary for as long as I can remember, and she was very outspoken, very vocal, and a leader. She
and my grandmother usually were leaders. For a time she would
do things my grandmother would hesitate to do. So when she became ill and couldn't go to church regularly, they began to look to
me. I felt uneasy about it at first, but now I am the choir president,
the lead singer, Sunday School teacher, and I help in making some
of the big decisions for our church.

Do you see yourself becoming an "Amen Sister?"

I do. I find myself standing up, not because of the "Amen
Sisters," because I have gotten up all by myself from time to time.
And it is really amazing just how good that makes you feel when
you do.

Is this like a testimony?

It is a feeling I get. When I get up, I am showing my support for
what's going on. If someone is singing and the song is inspiring, I'll
get up. I stand up, and I can sing along. If a minister is talking, it is
like more of a testimony to myself to stand up. If the minister is
speaking directly to me, I've got to show that expression. Some
women will raise their hands and give the "amens" and praise the
Lord. When I was little, these ladies were older; they were practi-
cally elderly. But now it is changing. A lot more younger people are
expressing themselves. At first I thought it was pretense. Then I
started experiencing it myself.

Tell us more about your involvement in the church?

I am the lead singer in our choir. There is something uplifting about singing and listening to spiritual music. There is not another feeling like it. When I hear music, particularly spiritual music, there is a certain peace and harmony about it that allows me to concentrate on what's bothering me.

It is a communication tool for me also. Since I am the lead singer, lots of songs come my way. Some people say I have talent; to me that is a compliment because, if I don't have anything else, I can give people enjoyment through my music. If I can make people feel good about themselves or some situation in their lives, there is nothing better than that to me.

What was your first awareness of God?

I was about thirteen years old, in junior high. Our school had taken a field trip to the cinema in Jacksonville to see the movie called "For Pete's Sake," a Billy Graham sponsored film. As I watched the film, there was something about it that was very sad, yet it had a lot of hope in it toward the end. I realized then that there could be something to all they had been telling us at Sunday School. At the end of the movie, a feeling came over me, and I knew that there really was a spiritual being. There was something about the movie which allowed me to understand things about Christianity that I had never understood before. An even fuller understanding of spirituality came years later when I realized that spirituality comes from inside an individual, not from what someone does in church.

What experiences led you to that fuller understanding?

I guess the first was when my brother was in a car accident. I was just nineteen, and he was a couple of years older. My mother got a call in the middle of the night saying that he had been in an accident. I remember feeling that this couldn't be happening to our family. I didn't want to believe it. When we got to the hospital, the doctor explained to us that my brother was still unconscious and that they were putting him in ICU.

I wanted to be brave for Mother, to show her how "adult" I was. I really felt God's presence then because I was able to be strong.

Mother was weeping, saying she was holding me up, but I was the one who was holding her up. My brother was in a coma for eleven days, but in all that time, I never gave up. Then we got a call late that Monday afternoon that they were losing him. I got there before Mother did. When I walked in and kissed him, I knew that he was gone, that he had left me. It took a while before I really realized what had happened and that there was nothing I could do about it, and there was only me and my mother now. But I had a sense, a feeling, that someone else was with me, and yet I felt abandoned too. I did much questioning of my faith at that time.

I lost my brother in November, 1978, and seven months later I lost my uncle, my mother's only brother, who was on the police force. About eighteen months later, almost two years to the day that my brother had died, my brother's son died. So there were three very important people in my life who died in a short period of time. Mother always told me the old saying that God doesn't put on you any more than you can bear. Through the years there have been other relatives who died—my grandfather, for example. I took his death hard because he never fully recovered after his son was killed. He had had a nervous breakdown, and we put him in Rusk State Hospital. After that he had a stroke, and we had to put him in a nursing home.

The final thing that convinced me that I was truly strengthened by God was when my mother became ill. When we found out that she had a terminal illness, we talked about it and made plans, even up to the very day that she died. That night she had a headache that just wouldn't go away. Over the months she had been ill, I had learned to accept that a headache didn't necessarily mean she was getting ready to die right then, so I did all the things I normally did whenever she had a headache. I drove her to the hospital after the medicine didn't work. We talked a little bit on the way there. The instant we got to the parking lot, I knew I was losing her because she couldn't talk. She never said another word to me after that. There was a moment of panic while I thought, "Am I ready for this—am I really ready for this?"

Over the next several hours the doctor told me three times that she had gone into cardiac arrest and they revived her each time. He finally looked at me and said, "We can keep her alive for as long as you want. When she goes into cardiac arrest, we can revive her. The hardest thing you'll ever have to do is what I am going to ask you right now: to sign the paper authorizing a 'no code blue.'"

I said, "No, I can't do it, I just can't do it."

And he said, "Think about it."

I talked to my aunt for a little while. I thought about all the times my mother had suffered and decided it would be very selfish of me to keep her alive like that. I must have signed that paper, but I don't remember doing so. I knew I was doing the right thing; she could die in some kind of peace. And then I knew that I could handle it.

I have no regrets, because I am a stronger person after having gone through all that. And I know that I didn't get strength from any of my family or my friends, but from God.

Have other incidents in your life forced you to find your strength in God?

Even as a child, I stood up for what I thought was right. Later, I even went so far as to join the NAACP for a time. I don't agree with everything they stand for, but I do think, as a black woman, it is important that I stand up for what I believe in.

When I was still living in New Summerfield, some incidents in the public school had many of the Blacks and other minority families upset. Someone said that the NAACP was good at straightening out things like that, so we contacted the chapter leader from Tyler. He helped us organize. We confronted the school administration about the things that were going on and made the community aware. In one respect this incident got families involved in the activities of the school. This situation has gotten much better. Things are not perfect yet, but we called attention to the fact that some things were going on that shouldn't have been.

The church has been of vital importance to Blacks for a long time, since long before the Civil War. We put ourselves in the children-of-Israel role, the mistreated—which is not always true—but we have put ourselves in that mold. Therefore, if we don't have a strong belief that God is really with us in what we do, then we don't have a prayer.

You said earlier that you got your strength from God. Tell us about your prayer life.

I pray all the time—even if I am not in the formal prayer position. I rarely wake up in the morning without saying "Thank you." When I go to bed at night and don't say thank you, I will wake up in the middle of the night and do it. I remember times when I was commuting to school at night, the whole time I drove through the backwoods between Jacksonville and Nacogdoches I was saying a prayer.

What kind of challenges lie ahead in your life?

I am now thirty-eight years old, and I lack about two semesters of college. Finances are the biggest thing I have to battle, because after I quit school, the student loans started coming due. If I can finish my degree in social work, I will be on the road to doing what I have always wanted to do—helping people. I think I got that desire from my mom. She was always so giving. She never achieved academically, or attained celebrity status, but a lot of people respected her. If I could have one thing from her, I want that ability to put people at ease, to give them encouragement.

I want to work as a case worker in the area where I was affected—dysfunctional families. When I made my decision to become a social worker, I volunteered and worked at a crisis center for a while. I did hotline counseling at the women's shelter in Tyler. I was educated into areas of dysfunctional families that I never knew existed. Physical abuse, child abuse, rape, all that kind of thing. I was green; I didn't know people went through experiences like that.

I want to help people understand that we can't control everything that happens to us, but we can control how much of it we accept. I basically want to get across to people the fact that even though something tragic might happen to them, the solution is in how they handle it.

But recently some things have happened in my life that have made completing my degree harder to achieve. I became ill a couple of years ago, and that really got me to thinking. I know my time is not guaranteed to me, nor is it guaranteed that I will ever be what I want to be. I am just going to have to do what I have to do and see what happens. I know those experiences didn't happen without a reason. I just have to accept the limitations I have right now and go with that.

Tell us about your health concerns.

It started in the summer a few years ago. I had just gotten out of school, and I really thought it was just exhaustion. I was working three jobs. I had just applied for another position in a school district in Nacogdoches so I would be closer to school to finish my degree. I woke up one morning and, as I took a shower, I had a tingling feeling in my right hand. I thought it was because I had slept awkwardly on it. Thirty minutes later the numbness and the tingling feeling were still in my fingers and had started extending up my arm. I began thinking heart attack, stroke. By the time it had traveled to my shoulder, it was accelerating pretty fast. I called 911, and when I heard the operator's voice and she asked me what was wrong, I really panicked. By the time the ambulance got to me, I couldn't walk, and they rushed me to the hospital. The doctors ran tests and determined that there was fluid on the brain, but there was no explanation for it. After a couple of hours the paralysis was gone, and no one knows why to this day. They are keeping an eye on it.

Strange things have continued to happen. Last spring I had an eye infection that turned out to be the result of an infection somewhere else in my body. Even though I have had several tests done, no one has come up with a reason why. So I am left in limbo.

This has put your education on hold?

It has because it seems to me that every time I start making plans, I have to go to a specialist, and it is expensive. My insurance is not adequate to cover all that, particularly the first set of emergencies that I had. It seems like everything is just kind of compounding. So now I'm paying off school loans and then paying medical bills. That has put my education on the back burner. I have often told my family and friends at work that if I am eighty years old, I am going to make that walk (for my diploma). It doesn't really matter when; it is just the idea of doing it. However, it is not the center of my life. I'm waiting really, waiting for that opportunity if it comes, but if not, it's not going to determine the outcome of my life.

In the meantime you are working as a teaching aide.

Yes. I am working right now as an aide in special education with handicapped three-yearolds—emotionally and physically disabled kids. It is demanding, but seeing any progress in a child makes it worth all the hard work. I have been here three years and have seen major improvements in the kids who have come through the program. One little boy, who was totally paralyzed from the waist down when he first came, has since learned to walk and is now in a regular class.

There are kids whose physical impairments will never allow them to function on a normal level, but our goal is to give them the courage and the tools to work within their limited abilities. We try to help them accept their limitations and go from there. A little Hispanic girl who came in last year has spina bifida and is in a wheel chair. When she first came, she couldn't communicate at all. Now, she is in a bilingual classroom and will talk you to death if you give her a chance. Now there is hope that someday she will walk. It is very satisfying.

What is your greatest strength spiritually?

My ability to accept things that really are beyond my control. Accepting death—I had to learn that the hard way. After mother died, which is just over three years now, there was no one else I could lose who could affect me. I want to pass on that ability to somebody else. People say that they can't live, can't survive without a certain person; that is just not true. And if people will learn to accept things as they are, their lives will be a lot better.

Susan M. Purtle

Susan M. Purtle, a young, single woman of Baptist heritage, has lived most of her life in Arkansas. She is staff attorney for Ozark Legal Services in Fayetteville, Arkansas, and also serves as their *pro bono* coordinator.

"I am a person struggling to come to grips with who and what I am. Hopefully, on the other side of this struggle lies joy—for me and those around me." Her mother's autobiography is also included in this collection.

Passageways

by Susan M. Purtle

How would you characterize your spiritual life?

Perhaps as a passageway. As a child I often dreamed about passageways underneath our church sanctuary. The entrance appeared in different places, but the same set of passageways was always there. Sometimes the tunnel would appear lighted, but only for a short distance; sometimes I peered into blackness but always with the certainty that I was traveling down a safe passage. This feeling of safety and exploration stayed with me for many years.

I am still searching for places of safety, looking for entryways to love, to the unconditional love of God and others.

What is an early spiritual passage that you remember?

One occurred the summer I was ten, even though church and the reading of Bible stories had provided a haven for me from early childhood. One night that summer at our local Baptist camp, I sat on a wooden bench in the open tabernacle-style building that is classic Baptist camp architecture. I sat there hot and sweaty and deeply depressed, feeling rejected, a misfit, not belonging. My school teacher did not like me, and two of my best friends had turned against me. I hated myself because I didn't measure up to what society wanted me to be or look like. I agonized over critical remarks.

As I stared down at the tabernacle floor I felt a call, a tug to come to Christ. When, as is common in Baptist churches, I walked down the aisle to the strains of "Just As I Am," I was welcomed by the older kids in the youth group. Their acceptance wrapped around me. After praying for Jesus to be the ruler of my life, I felt joy and release. I didn't have to carry my troubles any more. God could do it for me. My blind faith, coupled with conscious commitment, started there. It brought me happiness and kept me in touch with the bigger picture of my life in relation to God. This happiness lasted for many years

As you reached adulthood, how did your spiritual life change?

A blind lecturer at Ouachita Baptist University inspired me during my freshman year. He pushed me to be the best I could be, to pursue goals. And about that time I began to remodel myself, imitating a woman in the dorm who was loved by everyone. I developed a "sweet and nice" persona that worked and allowed me to be accepted. When I transferred to Hendrix University, I received acceptance and recognition as my persona and my self-doubt became repressed. Later, I spent an academic year abroad, studying at Oxford, taking difficult courses, entering new doors.

Then came law school and transition. I found friends there, male and female, and they accepted me. We supported each other, watched out for each other, studied together, bonding deeply in that adverse environment. I allowed my spiritual life and its development to coast. And I indulged in destructive behaviors, such as having simultaneous romantic relationships and not being honest about my needs.

About that time I remember watching a television special about the Dead Sea scrolls and the debate raging over them. That issue became a catalyst for my own underlying religious questions. Although I had come into contact with other faiths in earlier years, without giving much thought to them, I suddenly realized that other beliefs had as much legitimacy as my own blind faith. Caught in limbo, knowing that I must have blind faith or nothing, I simply waited. Spiritual questions hovered over me like trembling clouds while I interacted with non-Christians, who didn't seem to have any religious questions at all.

Have you experienced a dark passage, a painful or unsafe place?

Not as a single event, but more as a culmination of many events. My imperfections and weaknesses, all the qualities I don't like in myself—messiness, dishonesty, poor judgment, inappropriateness, my need for acceptance—began to overwhelm me in 1991.

The law office where I worked as an attorney was a war zone, a gaping canyon. I missed my close friends from law school and tried to find love and concern in the office. At times I found approval, but it disappeared quickly; even my "Sweet Persona" was rejected. Reprimands, snubs, wounds from the office and from my romantic relationship called up the wounds from the past. I felt doomed by some of my behavior traits, which seem to be linked to behaviors of my family. This unresolved family issue continues to create dark, painful passages through my other relationships.

At times, on a spiritual level, I have told myself that it was insane to let others define me. I have spent much time in self-examination, trying to understand myself and my spirituality, and in doing so have uncovered some painful truths. I don't think I have loved myself since sixth grade. Henri J.M. Nouwen says that the place we embrace our weaknesses is the place where Jesus walks with us and sends us his spirit. Examining my weaknesses is necessary if I am to learn to love.

Have you caught glimmers of spiritual light along the way?

On Easter afternoon in 1993, as I walked down the street near my house, I despaired over my imperfect condition. Suddenly I noticed a particular yard with beautiful flowers rimming the street. Quiet beauty filled the whole lawn. I stopped. In the middle of that natural beauty, I realized that Jesus had died for all my weaknesses, that he forgave the bad parts of me, so I didn't have to despair. I stopped and looked up, and suddenly thought out loud, "Oh, I get it. I understand Easter!"

Another time, after I had been practicing law for a while, I attended a jazz fest in New Orleans. At sundown, the Neville Brothers performed "Fly Like an Eagle." As the song began, I saw my whole legal career from law school to bar exam to my cases pass before my eyes. Along with the refrain about time slipping, slipping, slipping into the future, all the pain and joy and difficulty of my cases rose in me. Then came the line wanting to fly like an eagle to the sea with my spirit carrying me. And suddenly I was soaring, soaring like an eagle toward the sea, flying out over a cliff above the rocks with waves crashing on them. I felt the air undergird me as I soared with the wind.

After the song, as Aaron Neville talked to the crowd, I realized that if I could practice law as well as the Nevilles played music, everything would be okay.

Recently, a long-time close friend hurt me deeply by telling me that she no longer wanted me for a friend. That rejection, coupled with my boyfriend's statement that he would leave me if someone better came along, caused an emotional breakdkown. I lay on my side that night, wracked with sobs so agonizing that I actually felt pain in my body. I thought, "If they reject me, then there must be something really, really wrong with me." Their rejections echoed back down the corridors of years to second grade. I felt utterly, utterly rejected and alone.

At three a.m. that night I repeated to myself, "I know God loves me. I know God loves me." And then in my mind's eye I saw one of my best friends over the years, dating far back to childhood, Suzanne. I could see her clearly, and she was saying once again, "You and I like each other no matter what we do." She seemed to put her arms around me and hold me, and I could feel the strong bond of acceptance and love.

I mentally searched for anyone else who accepted me and thought of another long-term friend, Beth. Inside, I knew the truth—she accepted me for myself and loved me, too. With the vivid memories of Suzanne and Beth holding me, I quieted and was able to fall asleep in my pain. They got me through the night.

As you look to the future, what gives you encouragement?

Spiritual guides have helped me in the past; women I admire and respect have taught me from their experiences. As role models, they give me hope for my present and future. These women have blended their need for love into their professional lives and into their families. Spirituality is an integral part of their lives.

One of the women, Sarah Looney, loved God very much. And she loved me. She was old and lived near my childhood home. I visited her often and she filled me with Coca-Cola and her personal stories, stories of her childhood and young adulthood, to help me see that I was not the only one who felt as I did. I remember Sundays when the call for people to accept Christ as their Savior was given and Sarah would go forward in church. When I talked with her about it later, I remember her saying in her quavering voice, "Oh, Susan, I rededicate my life to Christ daily because I have to!" Then she laughed and drifted off with a smile on her face.

Rededication of my life to God on a daily basis is necessary for someone like me. I seem to do so many things wrong each day that I'm ready for a rededication by morning. The simplicity of daily rededication is appealing and gives me a clean slate for the day.

My mother is also my mentor. As I was growing up she took me to the library every Saturday and opened many books and opportunities for me. She never reinforced my self doubts and the rejection I experienced at school. She treated me as an adult, talked with me as her equal, and most of all, she didn't try to get her needs met through me. She let me be free to be myself. Spiritually, I gain strength from her religious history, the fact that she attended a Baptist college, worked at a church for a time, and focuses on serving others. As she continues to evolve as a Christian, she shares her quests with me. Her spiritual growth provides a bridge for me to walk across to other ways of being; it is a dynamic for my growth.

Another mentor of mine is Virginia Kirk, who was also a neighbor when I was a child and remains a real friend today. She accepted me, encouraged me. Her open, loving attitude toward people inspired me; she wove Christian virtues into her daily life. Her spirituality could be characterized as: "I'm here, Lord. Open a door for me and I'll walk though it." She doesn't try to plan what will happen a few days ahead, nor design a specific route for herself. At times when I have told her of trying to plan how a situation should or could be, she would tell me her college chemistry story. After taking one course and liking it, she took another one. Pretty soon she had enough chemistry courses to complete a major. Before long, she found herself teaching chemistry in college. She explained that when a door opened, she walked through it.

What discovery have you made about yourself and God?

I'm not in control of events and situations. All I can do is put myself in God's hands. Recently I've been undergoing a deep massage therapy called Rolfing, which brings out buried emotions and irons out muscles. At times it can be very painful, physically and emotionally. In these excruciating moments, in order to get through the pain without flinching, I picture myself as small and sitting in the outstretched hands of Jesus.

This reminds me of Virginia Kirk telling me about her father saying, "Jesus is just a hand away. If you'll just take Jesus by the hand, he'll walk with you." The image of being here on earth and being cradled by his hand is very reassuring.

Searching for safe places is a theme in my life. As I contemplate the passages that lie ahead for me, some safe and some frightening, I know it is critical for me to walk with Christ in the places where I embrace my weaknesses. I know that it is important to recognize that God is, and will take care of me.

SARAH F. HAYS

Sarah Hays is married and the "mother" of two golden retrievers and a tabby cat. She is in private practice of neuropsychiatry in Batesville, Arkansas, a small town in the foothills of the Ozarks. She was born in Dallas, Texas, but has lived most of her life in Arkansas.

She claims no religious affiliation, a position she came to after her childhood in a fundamentalist church and years of search for understanding of her spiritual needs.

UNKNOWING

by Sarah F. Hays

What is spiritual to you?

I connect deeply with nature. I know next to nothing about what exists outside mother earth, even though I feel slap-dab in the middle of the universe. Once, I threw my arms around a giant tree with new leaves and felt the bark rough against my cheek. No matter how hard I strained, my hands couldn't come close to meeting. I tried to imagine what it's like to be a tree—starting as a seed, cradled beneath the ground, sprouting roots, growing in one place, branch-like arms reaching for the sun. Who is to say that a tree has no consciousness? That tree is a partner in the universe with me.

And when it's dark, so dark that I can see thousands of stars and the brush of the Milky Way, I feel connected to "what's out there."

Does God fit into your thinking?

As a child my parents taught me many lessons about God, yet from a very early age I could not accept those ideas. There was not an authenticity about them for me. I spent years running from the thought of God and what I had been taught, simply ignoring the questions about spirituality or questions of that nature. At some point in my life, I quit running and developed a sense of peace about what I did believe and suddenly I found that God was not a part of that.

How has your experience as a neuropsychiatrist affected you spiritually?

I remember being a psych resident and interviewing a very psychotic patient who had just been brought into the state hospital by the police. He was a vagrant who roamed from state to state, disheveled and disorganized and sick. And yet there was something about him that I could care about and I think he knew that. I think he sensed it. I don't know if I have ever had a patient who was more disorganized than this young man. He could not complete sentences in a coherent fashion. He did not have a consistent basis on which to behave because his reality was so distorted. Yet, in a moment when he appeared ready to blow, to become violent toward me, he responded by stating he wanted to go into seclusion.

This young man had a totally different reality than mine and it was an eye opener for me, the psychiatrist. Even though there are people who have a different reality from our own, it doesn't mean we can't make connections with them in some way. I'm not naive enough to think I can help a person become something that he or she doesn't have the potential to be, but I can be there with those people to help them in what they have. I look at these people and I think—the Biblical God I learned about culls out these people. How can I believe in such a God? How can I believe that God would condemn these people because they have not been immersed in baptism for the remission of their sins?

In my experience as a neuropsychiatrist, I have come to know that neurochemicals are the core of our cognitive abilities and of our emotions. Nerve cell activity in the brain appears to be the underlying mechanism by which we think and feel. Our whole life is based on what we perceive or sense, according to what happens to the neurons in the brain. Reality is interpreted by us according to the messages that neurotransmitters send to different parts of our brain. All is based on neurochemistry. Can someone have a thought that isn't triggered chemically? Where is the Biblical God in this process?

But I wonder what happens after death. I have some problems about what happens when the heart stops beating, blood stops flowing to the brain, glucose and oxygen can no longer get to the brain and chemicals cease to react. I have watched many people die and it is a very dramatic change. A person is lying there; I can see that she is clearly alive, though deathly ill, and in a space of a few minutes her life is gone and her whole body has a different look. Something is gone and it is a puzzlement to me. What is that "something" and where has it gone? Scientists tell us that nothing is lost in the universe, so perhaps some underlying essence that engineered that life goes back to a part of the universe or a matrix.

We desperately cling to our individual consciousness. We make up stories to combat the fear of losing it. But what if the universal consciousness is better? Every part of our world has its place—the earth in the solar system, the solar system in the Milky Way, and the Milky Way wherever it fits. It is as if there is a giant web of life interwoven into a pattern. Things that happen in my life may affect things that happen in another's life; these changes are somehow a part of the tapestry of the universe.

Certainly there may be those who fight against the tapestry that is forming, trying to destroy it. But I think there is a power for its mending. All things seen and unseen could be part of an interwoven whole. A rhythm may exist in which we move without conscious awareness of its sound or feel. That is where the power or mystery of our existence lies.

Can you go back in time and trace how religion affected you?

Perhaps it started with the perception of good and evil. I had two older sisters—a middle sister three and a half years older than me and one six years older than me. There was always the sense that my middle sister was going to tattle on me to my older sister Nena. Once, they had both gone to school and I took a toy that was special to Nena and played with it all day. My sister Marcia saw me with it and could hardly wait to tell Nena about it. Well, Nena didn't mind a bit! I guess at that early point I began to observe in my own family that there was good and evil. I could see it in my sisters.

I grew up in a religious family and went to church Sunday mornings, Sunday nights and Wednesday nights. At times I accompanied my father to small rural churches, where he often preached. And I attended a school where we had daily Bible lessons. None of this ever sank into my heart. During my teenage years I went to a private Christian academy because that was the easiest thing to do; it wasn't a matter of conviction. When I decided to do things that I knew my parents disapproved of, I sneaked around and did them and didn't feel too guilty about it.

Later, I married a man who had a background in church like my own, and we went to church only on Sunday mornings. When we moved to Little Rock for both of us to attend medical school, we went to church on Sunday mornings, sometimes on Sunday nights or Wednesdays, but not often. Again there was no real meaning for me. As a child and as an adult, I sat in church waiting to feel something, something that never happened. Gradually we let church attendance go by the wayside.

Then during my medical internship I became really depressed. I realized I had to leave my husband. If I didn't, I would end by dying, literally. There was a darkness about him—a frightening darkness. And so, I moved out, taking some pretty severe emotional scars with me. I was unable to grab hold of anything spiritual and had no desire to go to church. For many years I just blotted church and God from my mind. Perhaps it was because I wasn't ready to look at what I believed. I think, unconsciously, I turned against my childhood religious training on a very deep level. I refused to have anything to do with religion for a long, long time.

Did something stimulate you to take another look at your spiritual life?

Peggy, the psychologist whom I went to see while caught in the quagmire over my marital breakup, helped me do this. Without pushing, in a very subtle fashion, she suggested that I buy a book titled *Politics of Woman's Spirituality*. It was a collection of essays that mentioned worship of the Great Goddess. This appealed to me tremendously. Worshiping a goddess made sense, because women are the ones who create. Babies come from the womb; they don't come from men. To me it made so much more sense to think of our world in terms of the bounty of the goddess.

I always keep track of the solstice and the equinox and I have some goddess replicas in my house which I feel very comfortable with. I don't actually worship the goddess, because I don't believe at this point in the personification of a deity. However, I think there is a lot of healing in goddess worship, an inclusive sort of spirituality.

For a brief period, only six weeks or so, I participated in a group, probably two or three years ago, where they performed rituals in connection with the Great Goddess. Circumstances arose where I was no longer able to attend, but I found it to be very fulfilling, a positive thing. I began to read books about the archaeological time period when the Great Goddess reigned—before the Sky God took over and people became warlike. It seems to me that from then on belief in a patriarchal god controlled the way people treated one another, trying to subjugate others.

Do you think there is a connection between your father and the patriarchal God?

My father was a professor in a Church of Christ college. As a child I had him on a pedestal, thinking he was almost God-like. There was something a step above human about him. Ninety percent of the time he was a Christian gentleman, a very kind, loving person. But I think he disowned his anger, kept it bottled up inside, and tried to make us children disown ours. He would gently say at times when I was angry, "Don't let your stinger out," or "That's the old Devil talking." He simply could not accept that anger is a normal, human characteristic that we all have. He disowned his anger until it consumed him, and he lost control.

I remember one such episode while I was a preschool child. I was standing in my parents' bedroom and my father was in my sisters' bedroom. His anger exploded all over them, his voice boomed and I could hear him whipping one of them with a belt. I started to cry, terrified. Mother held me and tried to comfort me, but my father had turned into someone I had never known. Mother had to stop him. Later I stood by the sisters' bed and cried, while Marcia put ice on the welts on Nena's legs.

Periodically, my father's rage erupted at family members, but never at me. I buried those episodes and tried to think about my father only in the best of times. Perhaps unconsciously I did think of him like the Bible stories of God—loving and gentle but suddenly wrathful and savage.

Later, I learned that my father had a bipolar disorder with depressions and occasional hypomanic episodes. The family existed around his illness, and I spent a lot of my life as a teenager searching for medicines and cures for him. I came up with a lot of things, in conjunction with a psychiatrist, that did keep him stable for a long, long period of time. Somewhere along the way my father fell off his "God" pedestal, and I can now view him as an old man and be kind to him.

Was there anyone who had a positive impact on your spirituality?

There was a woman in my medical school class. She and I became friends. Certainly in my sheltered life I had never run into anyone like her. She had a number of monogamous relationships with men and was extremely intelligent, extremely kind. She was never sharp-tongued, never spoke ugly about anyone, never seemed depressed or down. She was not neurotic and seemed happy with who she was, yet she had no religion.

For the life of me I can't imagine a God sending her to hell. This was one of the kindest women I have ever known in my life. I never met anyone at the Church of Christ who could hold a candle to this woman. I think she was important, very important to me.

What nourishes your spirit today?

Simple things—sitting in my chair on my deck, brushing my dogs, having a glass of wine, seeing my husband smile, sweeping my sidewalk, riding on country roads and seeing wild flowers— blues, purples, bright yellows, orange. I think being outdoors and seeing the beauty of simple things enriches me. At those times I just feel happy to be alive; worries or cares are gone.

I have this sense lately, and I don't know if it is because of the changing events in my life or not, that my mind is turning from introspection to just living my life. I am not sure what that means. I don't know what to make of it. I don't know if I am running away from something, or whether I am going through a different transition in my life, taking a more outward focus, with less need for inward looking. I don't know.

Carl Jung's writings have also nourished me. Not too long ago I felt at loose ends, not wanting to stay only in neurology, but not knowing what to do. One day I pulled out a book he had written that I had bought years before, but failed to read. The time for it was right. It provided a lot of insight into my inner life and afterwards I read other books he had written.

I particularly love Jung's theory that the Collective Unconscious connects us all at a very, very deep level. Underneath our personal unconscious mind is the base of the Collective Unconscious, a pattern of behavior and responses that connects all humans. Just as individual humans have genetic material they received from their parents, if we take one step back from that, there is something in our psyches, some genetic material, that also provides us with a universality as humans.

For a long time I have wanted to make connections with others. I experience this link when I write poems and people read them and say, "Oh, yes, you know what I feel." It's just wonderful to think that beneath our personal psyches there is a collective psyche that connects us all.

For Those Who Come After

FOR THOSE WHO COME AFTER

Since the Civil War the South has been distinguished by its women writers: Kate Chopin, Ellen Glasgow, Katherine Ann Porter, Eudora Welty, Flannery O'Connor, Alice Walker, Maya Angelou, Harper Lee. They, like their equally distinguished male counterparts, have demonstrated the strength of the Southern storyteller. They tell of lives held to the land, bonded to or estranged from their community's heritage, woven together with past generations. In love with words, these writers craft language into art forms that reveal new images of reality.

Through their stories they picture for the world the mystery and cohesiveness of the South as a region. Angelou in *I Know Why the Caged Bird Sings* brings readers to Stamps, Arkansas, weaving her story in such a way that we can never forget, we will always remember Mama and Bailey, and Henry Reed, leading the Negro national anthem on graduation day. In Harper Lee's *To Kill a Mockingbird,* we hear the unforgettable story of a girl's growing up in a small Southern town and learning the meaning of courage.

Our contributors, too, picture the South as a spiritual home where they belong and which they do not want those who come after to forget. If we are not to forget, their stories must find a voice and a form that portray the tenor and cadence of Southern ways, the nuances of Southern "being," the spirituality that is both collective and particular.

Images of the Southern landscape dominate the stories of Mary Brown, Karen Hendley, and Jane Purtle. Though restive there, they describe how they build on that landscape a spirituality that satisfies them. Liza Ely has to escape the Southern landscape, going on the road to find the meaning of her roots and returning to claim them.

Most contributors in this section naturally pick up a pen as they reflect. They search for a suitable word, an appropriate structure, a lyrical rhythm for their stories. Shirley Matthews, Lou Rodenberger, and Twyla Wright probe their creative imagination for forms in which to mold their particular understanding of spiritual experience. Matthews draws on the Biblical imagery of the Psalms; Rodenberger, on literary sources; and Wright, on contemporary forms of the literary essay.

As they molded the raw materials of their lives into images that express spiritual truth and beauty, these women, like the other contributors, have revealed deeply personal feelings, thoughts and events. With courage, they have made themselves vulnerable in order to leave behind their authentic spiritual autographs.

Their stories make possible *anamnesis*—the undoing of our forgetting. Someday, in the earthly hereafter, a grown child or gray-haired grandchild or a wondering stranger may pick up these printed pages and claim the legacy left her. With these stories, all who come after will be enriched.

Twyla Gill Wright

A freelance writer, Twyla Gill Wright is a Baptist and seventh generation Southerner, living in a woodland which has been in her family for one hundred twenty-five years. Married to Dennis Wright for forty-one years, she is the mother of two grown children, Darick and Tanya, and has a grandson.

She has written religious curricula and served as teacher and worship leader for teens on a national level. "My life is full of wonders—a loving husband who celebrates freedom, a circle of quilters who give companionship, a ring of spiritual questers who discuss ideas freely, and young ones in Children's Worship who feed me as we discover God. Enthusiasm and focused energy thread my life."

EPIPHANY

by Twyla Gill Wright

*B*eneath the dwarfed branches of an elephant tree, I sit alone, a bottle of water near my feet and gray coals from last night's fire beside me. For three days and nights I have gone without food or sleeping bag, without a human voice to call my name. I scan the cactus-covered mountains, then look out to the sea below. Several times during the past two weeks that rolling dragon threatened to swallow my kayak, striking me with terror. But the solo, with its bitter cold, its loneliness, its hunger, even its fly-covered boredom, dulls my spirit. Soon it will end and I will rejoin the others. I am more than ready. This place has not spoken to me.

I kick at a pile of stones, sending them scattering. Then, distinctly, I hear a voice roar within, "Little Pebble, are my creations beneath you? Are you so advanced above them? Enlightened above your own kind? Who do you think you are?"

My breath catches. The moment freezes. Suddenly the stones, the cactus, the elephant tree, the sea and I—a forty-year-old woman— become parts of a whole, connected to each other and God.

Throughout my life, epiphanies, moments when God covered me with Sacred Presence, have shaped my spiritual pathway. The earliest in my memory occurred before I was three. God's beauty drew me to him through a pink elephant toothbrush held in my chubby hand; light shimmered in its transparency. It dazzled me. Common objects—the insides of broken rocks, chipmunk bones and horsehair snakes, the sun through a clear marble—all surprised me with their treasures. An insatiably curious child, I explored our farm from daylight until after dark. A hidden world opened at night, if I sat still and waited for its creatures to move about.

On Sundays I attended, with my parents and younger brother, a tiny Primitive Baptist church in rural Colorado. No one taught me dogma. Communion, occurring only twice a year, filled me with excited expectation—God in the church-house—during those magical moments.

Epiphany of Mystery

The magic began in my grandmother's sunny kitchen on Saturday afternoon before the great day. Grandmother carefully measured ingredients into a stoneware bowl, while she visited with me. But as she rolled out the dough, she grew increasingly silent. I lowered my voice to a whisper, aware that our task was becoming holy. Grandmother scored the cracker-like dough into tiny squares. She placed it on a baking sheet, then opened the oven door to her wood-burning stove. I scarcely breathed as the crackers disappeared inside. Even the canary in its cage hushed its song. I rushed on tiptoe to take my station at the back door. And then she said it.

"Twyla, go get a jar of grape juice. Mind that it has a good seal and color." She wiped her hands on her apron.

In the muted light of the cellar I looked through the shelves of home-canned juice, and picked first one jar, then another, holding each up to the light from the open door. Purple grapes clustered in the bottom of each jar, spent from their task of coloring the liquid a clear red. I made my choice and proudly carried it to Grandmother. She washed off the jar, then sat silently to wait for the crackers to finish baking. At length, she rose and opened the oven door. Out rushed the strange smell of unleavened bread. It had become holy.

On Communion Sunday I sat in the church house next to my mother on a long, slatted bench. No ornament, no flower, no color decorated the sanctuary. This was the house of God, not of the world. All members in good standing had partaken of the holy crackers, and then it was time for the communal cup. The elder held up the crystal goblet and repeated, "This is my blood, shed for you." A shaft of light from a window pierced the goblet of grape juice, the juice I had chosen, and suddenly Mystery was in the room, hushing me into absolute stillness.

This childhood sense of wonder, this sudden, overwhelming sense of the mysterious is not unique to me. Rudolph Otto, long-dead, named this mystery the Numinous, and wrote about its universality in *The Idea of the Holy*. The Numinous surprises both the Australian aborigine and the erudite scholar, causing each to gasp "ah" or "ooh." The Numinous astounds me, sweeps me into mystery, through sudden, overwhelming space or light or darkness or silence or ringing bells, or even minor-key music. Sam Keen, in *Apology for Wonder*, says this mystery compels by its surprise and by being both fascinating and frightening. It fills me with hushed awe. It touches me with the Holy, the Sacred, with God. But must I wait for God's own timing for this sacred touch? Why can't I conjure God to my side?

Dear Heavenly Father, you're magical and strong. Forgive my sins and bless us all.

EPIPHANY OF ABSENCE

Late at night I knelt by the open window in my college dormitory room. Icy wind, moaning across the snow-crusted landscape outside, rushed in to bite my face, my bare arms and legs. Flagellating myself with the bitter cold, I forced my knees to stay in their penitent position all through the long hour of prayer. Focused, intense, I begged God, begged aloud, my words encased in fear.

I stared up into the vast black sky. I clasped my numb hands together and called out again and again, "Heavenly Father, show me that you are real. Give me a sign. Please!"

Silence. Nothing. And then, like a star that died long ago, God just disappeared, blinked out of being. Blackness from the night seeped through me, filled me with a bottomless abyss. Lost in terror, I opened my mouth to cry out once more, but no sound came. There was no God.

Over the next months I wrestled with the empty cosmos, hunting reasons for God's disappearance. I weighed my unworthiness. Perhaps God had cast me out of his garden because I failed to hold fast to the literal, creationist position of my adopted Conservative Baptist church. I had succumbed to a geology professor's disbelief in the Bible's creation record; doubt then tore my acquired dogma apart, brick by brick. However, it seemed more probable that God cast me into the abyss because of the invisible scarlet letter which I wore on my forehead. Married and divorced in the sixteenth year of my life, I was branded an outcast by the church.

But I did not leave the church. I chose to behave as if God existed, even if I could not sense him. I relied on my genuine acceptance of Christ when I was fifteen, and my baptism shortly after that. The Holy Spirit had seemed to light on me like a dove as I rose from that watery grave.

After college I married one of the church's finest sons, moved away, gave birth to our son. I prayed, taught Sunday school, read the Bible daily, presided over missionary meetings in our Southern Baptist church. Then a lump appeared in my breast. Once again God's absence confronted me.

I lay prostrate on our bed, terror squeezing the breath from me as I imagined a malignancy growing wild inside me, its tentacles fingering death into my lymph nodes and into every cell of my body. Biopsy and diagnosis lay two weeks away.

The air conditioner hummed. I reached for a pillow to comfort me, but discarded it, letting sobs tear their way to the surface. My husband and mother ran into the bedroom and huddled over me. I stared up at their faces and blurted out angry words, born from guilt and gestated long past their proper birth. "God is a wrathful, vengeful God, and he's going to kill me!"

Horror reflected in my mother's eyes, while my words echoed from the ceiling, bounced against the walls and came back to my ears. Stunned, I listened, entranced by the power of spoken words. They were not true! That rejecting God was not the God of the grape juice, sparkling in the shaft of light. If there was a God, he was not vengeance, no matter what the Old Testament said. I knew. Cathartically, mysteriously, I knew. My body relaxed; my breathing deepened.

Now I could leave the tattered remnants of my cocoon behind. Cocoons incubate new life, only to be broken apart and discarded. At hatching time, the hormone-weakened cocoon splits, and the butterfly struggles to emerge, to let its wings fully unfurl.

In the terrifying splitting of my cocoon, when God was no longer the familiar Mystery, Beauty, Magic—no longer even punitive power—his absence weakened and tore open the old. If I had ceased to struggle, if I had not emerged fully into the new, I would have died in outgrown strictures or crawled with crippled wings.

Martin Marty, in his *A Cry of Absence*, affirms those Christians who must abide in the winterly frost of God's absence, while others bask in God's summer sunshine. Some winter Christians pound and pound on God's door, demanding that he show himself, while others hold only to intermittent flickers of his light in the vast winter dark. The latter seemed my way.

Apostle Thomas lost his beloved master, doubted the Jesus-like specter before him, reached to touch the wounds, and received truth. Guilt drove Apostle Peter to accept forgiveness and dedicate his life to the one he cursed. And didn't Apostle Paul's blind eyes prepare him for faith? Can darkness, doubt, absence, give birth to new life? Can it?

Almighty God, who are you? Are you?

EPIPHANY OF LOVE

In the nursery of our new home, in my thirtieth year, I relaxed in a rocking chair, my abdomen swollen with our expected baby. For six years we had looked forward to having a second child; all was well. Around me in the small room stood a crib, changing table, and chest of drawers; all was ready. I smiled and rocked.

On that October morning, without sound or sighted movement, without prayer on my part, God suddenly appeared. My eyes widened; my chair ceased its rocking. Divinity flowed into the nursery, expanding, filling every atom of air and object in the room. Time stopped. Nothing existed, not even myself—only God. I saw nothing, heard nothing, touched nothing. Every fiber of my body lost awareness of itself, tuned itself completely to the overwhelming presence of God.

Then a stirring encircled me, softly, gently. It tightened into an embrace—a sacred hug. With my ears, but without my ears, outside and inside, I heard God whisper, "Twyla." His whisper breathed into my depths, consuming me. "I—love—you."

Unconditional, completely affirming, more enduring than emotion, God's love held me close. It coursed through my blood, my flesh; its breath merged with my breath. A portion flowed into my center, low in my chest. And then, slowly, God withdrew his presence, atom by atom. Space opened around me. Like a powerful, gentle hurricane, God dissipated, leaving me with the small portion of himself nestled securely in my core. The larger, active part of God slipped from the room as soundlessly, as invisibly, as he entered.

I came back to myself. Great joy, like a thousand songbirds, sang throughout my mind, my body. The yellow curtains shone more golden than before, and even the trees outside the window glowed with vivid detail. My reflection in the mirror told me I was still the person I had been earlier that morning. But I was not.

In the next months and years God's love drew mine to his, and flourished. It spilled over into Christian writing, giving me a bliss, a vocation. It splashed into the lives of church youth. I continued working in my church, silent about God's visitation, for it sounded strange to the few I told. However, at a Christian writer's conference one of the participants grew curious after observing me take the Lord's Supper. He asked me what I was experiencing at that time. Hesitantly, I explained that I sensed God in the cup and communed with him there. He smiled and called me a mystic. A mystic? What is that?

Books seemed to jump unbidden into my hands: *The Practice of the Presence of God, Search for Silence, A Testament of Devotion.* I thrilled to the words of a twelfth-century abbess, Hildegard Von Bingen, "God hugs you. You are encircled by the arms of the mystery of God." She knew what I knew, and far more! I discovered spiritual kinsmen who had experienced God similarly, who longed for and found union with God. Their phrases echoed in my heart, caused me to clasp their books to my chest with pure joy. I feasted on their words like a famished younger sister.

In the midst of this spiritual illumination, we moved to the Ozarks, land of my ancestors. There, I met someone, who through her probing questions challenged me to clarify and set my spiritual experience into words. She valued my attempts to explain, probed deeper, listened. Together we read the fourteenth-century *Cloud of Unknowing*, written by an unknown English mystic.

Christian mystics from past centuries tried to write their experiences of direct union with God, but words often failed them. Some saw visions, some connected to God without mental images, but all were drawn into God's consuming presence, uniting with him, never to be the same—St. Teresa of Avila, St. John of the Cross, Julian of Norwich. Thomas Merton wrote in *New Seeds of Contemplation* that when God's pure love comes, images vanish, concepts and words are silent, our whole being embraces the wonder and incomprehensibility of God's presence. But, I often wonder, why do some people have this mystical connection with God while others, desperate for such loving intimacy, never receive it? Why?

Heart of my heart, Abba, absorb me, breathe me into yourself and out to others.

Epiphany in the Desert

In contemplative silence I closed my eyes and focused on the spiritual center in my chest. I left behind any consciousness of my environment: the wicker chair in the bay window, the plants, the stained glass window to one side. In this receptive and relaxed state, I went down into God's dwelling place within me, as I had done daily for months. I saw myself as a tiny, naked figure swimming in a dark spring, the dark fluidity of God. No emotions, no words invaded the sanctity of our being together.

But something ominous waited this time in the interior darkness. I stopped swimming, aware that unexpected change pulsed in the depths. Stilled, I heard, without a sound, God's voice from a great distance inside me. He roared majestically, like a desert puma, wild and untamed. He said, "I take my name away."

Shocked, I kept my eyes closed, feeling panic rise. "Don't leave me," I pleaded. "How can I adore you without your name?" Sadness, so intense it seemed an agony, spread through me.

"Come into the wilderness," he roared.

Immediately, the image of a walled oasis in the desert appeared as a vision close behind my eyes. A low adobe wall surrounded the safe garden, its gate swinging open. Beyond it stretched a rugged, howling desert. Somewhere out there in the wilderness of myself, nameless God roamed without image, hidden from view, untamed.

Lonely, without the familiar God in-dwelling, and with no spiritual companion on this strange path, I searched for spiritual guidance. Prayer, without God's name, grew tortuous. No graven image could survive in my empty center, which God had left unlabeled.

Some weeks later, on Easter Sunday, I climbed the stairs to the balcony of my church, ready for the handbells to call me to God, ready to join others in worship. I sat down and focused my gaze on the altar, expectant. But a camera mounted on a tripod, like some grotesque robot, stared back at me from the baptistery, oblivious to its profanity. It focused its lens on all of us, ready to show the community how many people attended First Baptist Church. Stung to the marrow of my soul, unable to bear the inverted focus, I fled the church. Angry tears spilled as I rushed up the sidewalk, away from the profane. My thoughts spun. Where was I to worship? Was there no place for me?

As I turned a corner, a huge wisteria dangled out over the walk. It stopped me. I gaped open-mouthed at it. Holiness dwelt in its twisted vines, which wound over a trellis and up into a juniper. My gaze swept high up the tree. There at its top a wisteria tendril reached toward the sun. Me? Must I reach alone?

In Biblical times God led prophets into the desert, into a wilderness, to sense his unfathomable presence. At such a time Jehovah spoke to Moses in a burning bush, giving answer to Moses' request for his name, "I Am that I Am!" I must beware of trying to tame God, to name God, to mold God in my palm.

The desert tradition has given wisdom since the earliest centuries of Christianity. There in the bleak landscape, God roams undomesticated, free of description. Monks lived primitively in the Egyptian desert and found God's silent roar an answer to their deepest need. In *The Way of the Heart*, Henri Nouwen brought these desert mothers and fathers to aid me in walking the way of solitude.

Jesus went alone into the desert and returned to start his ministry; yet, he continued to worship regularly in synagogues with those who did not share his vision. Can I survive this desert and come back to worship as he did? Can I love this Wild One, even if he slays me, even if he does not give me healing, prosperity, peace, eternal life? I cannot stop myself.

Thou with no name, let me follow the echo of your roar.

EPIPHANY IN THE MUNDANE

Corn stalks cried out mutely for water, their leaves browning from the drought. All the garden thirsted in that summer of my father. Squash leaves, like collapsed umbrellas, drooped in the afternoon's heat. Not a breeze stirred. I checked for signs of raccoons and deer, and groaned.

This garden, my father's joy, would be his last. I looked toward his house, nestled among trees to the east. Inside, he lay stripped to the bone by cancer. The work of my hands, the harvesting and canning of my father's produce, the telling of his garden's growth, was the best gift I could give. I cleaned his house, tended him in the night, communed with him about love and death. But exhaustion threatened me. My heart broke, my muscles ached, my eyes begged for sleep.

I picked up a water hose to reset it on another row of corn. Numbed into simple-mindedness, I watched my freckled hand grasp the hose, the water cascading from it into the soil; I felt the ground under my feet, felt the connection surge up from my feet to my hand. All formed a cycle, inseparable from one another. I stood transfixed, immobile in the scorching heat. God permeated it all, quietly, without majesty, without mystery—a soothing salve to my soul.

Now, four years later, I stand at my kitchen sink surrounded by dirty dishes. To my right I gaze with delight into red-gold flames crackling on the stone hearth. To my left I look out the window into yellow leaves twirling from branches. Gladness fills me. I pick up a bowl, feel its smooth curves, the bits of hardened cereal clinging to it. I am conscious, yet unconscious, of God in every cell of my body, every molecule of the bowl, of the flames, of the leaves, of everything. Nothing is separate. No mystery or love overwhelms me, no distant roar calls me. No activity, no magic moment, transforms the ordinary into the holy. The Sacred and the Mundane intertwine as one.

A thirteenth-century Christian poet, Mechtild of Magdeburg, wrote that she saw all things in God and God in all things. She saw everything as sacrament—in God, but not being God. So it is with me. As I suspend thought, as I attend to that in my hand, that at my elbow, a Transparent Plane of Being bathes all in silence, in stillness, in joy.

In the silence . . . .

Jane Hill Purtle

Project director for this collection of spiritual autobiographies, Jane Purtle has been interested in the autobiographical writings of women for more than ten years.

She taught English in college for twenty years, managed the food service in a Christian retreat center for five years, and now works with developmentally disabled adults.

Jane lives in a log cabin near Bullard, Texas, about two miles from the red-clay hill where she was born. She and her cats, Happy and Lily, like to watch birds and work in the yard. "Friendship, growth, family, grandchildren, and solitude give meaning to this time in my life," she says.

QUEST IN TIME AND MEMORY
by Jane Hill Purtle

I once read a book by John Dunne, *A Search for God in Time and Memory.* As I reflect on my past, I realize that through the years of my life, I have searched in time and memory. For the first forty years I did not understand my quest, which I identified only as a deep restlessness.

The year I was thirty-eight my quest began to reveal itself to me.

On a spring morning in 1973, I left home with my mind swirling, much like the rainstorm I drove through to work. A few days before, I had tendered my resignation as an English teacher at a small Presbyterian college in Arkansas, hoping to slow down the frantic pace of my life. As I approached the college in my black VW, the sky darkened and the rain fell thickly. Batesville, twenty-five miles from a tornado alley, boasted that it had never been hit.

The college sits on a bluff overlooking a river bottom, but I couldn't see to the edge of the bluff that morning. I hardly looked around because my mind was intent on my decision, on my future, and on my crumbling personal life. My husband was a prosperous lawyer; we had two healthy, smart children; we were active in the local Baptist church and various community projects. I had a lot of nice friends, some pretty clothes, and a secure position on the faculty. I wondered why I had chosen to resign at the end of the school year. My husband wondered the same.

After my first class, out my office window, I watched the trees bend almost double and noticed that darkness had fallen, a green, eerie, glowing darkness. Something was dreadfully wrong.

My colleague across the hall looked out her door. "I think we better get in a closet," she said. "This looks bad."

I crouched in the closet. I had on a pair of navy wool pants and my favorite jacket; I noticed that my clothes were damp and smelled musty. I said to myself that this day wasn't going as I had planned, but maybe I wouldn't lose more than half an hour in the closet. Then, I heard a loud crack, felt the building shudder to its foundation, and knew that we had been hit. I stepped out of my office door to see, ten feet away, the entire back end of the building in rubble.

"I must find my children," I said to a professor friend as I rushed downstairs and out of the building into the rain.

"I'll help you," he said and ran beside me, shielding me with his umbrella. Outside, one car lay on its top where the tornado had flipped it, but mine was unharmed. We took first one street and then the other, searching for a way through the felled trees and loose power lines.

Finally, we found them at their schools, unharmed but shaken. Like me, they had felt the ground move under them.

In the fall of 1975, a few days before I was forty, a more devastating tornado than the one at the college struck my life.

One morning after the kids had gone to school, I was in the family room folding clothes when my husband passed through. I had a yellow towel in my hand when he said from the bathroom, "I plan to move out in two or three weeks when I can get a place to live."

"What do you mean, move out?"

"I don't love you anymore," he said. "I haven't loved you for years. I've been thinking about this for a long time."

For the second time I felt the foundation shift under me.

He left to go to work. In the next weeks, I pleaded and promised and cried. I lost ten pounds in ten days. I tried to reach him through memories, through the children, through his marriage vows, through the Bible. He was out there beyond me where no words or logic or emotion could touch him. He was gone.

I felt my life was gone too. My career, my family, my commitment to church and God as I had known them were shattered; the humpty-dumpty pieces of my life could not be mended. If I were to survive, I would have to start over and rebuild.

I did not understand these tragedies as calls to simplify or be creative. I saw them as they were—the outcome of a lot of bad decisions, resulting in intense suffering and lasting grief for me and my children.

I had friends, wise friends, who prayed and tried to keep me from complete despair. I could not pray for myself down in the dark pit, falling free, thinking there was no bottom to the darkness.

Sarah, an eighty-year-old member of my church, lived about a block from my house. On the darkest days of that summer, I walked to her apartment, sat close beside her on a shaggy beige couch, felt her arms around me, and wept the bitterest tears of my life. I had failed, and I could do nothing to change the situation. Sarah never cried; she waited patiently, sometimes half an hour or more, for the tears to exhaust me. Then she quoted the 37th Psalm—wait on the Lord and be patient.

One morning in February, 1976, the pain overwhelmed me. Upstairs, in our bedroom, I screamed, beat my head against the wall, and fell on the floor. In that unbearable pain, God met me— no voice, no image, just a call within me, saying,—Do you want your life? If so, it must be mine."

I said to myself, "I want it, and I give up to whatever must be." That moment was the beginning of my conversion.

In those dark months, I didn't analyze or reflect; I just tried to hold on. Then as I came out of the dark wood of my mid-life, I began to understand my search. I understood that I wanted to live more simply, but finding a way to support myself challenged me.

An offer came from a small spiritual community in Syria, Virginia, which sponsored a retreat center and paid fifty dollars a week, plus room and board. With the child support I would receive, it appeared to me, though to few others, that this was the answer to my prayers. I laid aside my career and joined the community as food service supervisor and occasional retreat leader.

At the Center I searched for new understanding—the right prayer, the right magic, the right stance with God which would make me acceptable, which would protect me from more tornadoes. I desperately needed to find a place of safety.

I began to read Thomas Merton, Thomas Kelly, Brother Lawrence, Dietrich Bonhoeffer, Teilhard de Chardin, William Stringfellow, Elizabeth O'Connor, anyone who could tell me more of God. I read the Bible hungrily, searching its stories for my own.

And I prayed. The darkest summer of my life, 1976, I prayed the Jesus prayer continually for days: "Lord Jesus Christ, son of God, have mercy on me, a sinner." And a prayer from "Ash Wednesday": "Teach us to care and not to care. Teach us to sit still." At the Center I learned discipline in prayer, learned that silence was for me the deepest and best prayer. In silence, I could momentarily reach the safe place where my heart longed to abide.

During the first years at the Center, I allowed the Blue Ridge Mountains, the tulip poplars, the Rose River, and a loving community to begin to heal the brokenness. But I was often intensely lonely and depressed; doubts about meaning, about who God is, about who I am, often haunted me.

Then another shattering, as devastating as the break-up of my family, shook the fragile new life I had begun to build. My son did well the first year at the Center, but he soon became rebellious and dissatisfied. Shortly before he was sixteen, I discovered he was forging checks for money to buy drugs. Monday of the week he was sixteen, I walked into the sheriff's office in Madison, Virginia, and signed the papers to have him incarcerated. Feeling like Abraham must have felt on Mt. Moriah, I saw myself twisting a knife in his heart, inflicting a wound from which he and I might never recover. It was the greatest risk of my life. After he came out of detention, I had to testify against him and see him placed on probation in my care.

In the months which followed he went into a residential facility in Richmond where I drove to see him every week. Two dark moments during his time there almost overwhelmed me. When he first came home on leave, he and his group sat in the living room to talk about their issues and explain to me what was happening with them in their program. Soon my son was cursing and berating me; his counselor reprimanded him, but he would not stop and became physically violent. The boys, who were trained to restrain each other, pinned him to the floor; then holding him completely immobile, carried him out the door and to the van, with him cursing all the way.

I did not see him for many weeks after that, not until he was willing to apologize and promise to work with me. He seemed to be making progress. Then one day the telephone rang; it was one of his teachers saying that my son had run away and they could not find him—though the boys, other counselors, and the police were searching Richmond. The hours of waiting were agony; but when he finally came back, the turning point had come. He began the slow process of doing his own rebuilding.

Even though this experience shook me as violently as the earlier tornadoes, I found internal strength not present before. And this time I could pray for myself.

During all the years of my childhood I lived inside myself—never telling anyone about the terrors or joys of my interior life. My mad dog dreams started when I was eight or nine. I would dream I was on a street in the lower part of Riverside, the wartime housing development where we lived in Orange, Texas. I was alone; the streets were filled with water, and on the sidewalk ahead of me was a large, dark dog, stumbling and foaming at the mouth. Usually, I wakened myself at that point, paralyzed by fear. Sometimes I managed to run away.

The summer I was nine, our pastor at Cove Baptist Church preached the first revival I remember attending. We met in the Cove School building every night, in a large lecture room with desks. He preached his usual hell-fire and damnation sermon, often shouting at the congregation, "You'll bust hell wide open."

That night terror filled my heart as I sat in the desk, feeling the spirit moving and seeing myself burning in the flames of hell.

I was immobilized. I put my head down on the desk and pretended to be asleep. Verse after verse of "Just As I Am" filled the room as people moved to the front and the pastor kept saying, "Make your decision tonight; you may die and go to hell before tomorrow."

When it was finally over, Daddy shook me and said, "Wake up. Time to go home, honey." Wide awake, I felt like a hardened sinner.

I was first baptized when I was ten. I remember the terror of it but not much else. The second baptizing when I was twelve was easier because I knew what to expect, but neither of them assuaged the guilt and self-hatred in my soul. I never felt my sins were washed away, as all the gospel songs assured me they would be.

As a child, I felt alone, and I looked for friends in books. I read Louisa May Alcott's novels and biographies about famous women. People like Jo March, Rose Campbell, Emily Dickinson and Amelia Earhart told me that other ways of life existed, but I had no idea how to get into those worlds.

When I went away to college in Abilene, Texas, new worlds began to open before me. Dr. Edwin McClain, my English professor, showed me the door into the world of the spirit—the door to people like John Donne, George Herbert, T. S. Eliot, the Brontes. In the fall of my senior year, Carlyle Marney spoke on campus. Dr. McClain encouraged me to hear Marney, and for the first time I listened to a minister who spoke truth to me.

I bought Marney's book *Faith in Conflict* and began reading it. Though I understood little of the content of the book, I sensed that other conceptions of spiritual questions, other interpretations and understandings of the Bible and God, existed, and that people like Marney could guide me into that new country. In the spring, I heard that Marney was coming back to West Texas to deliver a series of sermons in a Presbyterian church.

A group of us drove to Big Spring one night, arriving just as the service began. The church was dimly lit as we entered. Marney stood in front of a stained glass window with a large red cross glowing behind him. He was a rather large, stocky man with broad hands and a penetrating voice.

He preached from Isaiah 4 and 5—the vineyard passage and the promise of Jerusalem's restoration—explicating the passage verse by verse. It was as though the top of my head had come off. He spoke of God's condemnation and of God's love and compassion, and I realized the two could co-exist. His words hammered a crack in the wall of distrust I had built to protect myself from the teachings of my church. His voice also called me to look toward the far horizon, the distant hills of solid reality.

Through my childhood, my college years, my marriage, the years in Virginia, I searched for God in the experiences of my life and in the stories of others from the past and in my own time. My quest brought me to suffering and joy and community.

Suffering and joy are inextricably linked when the suffering is God-given; and when I see the end, I understand that all suffering is God-given. If I embrace the gift, it will transform me; if I reject it, it will torture me. When I claim the suffering, I claim the joy. Thomas Merton says that the more we seek to escape suffering, the more we suffer because insignificant things torture us in proportion to our fear. Etty Hillesum, about to die in a German concentration camp, wrote that it is a matter of living from minute to minute and taking suffering into the bargain.

I have come to understand that I feared suffering and pain so much I tried desperately to escape them. When the pain grew so intense that it was a burning bed of coals within me, I contemplated suicide. I did not understand that suffering tears us apart so that we can be remade. Just as the tornado which struck my college in 1973 made necessary the construction of a new and more beautiful college complex, the tornado which tore apart my family made necessary and possible a new life for me.

How does suffering become transformed into joy? T. S. Eliot says the fire and the rose become one. In 1983 as I began to understand my transformation, I drew pictures of fiery rose mountains and mandalas of black, swirling tornadoes. These gradually mingled into fiery rose spirals, ending finally in a pure rose center with one black dot. That image expresses better than words the conjunction of pain and joy.

This joy is not happiness, not a feeling. For me, it was first a momentary relief from suffering. Then it was a sense of freedom from myself, a knowing of Being beyond myself. Now I experience it as a subterranean stream where I can retreat anytime I withdraw into the center of myself. I sense its essence in the recurring images of Eliot's *The Four Quartets*—a mingling of transience and permanence, flowing until they find the end and the beginning as the same.

In these last years communities have embraced me wherever I have been, groups of friends with questions like and unlike my own, who share my longing to know God. Thomas Kelly calls this experience of companionship the "Blessed Community," an enlargement of the boundaries of ourselves so that we are within others and they are within us.

My friendships reach back to days at Hardin-Simmons University and forward to later years of companionship with my daughter and son, my mother and father, my brothers, nephews and niece. They extend over time and space, to women like Margery Kempe of fifteenth-century England; Louisa May Alcott; Mary Jane Dill and Lura Hill, my grandmothers I never saw.

I am also bonded with the creation around me. In my small log cabin in the country, I listen every day to the bird calls which signal the revolving seasons. As I write this spring, I am saying goodbye to juncos, white-throats, goldfinch, and pine siskens. This week I recorded the year's first summer tanager, painted bunting, and dickcissel. This morning, I watched a pileated woodpecker hammering on a dead pine in the woods a few hundred yards down my dirt road. For twenty years I have watched birds and let their presence, oblivious to my pain or joy, speak to the eternal movement of my soul.

As I walk the roads near my home, watch a Carolina wren hide in a hanging basket on my porch, respond to my cat's meow, wake from a dream which speaks to me, I feel, at least momentarily, "at home." At home, calm in the center.

LOU HALSELL RODENBERGER

Born in Texas, Lou Halsell Rodenberger says her rural schoolteacher parents were "profoundly aware" of their Southern heritage. Lou, a United Methodist, is married to a retired professor of engineering, and they have two children and five grandchildren. Now professor emeritus of English at McMurry University in Abilene, she writes reviews and essays about Texas women writers and is co-editor with Sylvia Grider of *Texas Women Writers: A Tradition of Their Own,* a history of women writers in Texas published by Texas A&M Press in 1997.

"I have a profound interest in what women writers have accomplished in the South. To be considered a Southern woman writer myself is intimidating, but the opportunity to explore autobiography with spiritual development as a theme provides irresistible incentive."

HEART KNOWLEDGE
by Lou Halsell Rodenberger

No two summer sunrises are ever the same out here on the Callahan Divide at the western edge of the Texas Cross Timbers. I smile when the sun's fiery crescent breaks over the ridge across our valley. God smiles back, offering me once again a shining gift—a daily miracle.

Some greats ago, a Cherokee grandmother added color to my mostly Scotch-Irish heritage. If Jung got it right, then surely my "collective unconscious" connects me with that forebear's spiritual oneness with God's natural world—"heart knowledge" a minister friend calls it. The heart's knowing attunes this country dweller to many daily miracles that lift my inner self and inspire feelings of well-being.

This morning, with coffee mug in hand, I watched quietly as four brilliant papa cardinals defended their feeder space in our backyard live oak grove. I savored the peace I felt, then thought: here is nature's poetry. I will say this to my ten o'clock literature scholars, who think they hate poetry, when I go to school later this morning. My quiet time became planning time as feelings dictated thought.

My friend who defines heart knowledge understands. She reminds me that it is only when heart knowledge converges with head knowledge that true understanding of personal spirituality emerges. As I look back over my life, recovering my spiritual biography then depends on how profoundly I recall those moments when heart response intensifies the experience of knowing.

As I look back on it now, my life as a rural schoolteacher's child seems culturally stark. Books were few. The best Christmas gift I remember added *Black Beauty* and *Old-Fashioned Girl* to my skimpy library. Music did not exist except for an occasional evening of listening to *The Grand Ol' Opry* out of Nashville if the radio battery held out. Country bands with fiddle players and steel guitar virtuosos provided the background for summer evenings of community news exchange after long days of hard work and heat.

Religious life depended on my Methodist parents, who either initiated union Sunday Schools in rural schoolhouses or drove to the country churches now considered picturesque by historical preservation committees. Whatever the weather, Sunday always brought its own special atmosphere. Sitting in one corner of the church, I would listen to a smiling teacher tell Jesus stories. As we filed by her to find a seat with our parents for church, our teacher would hand us small picture cards which retold the lesson story and provided entertainment for this restless child while the preacher droned on.

Those quiet moments before the singing began flash into my memory now as tableaux. Through unscreened windows opening onto a mesquite pasture, a mockingbird insists on opening the service with his persistent solo. The grown-ups sit quietly and wait for the song leader's instructions. An almost imperceptible breeze brushes past to cool the hot summer sanctuary as I look at the picture of Jesus on my Sunday School card and listen to the mockingbird trilling and whistling through his magnificent stolen repertoire. If an infant soul can meditate, surely the contentment I felt in those moments must have inspired in me, for the first time, a connection between the cardboard Jesus picture, my Sunday School lesson, and the reality of the grace and love of Jesus's life and death.

The poet Wordsworth believed that these "recollections of early childhood" provided "intimations of immortality." In his *Ode* he explores his philosophy that the child, in his innocence, reflects "God, who is our home." The venerable poet declares that as we grow away from childhood, our ability to perceive the spiritual in experience fades away.

Although this work of Wordsworth's is one of my favorites, I can trace my own infant soul's development into fuller spirituality. I can recall many events which happened after that transcendent moment inspired by a Sunday School card, and all are permanently etched on the sketchbook of my expanding consciousness. As disparate as those images are and reluctant as I may feel about examining *why* I remember them so clearly, those memories, which now I understand affected both heart and mind, hint largely of spiritual immortality.

Mine was a peripatetic childhood. My sister and I learned to "make the best of things"—my granny's term for accepting and improving, if you could, the situation you found yourself in. As children of the Great Depression, we accepted the run-down country houses, the long bus rides to school, and our limited social lives—without complaint.

My high school library shelved a set of reference books, a few novels, and not much else. But my mother, as a one-room schoolteacher, had the privilege of monthly access to the large closet in the county school superintendent's office, which served as library for the county rural schools. The books my mother checked out monthly from that dusty collection in the county courthouse offered me a kind of salvation. I soon found that books gave the imagination exciting and even exotic places to roam—places I intended to explore some day.

At sixteen, with high-pitched shaky voice, I delivered one of the four brief speeches honor students had been told to prepare for the high school commencement program that hot May night in 1943. My father had helped to write the eloquent purple prose I stammered through. I remember not a word of it. Nor do I remember any other part of the program. Although I must have been exhilarated when I learned I had achieved highest honors, no recall of rejoicing remains. Instead, I hear the sad lovely melody of "As Time Goes By," sung with great feeling by a trio of my classmates. We knew that night as we said our goodbyes that they might be final ones. World War II raged on despite our joyous celebration of adult beginnings. That very evening, nearly a dozen of my classmates would leave for military service where, as Marines, four were destined to perish in the South Pacific. A melody with words I no longer can recall poignantly expressed my own heart's response to the somber future no head knowledge could prepare us for.

Three months later, my father left me forlornly perched on my trunk on the porch of one of the co-op dorms at Texas Woman's

University (then Texas State College for Women), waiting for the noontime opening. Wartime tires made a risky adventure out of every automobile trip, so my father and sister wanted to be back in West Texas by nightfall. What lay ahead of me I had not the slightest notion. As it turned out, after a short bout of homesickness so intense I lost ten pounds, I discovered that college life offered sustenance for my narrow little soul as well as challenges for my eager mind.

President Louis Hubbard knew that the cultural backgrounds of many of us were limited. With the avowed aim to produce a fully educated young woman, he brought the best in music and dance to campus. For my untrained soul—which had depended on books, country music, and radio drama during my growing-up days—the fare proved almost too rich. Sigmund Romberg brought his orchestra to Redbud Auditorium stage that fall, and Isaac Sterns, Arthur Rubenstein, and Lily Pons all stopped off to share their talents with the Tessies. Critics John Mason Brown and John Rosenfield planted exhilarating ideas for later reflection in our uncultivated minds.

I soaked up culture like a Texas prairie at the end of a drought does rain. Had Dr. Hubbard known how successful his aims were met for this West Texas child, his heart, too, would have warmed. Spiritually, those four years were discovery years. My soul basked in the accomplishment of new experiences, even though my timid self often had to be prodded to initiate those happenings.

By my junior year, I finally found my way to First Methodist Church, where Jewel Posey directed the activities of the Wesley Foundation. There, in the church basement, students from both colleges in town met on Sunday evenings for supper and worship, all prepared by the members themselves. For the first time, I understood the joy of working on a team where members really cared for one another.

To conclude Sunday evening services we held hands and circled into a tightly wound spiral, singing "We are climbing Jacob's ladder . . . soldiers of the cross." I learned then that my spirit need not make its journey alone. Most of us left quietly for dorm rooms after we gave a friendly squeeze to the hands we held, but we went with the knowledge that communion of hearts expands heart response. We felt the warmth of Christian community that year perhaps even more as we spent long evenings painting the interior of the old house where students operated a day-care center with the guidance of Ma Holcombe, resident comforter.

I carried with me the need for membership in a community of believers when I arrived in Kerrville, Texas, in 1947 to begin what I thought then would be a lifetime career of newspapering. It was a magic year and a half. Barely twenty, I lived in an elegant boarding house on Earl Garrett Street run by the crusty, warm-hearted Miz B. The Beehive harbored an intriguing array of characters.

I was innocent in the ways of the world, as my granny might have pointed out. But somewhere in the lively Beehive my guardian angel found a hiding place and worked hard extricating me from tricky situations. Before long, she turned my reluctant feet toward First Methodist Church two blocks over from the Beehive. There, I found my spiritual boarding house, as lively as the Beehive and much more challenging to my soul. This time, I was drafted as one of the leaders in the Methodist Youth Fellowship and given the job of providing Sunday morning worship services before Sunday School classes met. Here head knowledge and heart knowledge were forced to converge.

I have delivered classroom lectures for nearly thirty years; I have spoken countless times to civic groups and at writers' conferences and professional meetings. None of the natural highs those experiences always inspire would have happened if I had not forced myself to stand in front of forty restless high schoolers one Sunday morning and deliver my first devotional talk. With Peter Pan collar buttoned, I knew the red blotches on my neck and face betrayed the terror which came near to immobilizing me. My voice shook perceptibly and my knees threatened to rebel. I don't recall text or talk, but it may have been from Ecclesiastes, already my favorite book of the Bible. Its author, the Preacher, spoke to my heart, and even at twenty, I already had first-hand knowledge of some of the attractive follies the Preacher spoke of. I also realized that my life's challenge would be recognizing the right time to cycle into the next stage of my adventure on this earth. I may have spoken that Biblical insight on that summer morning.

Whatever I said captured the attention of a young ministerial student, home from a missionary trip abroad, who rushed up later and congratulated me on my moving presentation. I stammered a thanks. That evening a strange combination of agony and elation kept me awake as I relived the low and high of that first effort to share the knowledge of my heart.

After eighteen months of writing up weddings and hospital news, fielding complaints about misspelled names and garbled phone numbers in the classifieds, and posting advertising income in the weekly's books, I reluctantly abandoned my newspaper career and the warmth of the Beehive, where I had first explored my then shapeless philosophy of life in all-night sessions in front of the fireplace with Cameron, who loved poetry and made wild, undisciplined, haunting music on Miz B's piano. There, when my summertime romance with one of the engineers flamed out, I had learned that the human heart can be treacherous. There too, I had learned the kindness of the human heart, when the gray-haired physical therapist down the hall dared to nurse me through a vicious bout with the flu after my roommate moved out for its duration. This heart knowledge would serve me well in my new job as high school English teacher in a far West Texas town. My spirit had learned the excitement of exploring ideas, the complexity of human relationships, and the definition of compassion.

My guardian angel went along for the ride to the flat, dusty High Plains. I became active once more in a Sunday School class, this one miraculously composed of young, single, college graduates whose piety was tempered by fun-loving spirits. My watchful angel soon pointed out that the engineer who presided over the class would be important to my future. We have been married forty-four years now. We have raised another engineer and another teacher, who have both made happy choices in mates and provided us five grandchildren to love. God has been good to us.

Intimations of immortality abound in recollections of our personal history. Those early years of marriage come back as a collage of sharply drawn images. Heart knowledge increased as I learned what it meant to become mentor and example to a creative, witty high school newspaper and annual staff. Punning, playing, and producing, these hard-working teenagers gave me love and taught me tolerance.

Soon the Air Force called in its reserves as the Korean War heated up, and my husband reported to Reese Air Force Base near

Lubbock. We moved to north Lubbock, sharing the roof of a green stucco duplex with friends who met, as we had, in that fateful Sunday School class. The warmth of that relationship comes back in memories of those Saturdays when we pooled groceries and ate together.

Our first child, a dark-haired daughter, arrived in yet another Texas plains town. I waited alone for her during the last two months before her birth, cultivating strategies for dealing with solitude in a new town. While my husband traveled on business in Europe and Africa, I embroidered an alphabet quilt, hand sewed baby clothes, read long evenings through, and let my heart have a say in what this child might bring to our lives. I learned for the first time that solitude is good for the soul. Lives need regular examination; so do hearts, I learned.

The spring of 1954, my husband took a job in the oil patch, where he was expected to report to work seven days a week. We moved into a tiny, unairconditioned house in the nondescript country town where the company was based. While we lived there, our firstborn, whose dark curly hair and big eyes stopped traffic on Main Street sidewalks, performed all of the natural feats so miraculous to new parents.

Those are smiling memories, prelude to that unforgettable night when I glimpsed, if only for a moment, the dimensions of heaven. The scene comes back as yet another of memory's tableaux. I sit nursing this warm bundle whose demanding cry has awakened me, holding her close and rocking quietly. Moonlight filters through organdy curtains floating in the West Texas night breeze. My soul knows utter peace and complete love in this moment. I say to God: "Now I know, Lord, what love is." This moment brings sure knowledge that for this one time in my life I feel God's presence. The mystery and joy of human love I feel for my tiny daughter this magical night previews for my heart what lies ahead for all believers.

In the forty years since that night, my heart's experiences have been rich. I have experienced the elation of watching a son and daughter grow in accomplishment and maturity. I have traveled. A French exchange student laughed and loved her way into our lives and hearts to become our "other" daughter. And I returned to the classroom as a student and then as a teacher.

I was one of the women who braved both frowns and grins to ignore sixty years of tradition and introduce a female presence into the classrooms at Texas A&M University. There I had the good fortune to enroll in a course on the British Romantics with an extraordinary professor. Even now, the image of him leaning forward over the podium reciting Wordsworth's "Michael," or Shelley's "To a Skylark," comes back sharply in my memory. But it was more than poetry reading he shared with us. He gave our minds new ideas to consider and taught our hearts the beauty of poetry.

Now, I drive eighty miles daily to share in a university classroom all that I learned during those years as a graduate student, but I am once again a country dweller. God's blessings have never ceased. As I write, a barn swallow swoops by on her way to a mud nest precariously stuck to our porch eave. I marvel at her grace— poetry in action. Quail couples feed daily under the feeder, gathering strength to care for their newly-hatched brood hidden under the junipers along the fence line. Whip-poor-wills call to one another all night on the moonlit hill rising behind our house. A great blue heron robs our fish pond of most of the goldfish, but I do not worry. Five remain. Already, hundreds of tiny offspring race the tadpoles around the edge of the pond. Daily miracles are not hard to come by here on our hill.

Wordsworth got it right when he recognized the intimations of immortality—heart knowledge—in memories of childhood, but his recollections stop too soon. Life would be pedestrian and prosaic if God did not continue all of our lives to surprise our hearts with glimpses of the hereafter reflected in nature's miracles and in human love and grace.

KAREN HENDLEY

Karen Hendley leads a varied and creative life. She lives in the woods of East Texas in a house she built with her husband, David. The family spends a lot of time together because David, potter, works at home, and children Hans and Lenora have done their schooling at home for the past ten years.

Karen worked as an art teacher before she had children and now works part-time as Youth Director at First United Methodist Church of Rusk. She is active in the Cherokee Civic Theater, where she has done everything from acting and directing, to fundraising and organizing.

Creativity runs throughout her life in her artistic creations, the family's handmade home in the woods, and a folk-rock trio of which she and David are a part. She lends her creative ideas to directing summer Bible school events and her work with the Cherokee Civic Theater.

BOTH SIDES

by Karen Hendley

There is a picture of me in the family photo album. Nearly all of the pictures in this album are of me, as I was an only child and the first grandchild. Our family was small; my dad was an only child, and Mother only had one sister. Even though most of the pictures are of me, this one of my fourth birthday party stands out. I am at the head of the table, the only child surrounded by adult friends and family.

None of those people are still with me, but in a very important way they shaped my future. Their living created a place for me in this world. Everything those people did in their lives makes a difference in mine. The void created by their deaths made room for more life. My beginning as a vital human being, as well as my understanding of God, came from the shadows of death and the never-ending cycle of creation of which I am a part.

Daddy knew about creation. He knew that death was the beginning. Born the son of a Jewish father and Christian mother, Hank Hirschfeld's Jewish name was a danger to him in Nazi Germany. He came to America at age 18 just before World War II, escaping the persecution which his parents remained in Germany to endure. For me the most significant part of his heritage lies in a story I remember so well. When he turned thirteen and his father asked him whether he wanted to be confirmed as a Christian or have a Bar Mitzvah, Daddy chose neither. At that moment, he became a seeker of the truth.

Choosing not to believe in a religion but to believe in God, he freed me to make choices, to question, to find my own way. This choice, however, did not end his search for understanding or his concern for making the world a better place. Following his lead helped me to be aware of the creative nature of my life and to understand that my choices were eternal.

Daddy often told me that he believed in miracles because I had survived several surgeries to correct a congenitally dislocated hip. I felt that he believed in miracles because I was even born at all, and because he was able to bring his parents to America after the war. He felt his life to be a miracle. He loved music and art, studied history and political science, and believed that books held the keys to the universe.

Loud music and lively discussions among his intellectual friends and business associates exposed me to very noisy and big ideas. Daddy was a participant, wanting to make sense of the world and experience the joy of it. Looking back, I realize that perhaps these deafening symphonies drowned out the pain of his struggle with his own spirituality. At the same time, I heard the music and felt God's presence in my life, real and tangible. Daddy's struggle became my rock, the foundation of my faith.

"Today's my father's birthday," I remember Daddy saying when I was about nine years old. I jokingly replied, "Why don't you send him a card?" Daddy was not amused as his father had died many years before. A discussion followed which I remember as my first awareness of death and what it means. I had always felt that my grandfather, whom I had never met, was alive, since he was so alive in my father's descriptions, in his photos and stories. My learning what it meant for him to be dead was a significant lesson. It made me want to know my grandfather even more, and led me to embrace the idea that people live on after death. That became part of what God was to me.

Mother was a Christian, a Methodist. Her father was dead, also, but she didn't talk about things like that. She was a quiet believer—acceptance personified. She just *was* religious, the embodiment of trust—no talk, just action. She took me to Sunday School and church because it was just what you did; there was no struggle. It was a community to which we belonged.

Mother always held me, happy or sad. She listened whether she agreed or disagreed, saying, "Always do the best you can," or "Use your best judgment." She just assumed I knew how. Mother loved art and music, but not as intensely as Daddy did. And she was creative. She made clothes, and she was rarely without her cross stitch or embroidery. Using her unique decorating style, she tried to make our house her own. She wasn't afraid to do unconventional things such as using foreign newspapers or wine labels for wallpaper. Her approach to life, practical and creative, had a great influence on me.

Mother too, knew that death was the beginning, and she knew about creation. Her knowledge came from the doctrine of the church and her faith from the story of Christ, that he died for us and that we must be born again for creation to continue.

Mother listened, Daddy talked. They showed me both sides of the spiritual life, the struggle mixed with trust and obedience.

I was baptized and confirmed in the Methodist Church when I was twelve because it was what you did at that age. My mother made me a new outfit, white pique with a floral over-jacket. My Daddy, who never came to church, even came for the ceremony. The minister sprinkled water on my head, and I repeated the vows. Ironically, it was at this time that I began to question. The whole idea of faith as taught by the church was elusive to me. How did anyone know that Jesus was really the son of God? How could anyone rise from the dead? By the end of my twelfth year, I quit going to Sunday School because my teacher couldn't answer my questions. My mother never made me go back.

Awakening to life, death, and the opposite sex, I was still oblivious to my own mortality. My friend Teri and I would ride the city bus to the Museum of Fine Arts, wearing our faded army-surplus fatigues and clodhopper shoes. We went often and soon had favorite paintings we sought time after time. I was not the intellectual type, and my well-read, studious friend was a great influence on me.

Occasionally we would spend some time in an old library. With its dark wood, tall stacks of books, and the quiet, it was a place where the creative lived and breathed. I was not a reader, but it didn't matter. The powerful presence of *the creative* moved me beyond my reality into a world where there were stories to hear and lives to know. I wanted to share in the creative force which so moved me in those places.

During this time of my creative awakening, Daddy was diagnosed with cancer; a malignant mole was removed from his leg.

"I've had that mole all of my life!" he said. "How could something you've had all of your life kill you?" I asked the question over and over as he got sicker, and our lives became consumed with hospitals, doctors, and treatments.

Mother was ill, too. She paced the floor with toothaches and headaches; neuralgia she called it. But she kept the vigil with Daddy and never complained if she was distressed or worried. She was just there, and we depended on her presence, never thinking that we would lose her first.

I remember the day she died. We had hugged and kissed, and I had cried the night before at the hospital where she was scheduled for "exploratory surgery." I don't think she told anyone that she had lung cancer. Trying to remove a lung, the doctor struggled to save her overworked heart. She died on the operating table, a tired and wounded angel.

That morning, sitting and waiting in the den of my aunt and uncle's house, I restlessly read a magazine. I remember the sun streaming in through the sidelights of the front door and an eerie feeling of peace. I remember that morning as the first time that I really prayed. I don't remember praying for things or outcomes, or for God to make everything all right. I just lost myself in God, for refuge. Praying like that seemed to clear the slate for the new life I was soon to lead. It was as if God called me to learn about prayer at that moment; lifted me up to see where I had been and where I could go and what hard work it would take to get there.

Daddy died five weeks later. I went to live with my aunt and uncle, and the search began. I saw everything with new eyes, with the eyes of someone much older. I had seen too much to think like an adolescent anymore. It was as if I had traveled to the "other side" to have a backward look, then returned to the place I had come from, forever changed. I read Thoreau, Anne Morrow Lindberg, Gibran; I wandered around the city, spent time in the art museum. I was looking for something to identify with, a religion maybe. I was looking for freedom.

My family didn't talk much and my friends didn't know what to say, so my grieving was mostly private. The loss had transformed me. I had an unarticulated knowledge of what life was about but didn't know what to do about it or with it.

My friend and I cruised Houston in her Fiat convertible. In that car, the wind blowing my hair, I felt like a bird out of a cage. We came to a stop light, and Suzy said, "Do you believe in God?" I didn't know how to answer, but somehow it was a welcome question. I said that I didn't know. She invited me to her church youth group at a Disciples of Christ Church.

It was there that I met Mary, the education director and my messenger from God, who taught me the meaning of Christian love and sacrifice. She taught me what God is like. I can see her standing there in the hallway, her arms outstretched, and the expanse of waxed linoleum spread out before her as I envision Jesus would have looked to so many people in need. Mary encouraged us to share our doubts and concerns as she shared with us the kind of Christian life she hoped we would all come to live.

Through the church, our energies were channeled into mission work. I tutored at a community center after school and helped sponsor a camp for underprivileged children. We washed windows at a nursing home and visited the residents. I felt tremendous resources within me. They seemed to come from the cavity of loss. The more I gave, the more I seemed to receive in the form of gratitude, love, and support.

Mary encouraged me to share my story because she knew that I needed to clarify my feelings if I were to resolve my inner struggles. She saw who I was and, through many conversations, searched my heart. Over time, she helped me reach the goal, a goal I had not realized I was trying to reach until I arrived.

I remember the night that the tears came. At a work retreat to clean up our camp for summer, we had a worship service in the rustic old dining hall which felt intimate, filled with so many loving people. I was invited to sing the Joni Mitchell song "Both Sides Now." One line of the song struck me as a revelation of truth. That line, which speaks of looking at life from both sides but seeing only cloud illusions, acknowledged the difficulty and struggle in trying to understand life. Like my daddy's constant efforts to make sense of things, and my mama's gentle acceptance of things as they were, I realized that it would take both ways for me. Maybe I wouldn't ever find more than illusions, but the search would be fulfilling. I also knew that I needed God.

Mary came to hug me, and I suddenly felt able to give her all of the pain. She held me and accepted me. That moment was my conversion experience, a powerfully emotional and spiritual one, and yet, clearly grounded in the reality of the world.

Since that conversion experience, my life has flowed in a continuum. I feel that my life as a whole is to be creative and that creativity is not limited to the arts, but is the work of God through us in everything we do. The idea that my life is part of God's creative force is at once liberating and limiting. My struggles have not been about the existence of God or how God works, or which church or religion has all the answers. I've wrestled with choosing the best ways to be God's instrument, and the church community has provided support and encouragement toward that end

Every day, I rejoice in the fact that I live and can share this time and space with people I care about. Dealing with the finality of life, while rejoicing in it, has made my life rich. The powerful voice of the creative, which spoke to me those many years ago in the museum, seemed so close to God. And I now realize that the power is within reach, as I strive with God to make this work of art which is my life.

LIZA ELY

Liza Ely, an educator and Licensed Professional Counselor, is the mother of two daughters. She owns a contemplative retreat center where she and others offer retreats and workshops. She also consults with holistic medical practitioners and offers workshops around the state and country. Liza, who is a Unitarian-Universalist, explains that she strives to "live my life work of sharing the message of peace, wellness, and simplicity. Living in the woods in East Texas keeps me close to nature and reminds me of my spiritual ideal of living love."

On the Road With the Divine
by Liza Ely

*T his morning I stand shaking at the phone booth, sobbing
after I hang up—Kreelene is dead. What a gift she was in my
life. She was the one who could best help me sort through a difficult
decision. She affirmed me so well.*

*I return to Blossom, my Volkswagen van, and have a quiet cer-
emony inside, lighting a candle and saying a prayer for Kreelene and
her family. It is almost exactly one year since I lost my husband Austin
in the fall of 1991. I go through the rainy, dreary day, crying off and
on. I fantasize stopping at a church on this Sunday morning and
announcing, "I have just lost one of my dearest friends. I lost my husband a year ago. Is there someone here who will just hold me?"*

*I park on a wilderness road in a national forest in Vermont. It's
already dark. I sink, spent, into my safe haven, my cocoon, my Blossom.*

I remember how excited I was when I found Blossom. She sat
in a mechanic's field, lonely, like the last child picked to be a member of the softball team. She captivated me. Month after month as
I passed by her on my way from work, I questioned, "What's her
story? Why is she still there?"

On a cold, rainy February day in 1992 I drove home, the rain
on the windshield mirroring the tears on my cheeks. This had to
end, this overwhelming grief over Austin. Something had to change
in my life to give me some hope and challenge. On impulse, I
stopped suddenly on the wet pavement, pulling into the turn lane
and into the parking lot next to the mechanic's field. The van still
stood alone, majestic but dejected.

I questioned the mechanic, "Tell me the story of that mustard-colored Volkswagen van." She needed a new motor, he told me, but her owners had no spare cash. I called them to inquire about buying it.

I remember the moment her wide door opened and I saw her insides—her heart—worn and tattered. But the moment I was inside I knew I was home. I could not fake a poker face designed for negotiation. I was in love. She was to be my home, my refuge, my comfort. She was to carry me on my travels, on the journey I had dreamed about for seventeen years. Austin and I had just begun making definite plans for the trip when he died. Now it was me. Just me.

Discarding Fears

Independence Day, but it was hot in Colorado—where I had heard people went in summer to escape the heat. Glenda had joined me for the first leg of my journey, two weeks of bliss—talking for hours, exploring new territory, jumping up to watch the sunrise, laughing, catching up. I took her to the airport to return to Dallas, the same airport that Austin and I had flown out of exactly one year earlier.

I watched her plane take off and cried as I walked back to Blossom. Painfully, I released the physical presence of my husband and my friend. Hundreds of miles from family and friends, I was now anonymous, alone. Yet, I felt a strong inner knowing, a knowledge that I was supposed to take this solitary journey, and not question. On this day of freedom, my sadness held hope, anticipation. This was my Independence Day—July 4, 1992.

Following vague instructions and looking at the broad green area marked on my atlas for Gunnison National Forest, I searched out the Rainbow people. I had heard of them a few years before when my daughter commented on a man being interviewed on the news. "He sounds like you!" she had said.

On the television screen, a bearded man in a colorful, crocheted hat was trying to explain to a conservative East Texas reporter why the Rainbow Family wanted to meet in the national forest there. The camera footage of the people looked like something left over from the 60s. The bearded man said they have an annual silent meditative circle for peace at noon every Fourth of July.

When I learned they were gathering in Colorado this year, just a couple of hours drive from the airport where Glenda left, I knew I had to attend. My resolve weakened as I became certain that I was really on the right road. I had never seen so many barely-functioning cars packed with people. These were interspersed with the stark government cars of the forest rangers. I suddenly remembered media reports about problems that can arise when 25,000 people gather. My stomach tightened; my scalp tensed as I questioned my judgment. If this was safe why were there so many patrol cars? My other voice, the one that propelled me on, told me it was safe because there were so many patrol cars. I drove forward, my right arm tensed, ready to pull off the road and turn around with any provocation. Fear, fear of differences.

I was allowed to pass through with Blossom, to go to "Van Land." Bright vests, hats, socks, scarves, bare feet, dirty fingernails, backpacks, bedrolls, water jugs greeted me in the "village." Thousands of people in their 20s, 30s, and 40s, surrounded me, gathering in celebration and unity. My torso, legs, arms, neck stayed tense as I searched for a place to park Blossom. I passed a man with a small backpack, 40ish, more "traditional" looking. I told myself that I finally saw someone more like me. Some tension dissolved. Maybe it would be okay.

I parked, but sat still, scoping out the area before I ventured from the safety of Blossom. A knock on my window startled me from my thoughts. The man "like me" encouraged me to drive a little further and park in another area. He thought I would be more comfortable there. I moved on.

Walter and his camping buddy, two businessmen from California, became my companions for that adventure. It was dark, except for the stars and the circles of campfire lights scattered about the forest land. Walter invited me to join him and visit some of the campfires. We walked across the dam, found a log at a campfire, and sat to listen to the sounds of drums, guitars, cymbals, voices.

The face of God is pure, is white, is clean, is chaste. Is it not? Why was it as I sat on a hard log in the dirt and grime, with smoke blowing across my face, hair, and into my nostrils, that I saw God in the faces about me? In faces worn with wrinkles that could come only from years of sun and cigarettes. In the husky voice asking, "Did you write that song, man? Good job!" In the unmanicured, rough hand patting a stranger on the back.

After five days in the forest, bathing with a washcloth dipped in my van sink, hair and skin gritty, sweaty, I was ready for the refreshment of cool, fresh water. I tidied myself up as best I could before venturing into civilization. I stopped in the small town at the entrance to the forest, a town inundated by the Rainbow People. A little girl stared at Blossom and me, intrigued. Her mother pulled her close protectively, warning her not to respond to my wave or smile. With tense torso, arms, legs, she was ready to move away quickly with any slight provocation. Fear, fear of differences.

EMBRACING TRUST

Something was wrong with Blossom; she needed help. I found a mechanic in a small mountain town in Canada. He was busy with the summer, in-a-hurry tourist trade. When he did check her out, it was not good. She needed major engine work, requiring parts from California. Frustration, anger, concern for the unexpected expenses shook me. I was stuck on a cement parking lot, waiting, waiting.

But what a parking lot! A dumpster sat right beside me; I could simply roll down the window and toss my trash inside. A streetlight offered exactly enough illumination for reading at night. A mall, just a block away, offered a cool respite from the heat, a phone, restroom, and a grocery store. The library was only a few blocks up the street.

I walked to the Mental Health Center and offered my services as a volunteer for two weeks. Talking with the director, I discovered some needs of their organization which coincided with my skills and expertise. I presented workshops to the staff and clients and was blessed with a much needed and unexpected check for my services. The director drove me to her unoccupied cabin deep in the woods and gave me some time away in the solitude of nature.

The mechanic and his wife, Arno and Vivian, "adopted" me into their family. With them, her aunt and uncle, and friends of theirs, I was treated to meals, a camping weekend, a massage, a haircut, laughter, and hugs. I fixed my "family" an authentic Tex-Mex dinner, trimmed roses, mowed lawns, talked and shared.

I was learning. One of the major purposes of my journey was to experience different places, to get to know people from different parts of the country, to understand how we are all different, how we are all the same. But I had begun to rush along, spending only a couple of days in one place. Blossom made me stop. She made me spend time being with people, to experience their goodness. She helped me to trust the process. She helped me to see the more I gave, the more fullness I had in my life.

Dancing With Nature

In the Hoh Rainforest ancient trees sweep to the sky, their branches serving as shelves for long, wispy moss. Lots of greens, sparkling, gleaming, radiant. I expected to see flower angels, fairies, jump out any minute to dance on the moist floor.

I came upon a nurselog, a tree that had fallen and become the nurturance for new trees. Three "babies" had taken birth there and grown, now old and filled with wisdom. The Trinity—Father/Mother, Son/Daughter, Holy Spirit? Or Mind, Body and Spirit? Three beings, separate but joined, flowing harmoniously as one. I stood next to the trees and looked up into the canopy of limbs, branches, and moss, saying a prayer. I sought their wisdom, asked them to share their knowledge with me.

My hands moved forward, pulling my arms up. I felt their tingling energy. I released my will and moved with them, dancing with the wise ones. I was only slightly aware that I was on a public hiking trail, that others might come along and question my sanity. Our privacy was not invaded. I knew when the sharing, healing, was over. My hands stopped over my heart. I gave a bow with hands prayerfully folded and honored the good in my friends with a parting "Nameste." I blew a kiss and my hands moved back to my cheeks, a kiss returned. I felt blessed.

I drove on then, deep into a national forest, over miles of bumpy, uneven, narrow gravel road. Summer over, the crowds were gone. Aloneness and quiet, nothing but quiet. Then slowly I heard the sounds normally drowned out by the hum of machines, the ring of phones, the roar of the heater, the words in conversations. The wind whispered and roared, the raindrops made music on the metal of Blossom, the birds conversed in the trees, their wings whispering in the still air.

But a restlessness surfaced and my thoughts spun out questions and answers. Where was my home? My nomadic existence made me feel rootless, rootless in not knowing where I would be each day, not having the security of a filled appointment book. Where is my home, my security? My physical home is the shell of a body—five feet, eight inches, one hundred thirty-five pounds, graying brown hair, moles and freckles, bones and flesh. No. My home is my spirit, my soul. It is singing, sobbing, flying, sinking flat and tired. It is loving. It is hugging people, trees, mountains, life. It is sand between my toes, digging in, sliding off. It is being with squawking birds, bright moons, silent and wise rock people. It is looking at a wasp eyeball-to-eyeball and inviting it to move on. It is sinking into the gaze of another's spirit, losing all judgments, differences, all separateness.

The sadness is still heavy the morning after the phone call. I gasp and hold my aching heart as I remember yesterday, the loss of Kreelene. I pull out a basket that friends gave me before I left on my trip, a basket full of notes and poems for me to read when I need to feel their presence. I pull out a poem by James Dillet Freeman about bridges: how as we come to rivers our bridge might be a loved one, a stranger, an incident, or a prayer.

I take a walk down an isolated, narrowing path and pull strength from the golds, reds, greens of the trees. I think how, at this moment, nature is serving as my bridge. I think of the kindness, the generosity, the blessings from the strangers I have met. I think of the strength and lessons from the unplanned, unscheduled events of my journey. I think of the times when I was enveloped in peace while in the silent center of prayer.

I turn the bend in the road to discover an actual bridge. It is old and wooden, no longer useful except for foot traffic. I stand in the middle, over a fast moving creek, rocks poking up and casting the water in swirls. I close my eyes; I breathe deeply into my chest, my abdomen, down to my toes. As I hear the rush of the water, smell the freshness in the air, I feel the power of the water as if washing over my body. I feel healing. It is clear now. The whys are being answered. My travel is serving as a metaphor for my spiritual quest, my journey into the sacred, the recognition of Divine Omnipresence.

I walk back and the sun makes its first appearance in three days, shining its brilliant light across my face. It penetrates my body. I look to it. I praise it. I thank it.

SHIRLEY W. MATTHEWS

Shirley Wittman Matthews, Professor Emeritus of Art, Lon Morris College, Jacksonville, Texas, taught in Texas public schools and served as a local church director of Christian education prior to going to the college. One of her major interests has been the study of art history and the interrelationships between religion and the visual arts.

She and her husband have a son, a daughter and son-in-law, and two grandchildren. In retirement, Shirley enjoys reading, gardening, birdwatching, writing poetry, and hiking in the Texas Hill Country with her family.

PSALM OF GRACE
by Shirley W. Matthews

*O Lord, my Lord, you are my strength
and my salvation;
In you alone, Lord, will I put my faith
and trust.*

Thunder and lightning shook the morning sky, as an unexpected August storm poured heavy rain over the city,
turning streets into flowing streams. The year was 1992. Inside,
surrounded by the sterile whiteness of a hospital delivery room,
I stood beside my daughter's bed anxiously awaiting the birth
of my first grandchild. My daughter held tightly to her husband's
hand as he stood on one side of the bed, and with her other hand
she grasped mine. Each pain she felt became my pain, and I longed
for her labor to be finished. My heart raced with fear.

"Gracious God, be with her, help her, strengthen her," I prayed.
"Lord, be with her; God, be with her," silently, with my eyes wide
open, I prayed over and over again. As I continued to pray, a sense
of peace flowed over me. The stark whiteness of the room warmed
to a golden brightness, enveloping all of us. Like Moses before the
burning bush, I knew I was on holy ground, that God was in that
place. My fear vanished. I felt God working in and through each
of us, working to bring this child safely into the world. And then,
in the miracle of that moment, my tiny grandson was born, healthy
and beautiful, and soon was laid in his mother's waiting arms.

I knew that God had been present in that hospital room even
before I had begun to pray. The light that illuminated the room

had also illuminated my life and my understanding. My memory slipped back to an earlier, similar experience, when I was lying quietly on my bed in a hospital room a few hours after the birth of my own first child. I was alone. A bright, golden radiance flooded the room around me, and I sensed, in that brilliance, the presence of the Holy Spirit. I felt completely secure, wrapped in that divine presence, and rested in the assurance that God would continue to comfort and sustain me. In the experience of heightened awareness in my daughter's hospital room thirty-four years later, I gained renewed assurance that the creator of the universe, like both loving father and nurturing mother, cares enough to be with me in both joy and sorrow, even to suffer with me.

I am well acquainted with suffering. I have known the anguish of despair. In the early years of my marriage, just as the joys of motherhood were finally mine, depression crept into my life, spreading its dark wings over me. My days were filled with dreary shadows, and the joys I should have known came only in small glimmers. After only a few months, the darkness lifted, and daylight filled my life again.

But soon, the shadows returned. Depression hovered over me again, casting its dark distortions into every corner of my life. My shaded existence wavered between life and death, and death often seemed the sweeter. In my despair I cried, "Why was I ever born? If you are there, God, why do I languish so?"

I felt alienated from those I loved. I remember feeling very tired, lying across the foot of my bed, listening to the joyful sounds of my family as they sat around the table, eating the evening meal, talking and laughing. But, like a lonely bird in the night, I felt alone, angry, hurt, without understanding why. My perspective was skewed; I made false assumptions. I felt unloved and afraid to trust those I loved the most. And yet, I carried on my daily life with people around me unaware of how I was suffering. I told no one.

Finally, the dark shadows disappeared. I savored each new day in the light and, in celebration, returned to school, completed my degree, and began teaching art. Teaching was both a challenge and a joy, but after several years, an increased number of classes and other added responsibilities left me no time or energy for doing anything creative. Often, I would lie awake at night, mentally working out ideas for a composition to draw or paint, but exhaustion would overtake my body, and I would soon fall asleep. My creative ideas no longer took physical form.

After a dozen years of denying my need to paint or draw or write poetry, creativity seemed to leave me, and into the void came that dreaded companion, depression. It dulled my senses, causing me to doubt all my abilities. The image in my mirror reflected neither creativity nor intellectual ability; it reflected only inadequacy. But I continued to teach, even though I lost sight of who I really was. And like the psalmists of old, my heart poured forth its own lament:

> Hear my cry, O Lord;
>> turn not away from me.
> Alone I cry in my despair,
>> but no one hears my cry.
> My own reflection is empty,
>> and no one knows my name.

Into that fragile scene moved fierce new enemies. Like hungry lions waiting in ambush, serious threats to my health appeared. As quickly as I escaped the pursuit of one, another met me face to face, its angry eyes set for the kill. First came the pain in my hands. As I was driving home from a neighboring town, my right hand began to throb with pain. My fingers tingled with numbness, but the agony persisted. I could do nothing to stop it. At home the pain continued, and soon my left hand developed the same symptoms. The pain was severe, especially during the night. I would leave my bed, go into the kitchen and, while sitting on a high stool, fling my arms wildly around and around with as much force as possible, trying to alleviate the excruciating pain. But it remained with me from night into day. Doing any kind of art work, even a classroom demonstration, was impossible. I consulted a neurologist who diagnosed the condition as carpal tunnel syndrome. He sent me to a surgeon who operated on both my hands.

The pain was gone, replaced by healing incisions. But then came a new diagnosis. On the day the surgeon removed the last stitches, he informed me that the results of a tissue biopsy taken from my hands during surgery indicated amyloidosis, a serious condition. The rheumatologist explained that if that condition were truly present, not even chemotherapy could stop its progression. There was no cure.

At home during the Christmas holidays, I read book after book, seeking guidance for overcoming this threat to my very existence. I was anxious about the frightening diagnosis and miserable from the pain of newly developed rheumatoid arthritis. Unable even to dress myself, I was totally dependent upon my husband's care. But I continued to read, and I prayed. Finally, after months of testing, the rheumatologist determined with near-certainty that amyloidosis was not now present. I rejoiced. I was willing to accept his diagnosis and get on with my life. Cortisone had helped relieve the difficulties of arthritis, and I looked forward to good health again.

Putting my fears behind me, I was determined to change my lifestyle, to simplify my life. But the dilemma remained: how could I take time to be creative?

As the school year came to a close that spring, a new problem appeared. Leukoplakia, a precancerous condition, developed. Following surgery, the condition returned, followed by more surgery and then by continuing recurrences and one surgical procedure after another. Weeks turned into months, and the problem persisted. I could not believe what was happening. The words I kept hearing were devastating: precancerous, malignant, biopsy, life-threatening. I felt caught in a situation with no possible escape, much as I felt in a recurring childhood dream. In my dream, I was in an open grassy field with a red picket fence running in one direction. A large brown bear was chasing me, but my small legs were unable to move. The only way to escape was to pull myself along the fence by grasping one picket after another with my hands. I struggled with all my strength to get away, but the bear ran faster and faster, his huge dark form coming closer and closer to me. Then, just before the bear could catch me, I woke up, safe in my own bed but filled with fear.

Finally my life seemed to return to normal. But the experiences of the past several years had changed my perspective. I made plans to retire. Determined to connect my creativity with my religious convictions and practice, I returned to writing poetry, published some poems in the college literary magazine and began a design project. It was a small creative beginning, a timid one.

But then, in the spring of 1991, just before my retirement from teaching, a severe reaction to asthma medication sent me rushing to the hospital emergency room. That, and the fact that my whole system was out of balance, required a week-long hospital stay followed by several months of recuperation. It was as if God had said to me, "Slow down; stop running. In stillness and in quiet hear my word to you." And in those months of rest, I came to terms with who I am in relation to God, to my family, and to others.

With the guidance of a perceptive psychologist, whom my physician had recommended for help in dealing with stress, I gained new insights into the biological aspects of my depression. I came to understand that my intellect, which I had doubted, was not inferior, that my sensitivity, which I had devalued, could enrich the intellect; that feeling and contemplation were natural to my being. He then suggested that I look back at the child, the young person I had been.

> *When I was but a child, Lord, you called to me;*
>   *when I was but a child, you called my name.*
> *As in a waking dream I knew your presence;*
>   *you encompassed me with your radiant holy light.*
> *Though I saw no one nor did I hear a voice,*
>   *I felt your presence, O Lord of my youth*
>   *and heard you call my name.*

When I looked back, I saw again a quiet, shy little girl. I remembered how, as a child, my heart was always tuned to the beauty of the world around me, to the joyful song of the mockingbird, to the coolness of early spring grass beneath my winter-softened feet, to yellow buttercups in a sea of green grass, to the music of rain on a tin roof.

My childhood was enriched by many people, especially my family. My father, sharing his many long-remembered poems, songs and stories with me; my mother, caring for me with her gentle touch and soft voice; my two older sisters, singing together, sewing dresses for me, drawing pictures, making special treats for me; my brother, spending a summer's day with me on a makeshift raft, pretending to be floating down the Mississippi River, with his playing Huckleberry Finn to my Tom Sawyer—all inspired my imagination, intriguing me with thoughts and words and images to last a lifetime.

I liked the pleasurable sound of words set together in poetry and listened intently when my father recited poems to me. I liked to draw and was inspired by the artistry of my sisters. Soon a drawing tablet and pencil became necessities for me. I liked quiet times of contemplation and imagination. I liked lying on my back in cool grass outdoors, watching the changing shapes of clouds, and I liked lying on my back indoors, looking up at the ceiling, imagining that it was the floor. I imagined how, in such an upside-down world, steps would be necessary to get up to the doorways, and hanging light fixtures became unusual standing floor lamps. In my imagination I created new and fascinating worlds.

Just as my family inspired my imagination, so did the church inspire my faith in God. The love I knew in the fellowship of the church, the Bible stories, prayers, and songs I heard there all spoke to my heart. I liked especially the Psalms of praise and thanksgiving, and I began memorizing them.

As a child of eleven or twelve, I felt that God had a special plan for my life, and I knew I wanted to be baptized. On a sunny Sunday morning when the invitation was given, I walked down the aisle to the front of the church. Light flooding through the windows filled the sanctuary. As I stood at the chancel rail before the baptismal font, I heard and responded to the minister's words, but I saw behind him the tall stained glass windows leading my eyes upward. I felt myself reaching out toward God and felt the light surrounding me as if God were enveloping me.

Throughout my childhood and youth, I kept in my heart the feeling that God was always present with me. One Sunday before the evening worship service, I left my teenage friends and went alone to the prayer chapel for a few moments of prayer. As I knelt at the prayer rail with my eyes closed and my head bowed, I sensed another presence in the small room. Since I had heard no one come in, I turned to see who might have been there before I entered. I could see no one, and yet I felt a presence, as if someone were

placing a comforting hand on my shoulder. With an intense awareness of the Holy Spirit beside me, I returned to prayer.

Such was my life as a child, as a youth: my days were filled
with church and school and a continuing love of art and poetry.
My desire was to respond in every part of my life to God's claim
upon me.

As I looked back at the experiences of my childhood and youth,
I realized that, as an adult, I had denied the child I had been. I
could see that God had been leading me toward wholeness, even
when I was a child. I began to understand that for me creativity
must be a way of life, a spiritual path, a means for serving God.
Regardless of any artistic work I might produce, living creatively
would help me to understand who I am as a child of God. It would
help me to relate to the mystery and beauty I knew as a child. I had
confronted, once again, the quiet, imaginative child, the sensitive
young person I had been, and—liking the person I saw—I took
her in.

The inner movements toward creativity that had begun earlier stirred within me. I wanted to create—with words, with colors
and shapes and textures. I wanted others to enjoy my works. I began to write poetry again and shared several poems through literary
publications at the college. My desire to create a large work of art
to share with others led to an unusual decision: my yard would be
my canvas, and the plants and flowers I had loved since childhood
would be my pigment. My garden would be a living, on-going,
changing work of art, eventually encompassing the whole yard.
Such a project would require horticultural study, planning, time,
and a great amount of physical labor; but with the help of my
husband, I began. Soon, yellow columbines, purple coneflowers,
blue salvia, autumn asters, Shasta daisies, and violets filled a small
garden. Gradually, other parts of the design came to life with
splashes of color—magenta, lavender, silvery gray, green, and snowy
white. My art project was underway. I was creating again.

Through the years, I have often ignored the workings of God
in my life, allowing the demands of my work and expectations of
others to crowd my life with complexity. My priorities have now

changed; the simplicity I longed for is within reach. I cannot ignore the workings of grace in my life: God has led me when there
seemed to be no way out. My cries "out of the depths" have resolved into a hymn of hope and praise. Now, impressions of those
moments of divine presence merge with the dailiness of my life,
and I am keenly aware that in my every moment I stand on holy
ground, that God is in this place.

The mystery of God is too much for me to comprehend; yet, I
know that the one who is with me today, in my joys and sorrows,
is the same God I knew in the beauty and mystery of the world
about me as child. And I give thanks:

> *Lord, even when I turned from you,*
> *when my heart was filled with doubt,*
> *You waited for me and my safe return;*
> *like a longing mother, you waited for me,*
> *And when I returned, you came out to me;*
> *with outstretched arms you took me in.*

> *Your steadfast love sustains me, Lord.*
> *In the midst of tribulation*
> *it is you who comforts me.*
> *My heart is filled with your praise, O God;*
> *With thanksgiving I sing a new song*
> *while my heart rejoices always*
> *in your steadfast love.*
> *For you, O God, are my strength*
> *and my salvation.*
> *In you alone, Lord,*
> *will I put my trust.*

MARY EVANS BROWN

Born the middle of three daughters to a house painter and homemaker, Mary Evans Brown continues to live near her birth place among the East Texas piney woods. She struggles to balance her strong call to social justice issues and her desire for a peaceful life in the country with her family. She and her husband, Jim, have two sons, Troy and Jeremiah, and a daughter-in-law, Janie.

"In my story I share the strong effect my grandmother and grandfather had on my early life," Mary notes. "As an adult, many women have taught me valuable life lessons. Among them Hazel Decker, a strong United Methodist and leader in United Methodist Women, stands out as a role model for acting on one's faith during troubling times."

QUILTS AND MOON FLOWERS
by Mary Evans Brown

The Wind stirs the soul into discontent
The Voice surrounds with silence and waits
> *for the rainstorm*
> *for the falling leaves*
> *for the owl calling in the night.*

Wandering through the rooms of my childhood, looking for the beginnings of my spiritual understanding, evokes memories which lie dormant in the closets and boxes. Memories flash to the surface that lead to other thoughts and images.

From my window, I look into my grandmother Evans' window and remember sitting with her in front of the space heater. She would sit in her rocking chair and I on the floor as we tore newspaper backing from completed quilt tops. Methodically, carefully, and quietly she had pieced together the small scraps of cotton and made the quilts she passed on to her grandchildren. I received the red and white one with over a hundred small pieces in each block. Each time I look at it, I think of how, without pretension or complaint, she finished raising her brothers and sisters when her mother died young, how she worked in the cotton fields between the births of her six sons, how she read her Bible daily and accepted the sometimes hard life she was given with grace and a gentle smile.

My grandfather Smith didn't leave such tangible evidence of himself. He was a man of action and felt that I should experience life. His legacy consists of stories about his outspoken stand against the Ku Klux Klan and the many moves the family had to make as a result. A man interested in history, he took me to see the last local cotton gin before it closed its doors. But he also taught me about things close to home. He taught me that putting freshly laid hen eggs into the water bucket in the well would keep them cool, and that waiting patiently for the moon flowers to open on warm summer evenings would eventually allow me to witness their one night of glory.

Through the years I have unconsciously drawn from my grandparents' lives to form my values for daily living. Grandma Evans' quiet honesty and spiritual aura combine with Grandpa Smith's passion and action as I find my own spiritual voice. I grew up in a small East Texas town with a tiny Methodist church. I often think now that my childhood resembles more closely that of someone a generation older than I actually am. Electricity came to our house shortly before I was born, but an indoor bathroom was still years away. I wore feedsack clothes and went barefoot to school, where there were two grades in each classroom.

My first year of school was marked with many "sick" days as I ran from a bully who constantly threatened to me. My teacher and parents must have known that I was not ill, yet continued to allow me to miss school until I was able to stand up to my predator. When it finally came, the physical blow was far less painful than the emotional pain of the preceding months had been.

Morrow Grocery in Flint, where Dad would sit on the bench with other men discussing their vision of the world, occupies an important place in my memory. On Sunday afternoons we went there for an ice cream cone, and I listened to the adults talk about what the preachers said at the Methodist and Baptist churches and who should have been there to hear it. If I had been more astute, I would have realized then the subtle rewriting of the scriptures taking place at Morrow Grocery. I would have known that the golden rule and the ten commandments had different interpretations on Monday morning—depending upon the person they were applied to.

My dad and his twin brother were house painters, and we picked Dad up from work at the small store each day. I was surprised when Dad was angry with me one day on the way home.

Why, he wanted to know, had I called that black man *Mr.* Sampson. Was I trying to embarrass my dad? Didn't I know better than to address a black man the same way I addressed white people? I was bewildered. Left to cope with this confusion alone, I continued to think of the man as Mr. Sampson; I was beginning to reject the rewritten scriptures of my elders.

When I was about ten, I again had to protect myself. It was a more difficult and a more serious task than the event that had taken place when I was younger. For one thing, my abuser was several years older than I. The details are not important here; neither is blame or revenge. The significance lies in the emotional pain that did not end with the encounter and with which I had to cope alone.

As a child trying to understand what was happening to me, I became acquainted with guilt and reward and punishment. The scriptures talked about rain falling on the just and unjust, but I heard conversations on the bench at the store about "just punishment" for unacceptable actions and about rewards for "living right." Were the events that happened to me my fault? Was this my punishment? What the Bible said and how the men on the bench interpreted it made understanding difficult for me—especially when I thought of my grandmother Evans. I remembered her rocking quietly, reading her well-worn Bible each day. I knew she was a kind, saintly person whom everyone liked. What I didn't understand then was that she had had a son die in early childhood, and that she raised a child who was mentally handicapped. Certainly these trials were not a reward for her life. Nevertheless, the feeling that bad things happen to people because of their sins lingered in the shadows of my understanding. Even now I find myself wondering if I am being punished when I experience hard times.

My defenses against emotional pain became stronger during my six years of junior and senior high school, when I rode a fading yellow bus to an oil-rich campus filled with convertibles, letter jackets, and cashmere sweaters. I convinced myself that I had neither need nor desire to spend nights at a friend's house; that being a drill team member was a frivolous waste of money; and that wearing nice clothes was unnecessary. I grew used to being alone— an outsider.

During my semester as a library aide, another aide confided to me that he was homosexual. Naive as I was, I hardly knew what he meant, but I did know that he was treated worse than a poor country girl who rode the bus to school. Not knowing how to help him with his ultimate question of acceptance by God and family, I did what I could by taking his place each time he was told to take films or books to a classroom. My defenses were greater than his, and rejection by the students was less painful for me.

I didn't see my intervention as from God. It was what you did for someone in need. My grandmother Evans was kind, and I should be also. But the lessons I learned in my early childhood stayed with me. I knew that while my church and teachers of the faith had taught me the golden rule, they would not approve of my acting it out in this situation. I kept my friend's pain to myself.

All the Sundays I had lived at home, I had gone to church. It was only natural for me to seek a church when I went to college, and I soon found the Wesley Foundation. Reverend Jack Shelton, the campus minister, had ways of conducting worship that seemed accepting of me and my spiritual path. There were people there who agreed with my ideas, who were struggling to find a place to belong also. I didn't feel as alone as I had before, and the solitary decisions I had made were affirmed.

This experience was pivotal for me. Since that time, I have had a continuing struggle with the institutional church—have wanted it to be a consistently affirming haven for me. It cannot be. But my experience with Reverend Shelton and with the ministers at Lamar University, where I later finished my degree, showed me that the church has promise, so I am not able to simply abandon it. In a sense, my struggle with the church has pushed my spiritual search forward, forcing me to listen and struggle to become what I want the church to be.

My grandfather Smith's model of action began to overtly play itself out in my life during my last two years of college. The Methodist Church and Wesley Foundation at Lamar continued to validate a faith of conviction and action. There I became part of a group that racially integrated the dorm rooms and questioned the gender-biased policies of the campus which required different dress codes, curfews, and public behavior for female and male students.

My awakened call to action merged with other values and concerns as I moved into adulthood. I worked with children in foster care, adoption, and multi-handicapped special education classes and with residents of nursing homes. My need to serve as an advocate for voiceless people was perhaps born out of my need for someone to speak for me when I was a child.

I was also called in directions which pulled me back to my solitary country roots. Five years in Montana, in the distant shadow of mountains and on the banks of the Big Horn River, had strong spiritual impact on me. The overwhelming magnificence of that sparsely populated land, the diversity and strength of the people, enriched my earliest memories of the plowed earth and the tall pines of my childhood. Taking care of the planet became a priority. With this desire, my husband and I moved back to Texas, to twenty-five acres of land, and built our passive solar home.

Living in a tent for a year and a half while we searched for the recycled lumber for the house was both struggle and reward. We put water in the refrigerator to keep it from freezing at night and pans on the floor to catch it when it leaked through the roof. In the spring, the moon flooded through the tent sides while the coyotes howled in the creek bottom. Bats, wild turkeys, armadillos, and every kind of insect became common companions. Before the roof and wall studs were covered with plywood, we spent a night in our sleeping bags on the second floor with the trees bending over, the stars peeking through, and the cicada talking from the woods. If we could have found a way to put a glass roof and walls on the rest of the house, we would have. That time in the tent reinforced the decisions we had made about building our house in the country and striving for simplicity of spirit.

Recently, at a funeral for a young woman who had taken her own life, the minister struggled to interpret for the mourners her success and failure, her joys and suffering. He said he was looking for the "fullest expression" of her life. I was struck by his words, for that is what I am trying to do—to find the fullest expression of my spiritual voice.

My spiritual voice continues to articulate itself in the country as we complete our home, protect the trees and wildlife from destruction, and sit on the deck in the late afternoon listening to the coming of night. My soul has been stirred, I have heard the Voice, and I struggle to respond to the call to proclaim the church's mission in the midst of the politics of the institution.

Verbalizing the needs of battered women and of families in need of health care, as well as actively participating in activities of my children, are other ways I respond to the Voice of the spirit.

Sitting on the screened porch on a summer evening hearing the chuck-will's-widow calling her mate reminds me of the evenings with my grandfather waiting for the moon flower to bloom as the moon slipped up from the horizon. The quiet time in the still of the evening invites the stirring of the soul and spirit and summons the Voice to come near. I wait in silence for the time to speak.